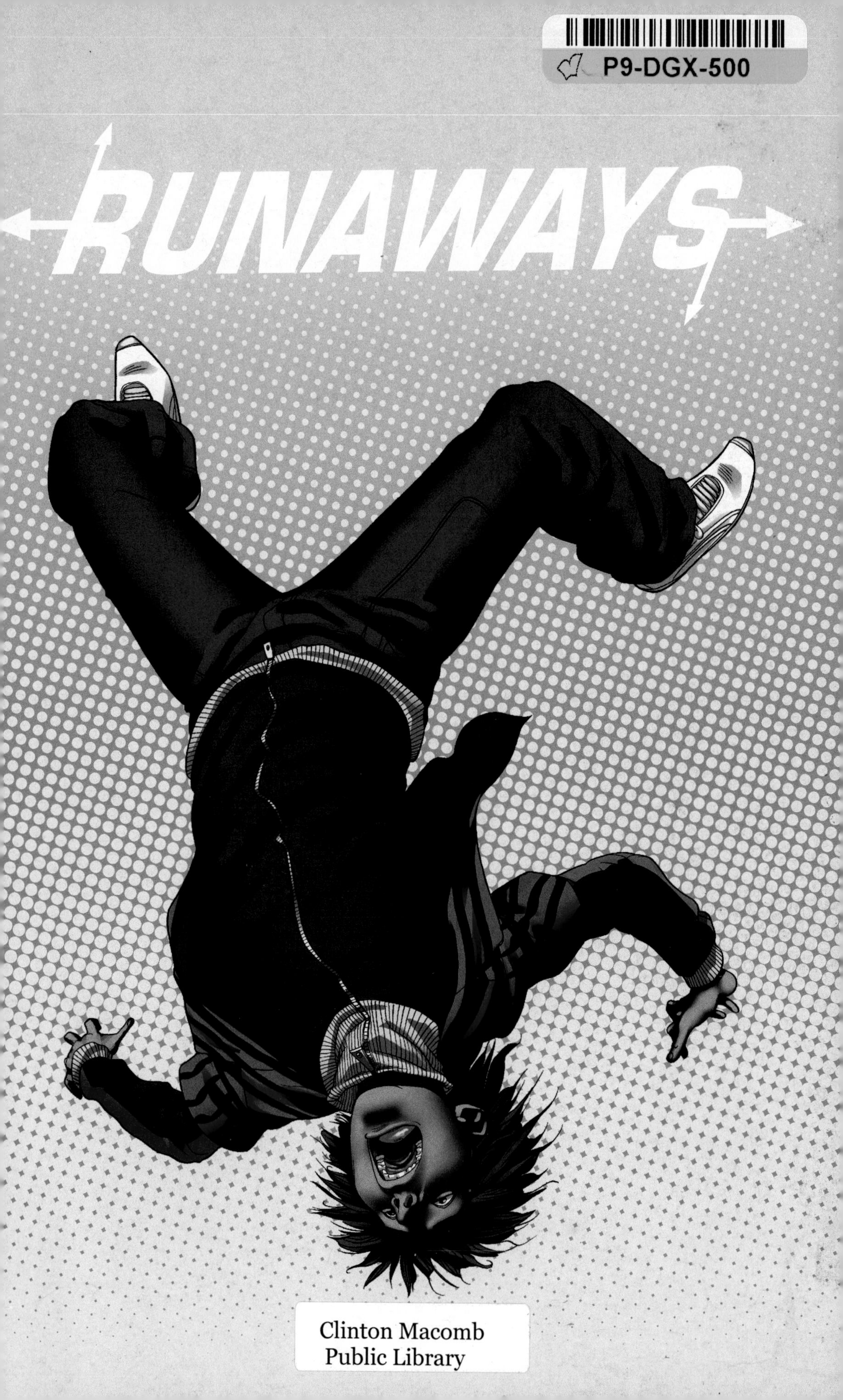
RUNAWAYS

RUNAWAYS

LIVE FAST

WRITER: **BRIAN K. VAUGHAN**

PENCILS: **MIKE NORTON** (#19-21) & **ADRIAN ALPHONA** (#22-24)

INKS: **CRAIG YEUNG**

COLORS: **CHRISTINA STRAIN**

LETTERS: **VC's RANDY GENTILE**

COVER ART: **JO CHEN**

ASSISTANT EDITORS: **DANIEL KETCHUM, SEAN RYAN** & **NATHAN COSBY**

EDITOR: **NICK LOWE**

SPECIAL THANKS TO C.B. CEBULSKI & MACKENZIE CADENHEAD

RUNAWAYS CREATED BY
BRIAN K. VAUGHAN & **ADRIAN ALPHONA**

RUNAWAYS VOL. 7: LIVE FAST. Contains material originally published in magazine form as RUNAWAYS #19-24. Second edition. First printing 2017. ISBN# 978-1-302-90872-0. Published by MARVEL WORLDWIDE, INC., a subsidiary of MARVEL ENTERTAINMENT, LLC. OFFICE OF PUBLICATION: 135 West 50th Street, New York, NY 10020. Copyright © 2017 MARVEL No similarity between any of the names, characters, persons, and/or institutions in this magazine with those of any living or dead person or institution is intended, and any such similarity which may exist is purely coincidental. **Printed in the U.S.A.** DAN BUCKLEY, President, Marvel Entertainment; JOE QUESADA, Chief Creative Officer; TOM BREVOORT, SVP of Publishing; DAVID BOGART, SVP of Business Affairs & Operations, Publishing & Partnership; C.B. CEBULSKI, VP of Brand Management & Development, Asia; DAVID GABRIEL, SVP of Sales & Marketing, Publishing; JEFF YOUNGQUIST, VP of Production & Special Projects; DAN CARR, Executive Director of Publishing Technology; ALEX MORALES, Director of Publishing Operations; SUSAN CRESPI, Production Manager; STAN LEE, Chairman Emeritus. For information regarding advertising in Marvel Comics or on Marvel.com, please contact Vit DeBellis, Integrated Sales Manager, at vdebellis@marvel.com. For Marvel subscription inquiries, please call 888-511-5480. **Manufactured between 9/15/2017 and 10/16/2017 by QUAD/GRAPHICS WASECA, WASECA, MN, USA.**

10 9 8 7 6 5 4 3 2 1

LLECTION EDITOR: JENNIFER GRÜNWALD
SISTANT EDITOR: CAITLIN O'CONNELL
SOCIATE MANAGING EDITOR: KATERI WOODY
ITOR, SPECIAL PROJECTS: MARK D. BEAZLEY
PRODUCTION & SPECIAL PROJECTS: JEFF YOUNGQUIST
P PRINT, SALES & MARKETING: DAVID GABRIEL

ITOR IN CHIEF: AXEL ALONSO
IEF CREATIVE OFFICER: JOE QUESADA
ESIDENT: DAN BUCKLEY
ECUTIVE PRODUCER: ALAN FINE

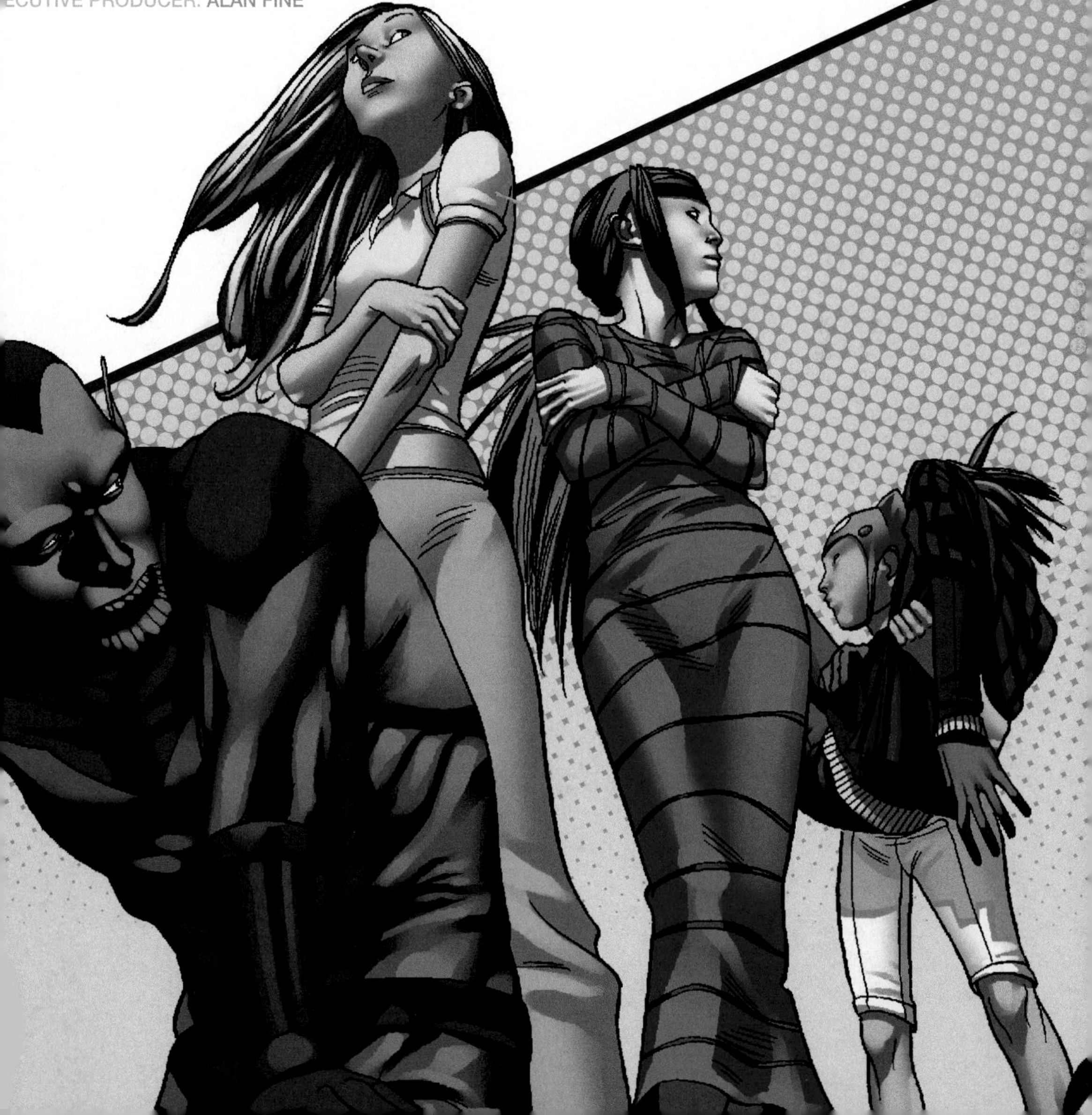

PREVIOUSLY:

AT SOME POINT IN THEIR LIVES, ALL KIDS THINK THAT THEY HAVE THE MOST EVIL PARENTS IN THE WORLD, BUT NICO MINORU AND HER FRIENDS REALLY DID.

DISCOVERING THEY WERE THE CHILDREN OF A GROUP OF SUPER VILLAINS KNOWN AS THE PRIDE, THE LOS ANGELES TEENAGERS STOLE WEAPONS AND RESOURCES FROM THESE CRIMINALS BEFORE RUNNING AWAY FROM HOME AND EVENTUALLY DEFEATING THEIR PARENTS. BUT THAT WAS JUST THE BEGINNING. TOGETHER, THE TEENAGE RUNAWAYS NOW HOPE TO ATONE FOR THEIR PARENTS' CRIMES BY TAKING ON THE NEW THREATS TRYING TO FILL THE PRIDE'S VOID.

AFTER A FEROCIOUS BATTLE WITH AN ALL-NEW PRIDE LED BY A TEMPORALLY DISPLACED GEOFFREY WILDER (FATHER OF THE LATE ALEX WILDER, THE RUNAWAYS' TRAITOROUS LEADER), GERT YORKES DIED IN THE ARMS OF HER BOYFRIEND. WITH HER FINAL BREATH, GERT "WILLED" CONTROL OF HER TELEPATHIC DINOSAUR TO CHASE STEIN, JUST BEFORE THE DEVASTATED YOUNG MAN STOLE A DECODER RING AND WILDER'S COPY OF THE ABSTRACT, A MYSTICAL TOME CONTAINING POWERFUL SECRETS.

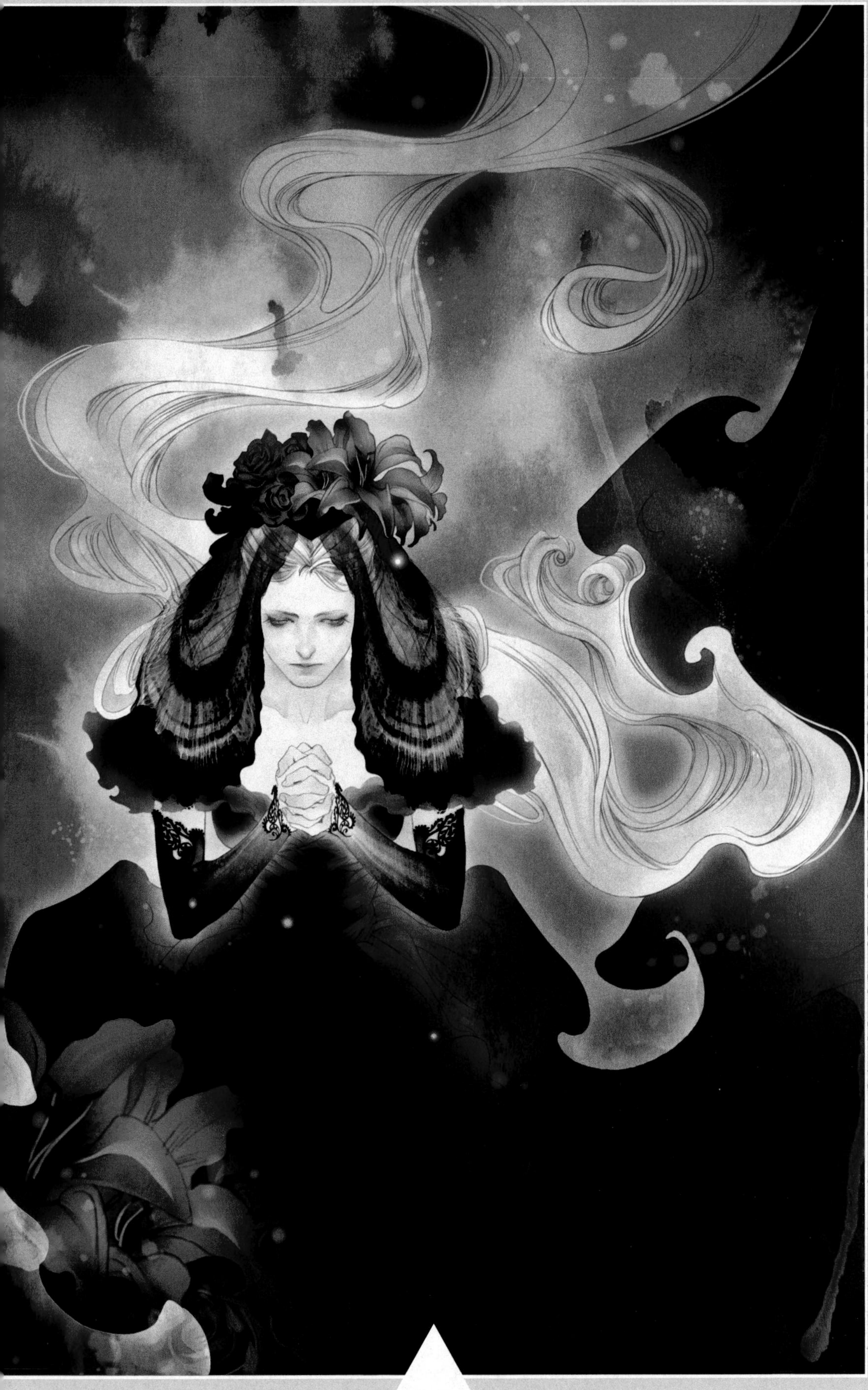

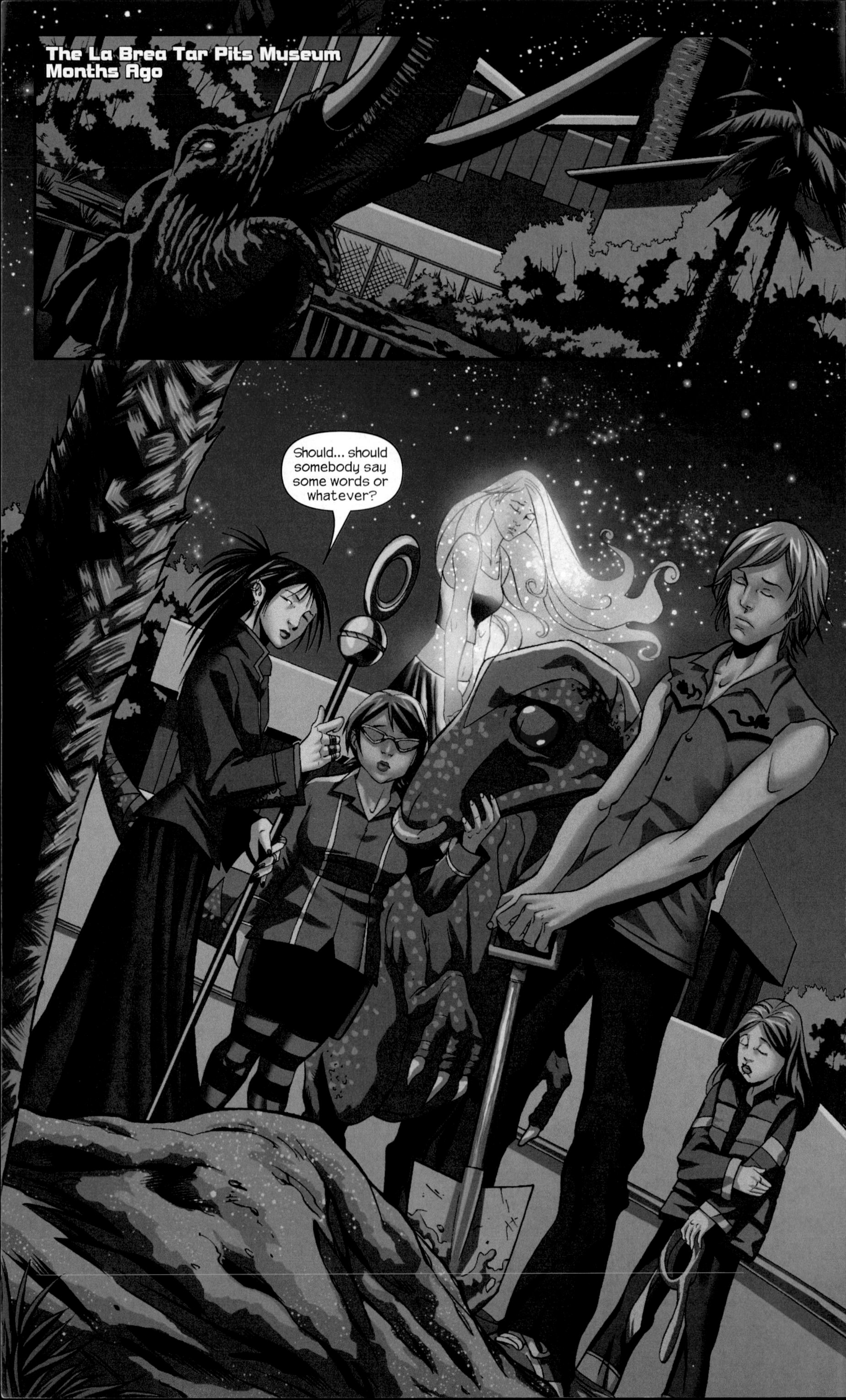

The La Brea Tar Pits Museum
Months Ago
Should... should somebody say some words or whatever?

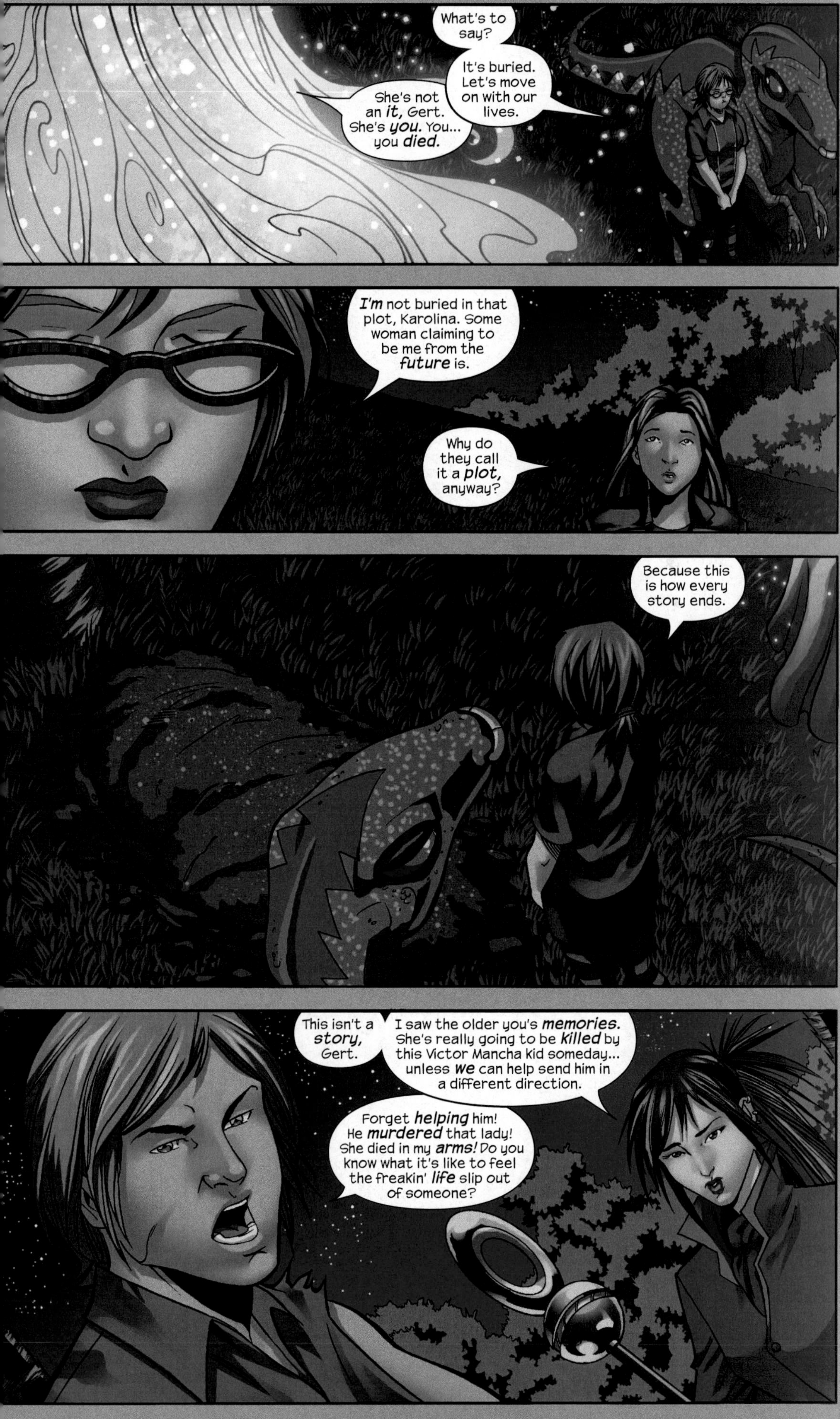
What's to say?
It's buried. Let's move on with our lives.
She's not an *it,* Gert. She's *you.* You... you *died.*
I'm not buried in that plot, Karolina. Some woman claiming to be me from the *future* is.
Why do they call it a *plot,* anyway?
Because this is how every story ends.
This isn't a *story,* Gert.
I saw the older you's *memories.* She's really going to be *killed* by this Victor Mancha kid someday... unless *we* can help send him in a different direction.
Forget *helping* him! He *murdered* that lady! She died in my *arms!* Do you know what it's like to feel the freakin' *life* slip out of someone?

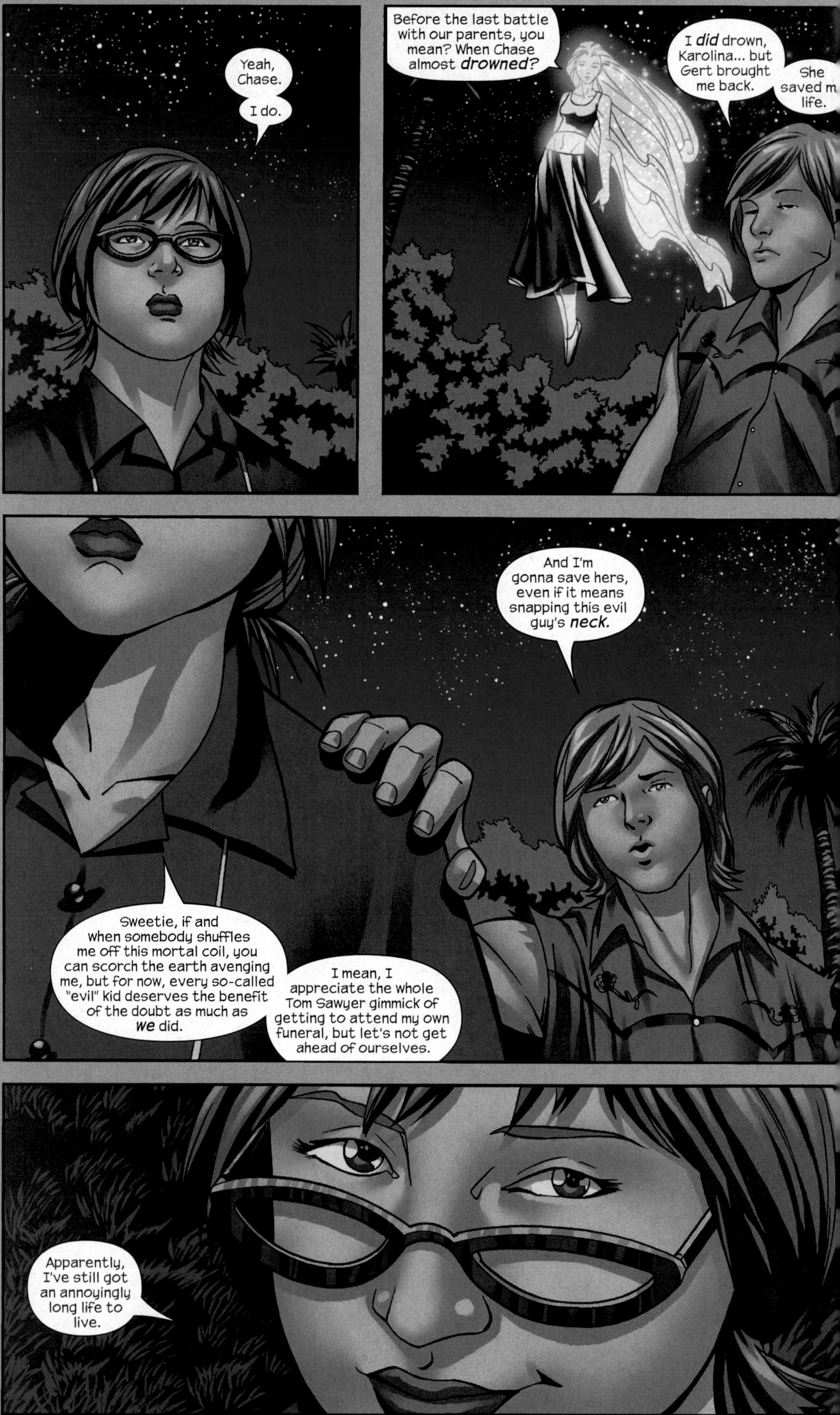
Yeah, Chase.
I do.
Before the last battle with our parents, you mean? When Chase almost *drowned?*
I *did* drown, Karolina... but Gert brought me back.
She saved m life.
And I'm gonna save hers, even if it means snapping this evil guy's *neck.*
Sweetie, if and when somebody shuffles me off this mortal coil, you can scorch the earth avenging me, but for now, every so-called "evil" kid deserves the benefit of the doubt as much as *we* did.
I mean, I appreciate the whole Tom Sawyer gimmick of getting to attend my own funeral, but let's not get ahead of ourselves.
Apparently, I've still got an annoyingly long life to live.

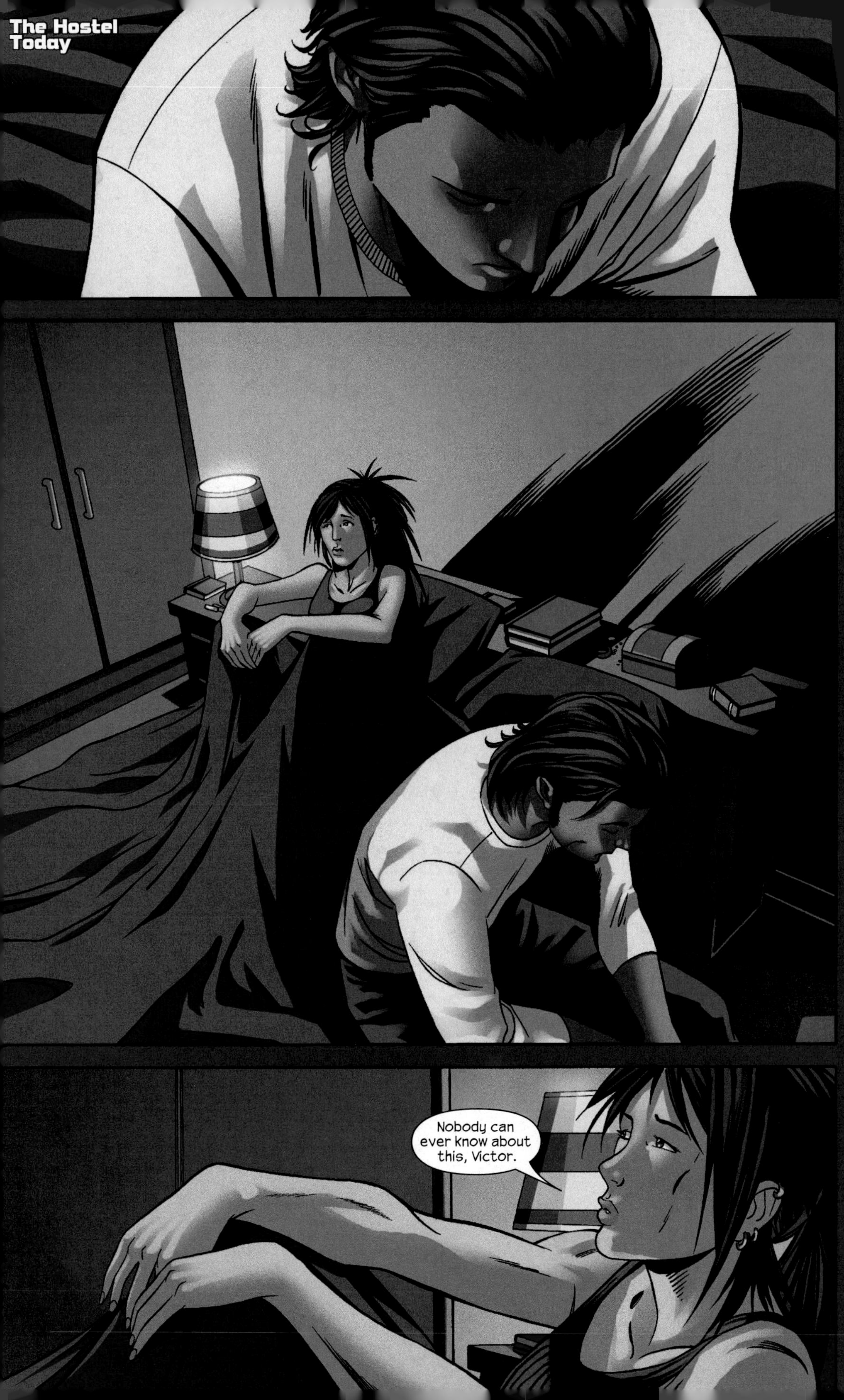
The Hostel
Today
Nobody can ever know about this, Victor.

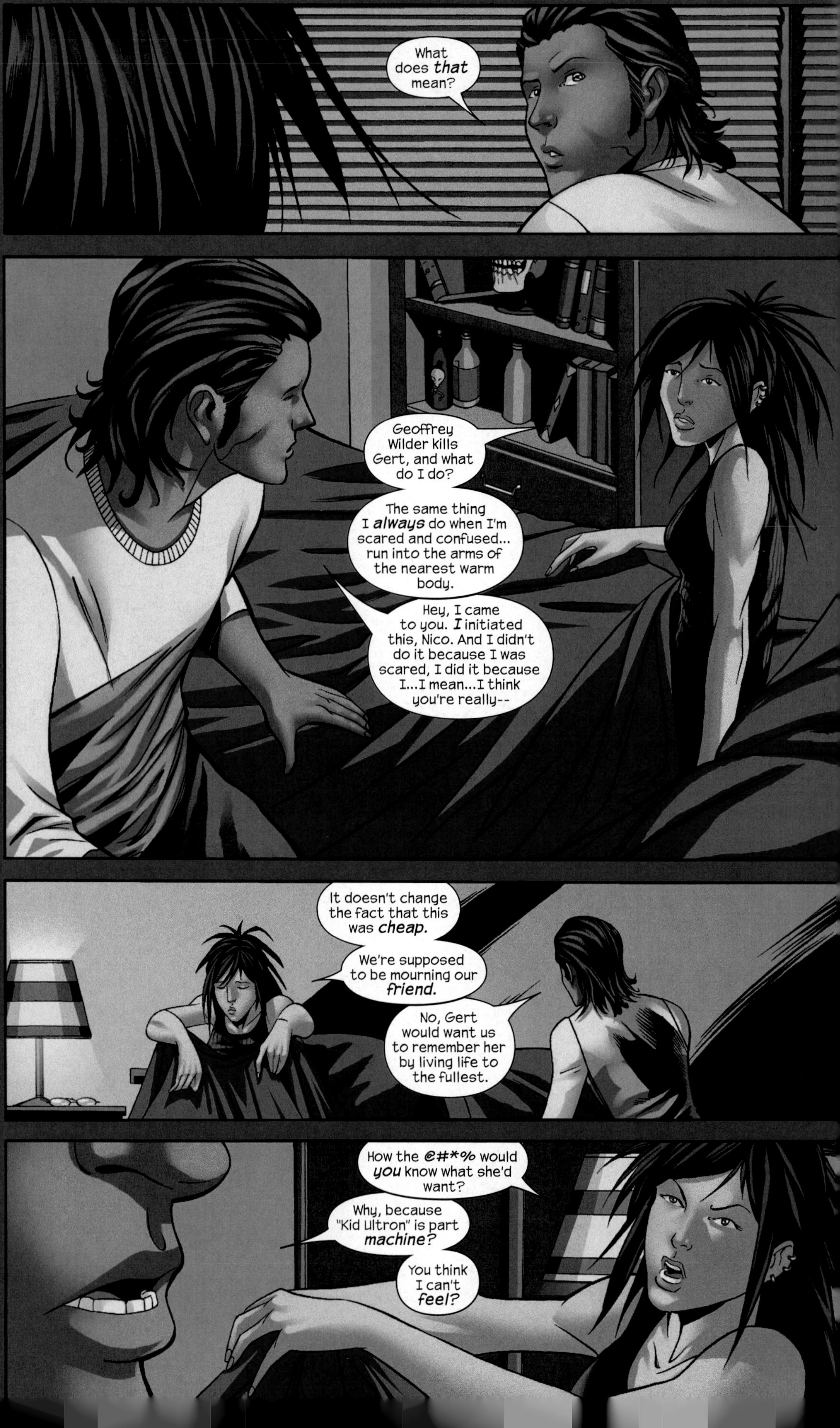
What does *that* mean?
Geoffrey Wilder kills Gert, and what do I do?
The same thing I *always* do when I'm scared and confused... run into the arms of the nearest warm body.
Hey, I came to you. *I* initiated this, Nico. And I didn't do it because I was scared, I did it because I...I mean...I think you're really--
It doesn't change the fact that this was *cheap.*
We're supposed to be mourning our *friend.*
No, Gert would want us to remember her by living life to the fullest.
How the @#*% would *you* know what she'd want?
Why, because "Kid Ultron" is part *machine?*
You think I can't *feel?*

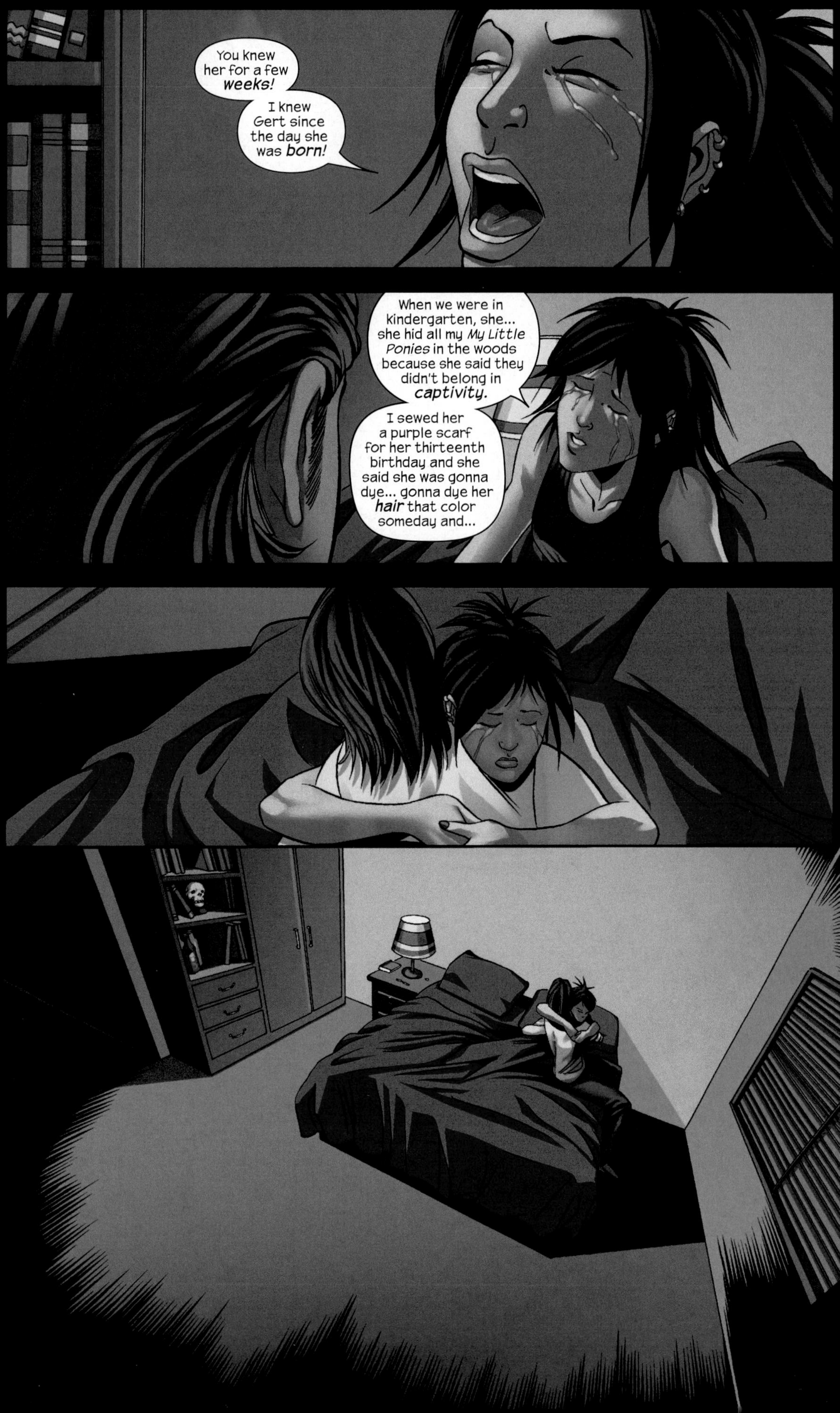
You knew her for a few *weeks!*
I knew Gert since the day she was *born!*
When we were in kindergarten, she... she hid all my *My Little Ponies* in the woods because she said they didn't belong in *captivity.*
I sewed her a purple scarf for her thirteenth birthday and she said she was gonna dye... gonna dye her **hair** that color someday and...

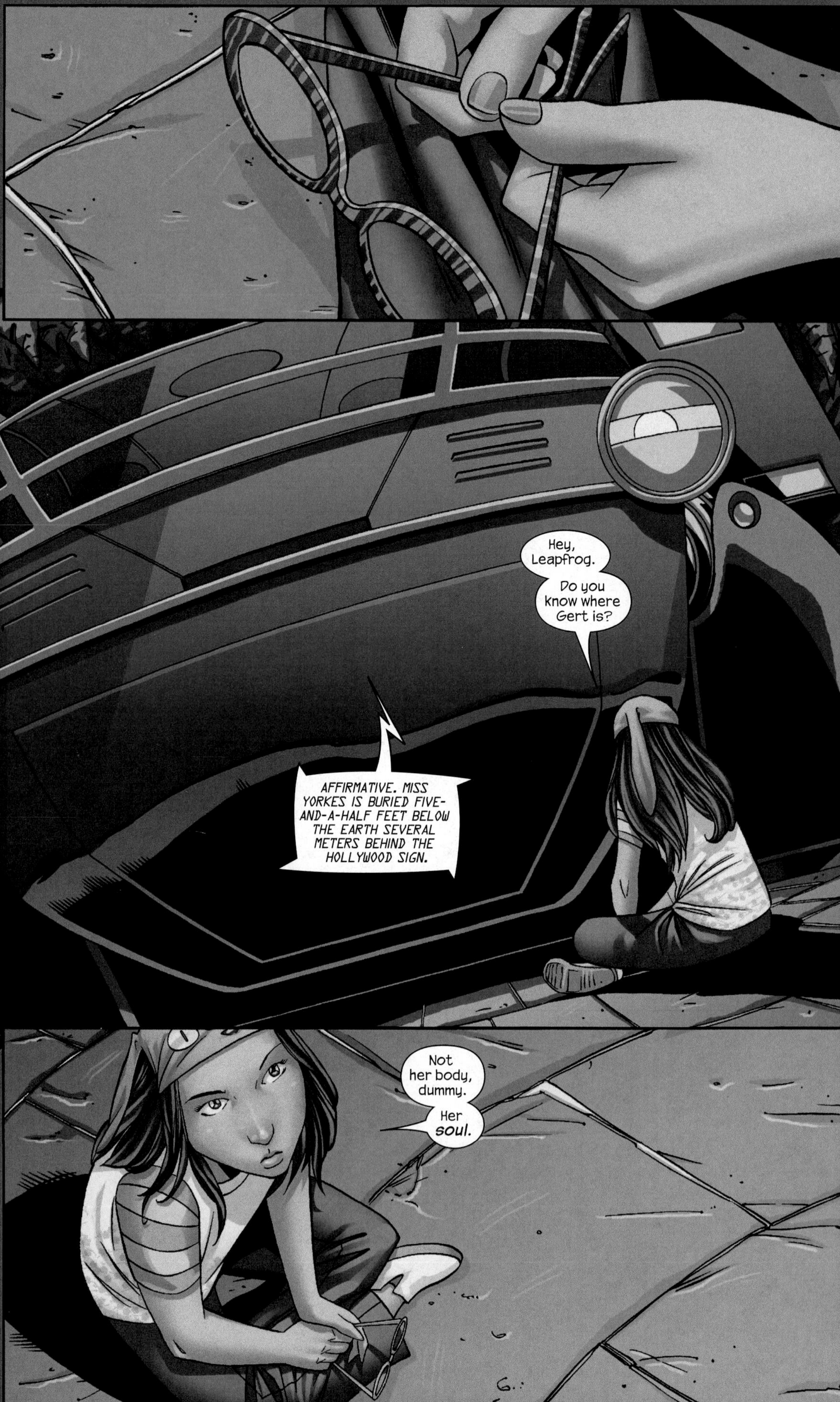
Hey, Leapfrog.
Do you know where Gert is?
AFFIRMATIVE. MISS YORKES IS BURIED FIVE-AND-A-HALF FEET BELOW THE EARTH SEVERAL METERS BEHIND THE HOLLYWOOD SIGN.
Not her body, dummy.
Her soul.

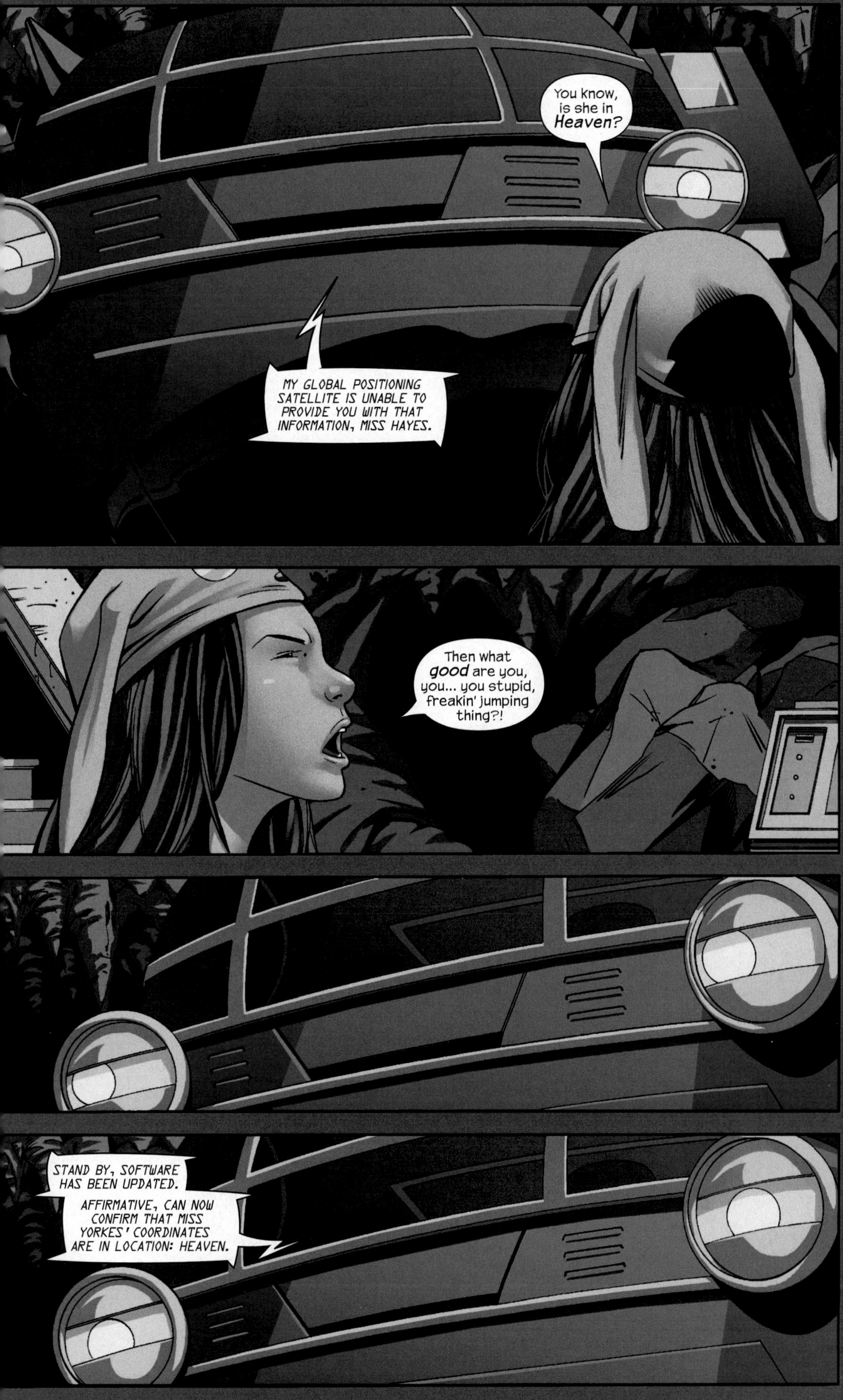

You know, is she in Heaven?
MY GLOBAL POSITIONING SATELLITE IS UNABLE TO PROVIDE YOU WITH THAT INFORMATION, MISS HAYES.
Then what good are you, you... you stupid, freakin' jumping thing?!
STAND BY, SOFTWARE HAS BEEN UPDATED.
AFFIRMATIVE, CAN NOW CONFIRM THAT MISS YORKES' COORDINATES ARE IN LOCATION: HEAVEN.

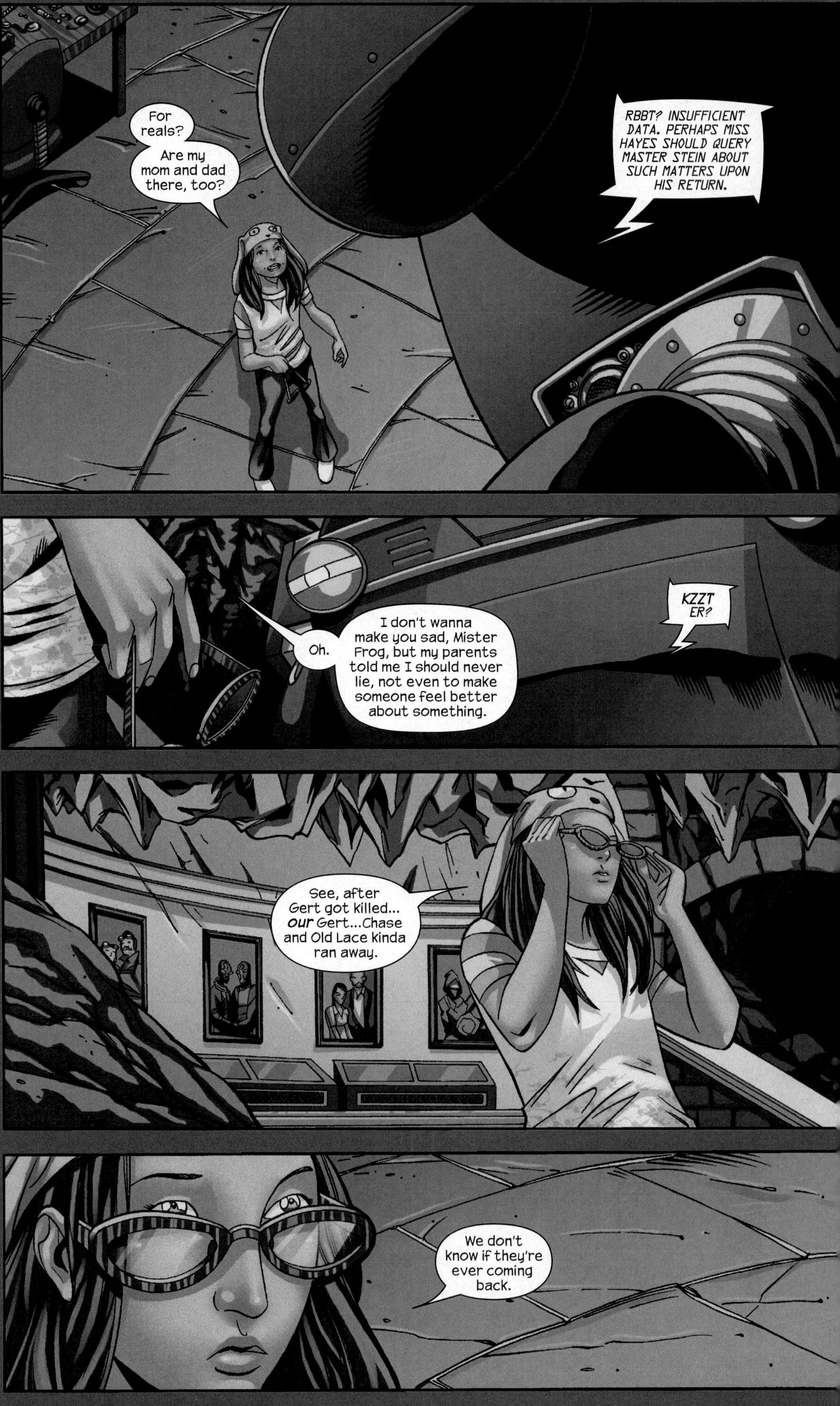
For reals?
Are my mom and dad there, too?
RBBT? INSUFFICIENT DATA. PERHAPS MISS HAYES SHOULD QUERY MASTER STEIN ABOUT SUCH MATTERS UPON HIS RETURN.
Oh.
I don't wanna make you sad, Mister Frog, but my parents told me I should never lie, not even to make someone feel better about something.
KZZT ER?
See, after Gert got killed... our Gert...Chase and Old Lace kinda ran away.
We don't know if they're ever coming back.

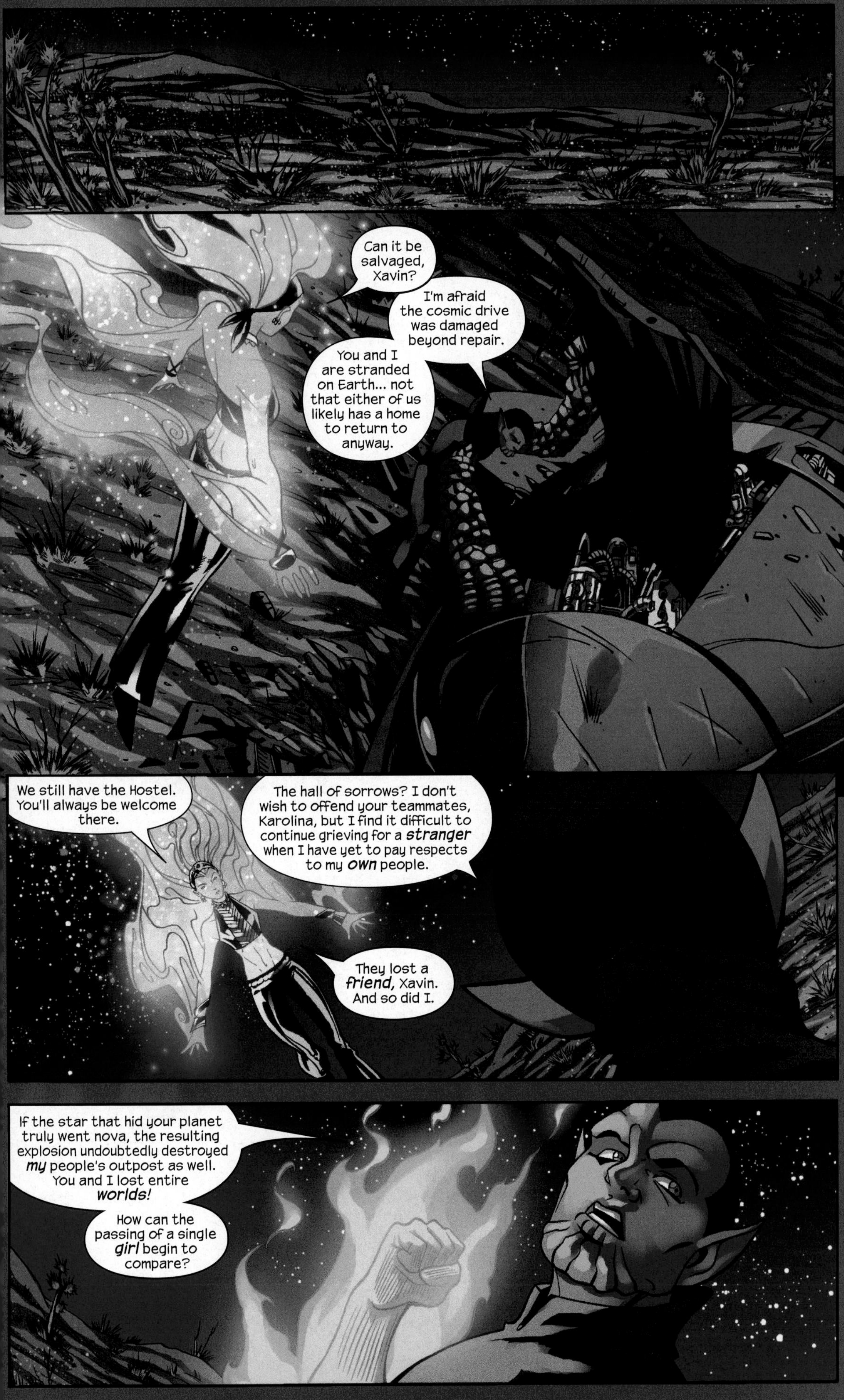

Can it be salvaged, Xavin?
I'm afraid the cosmic drive was damaged beyond repair.
You and I are stranded on Earth... not that either of us likely has a home to return to anyway.
We still have the Hostel. You'll always be welcome there.
The hall of sorrows? I don't wish to offend your teammates, Karolina, but I find it difficult to continue grieving for a stranger when I have yet to pay respects to my own people.
They lost a friend, Xavin. And so did I.
If the star that hid your planet truly went nova, the resulting explosion undoubtedly destroyed my people's outpost as well. You and I lost entire worlds!
How can the passing of a single girl begin to compare?

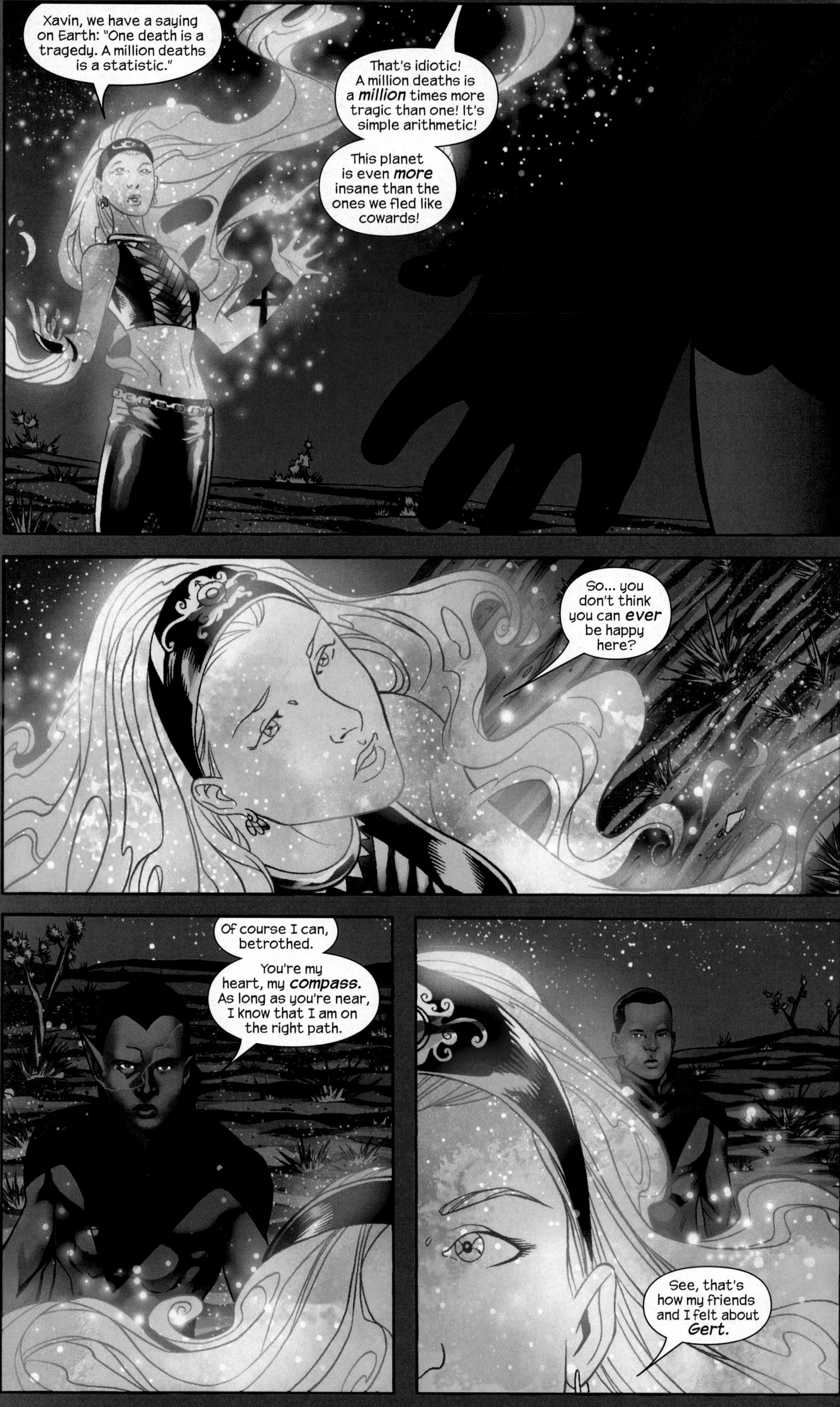

Xavin, we have a saying on Earth: "One death is a tragedy. A million deaths is a statistic."
That's idiotic! A million deaths is a *million* times more tragic than one! It's simple arithmetic!
This planet is even *more* insane than the ones we fled like cowards!
So... you don't think you can *ever* be happy here?
Of course I can, betrothed.
You're my heart, my *compass.* As long as you're near, I know that I am on the right path.
See, that's how my friends and I felt about *Gert.*

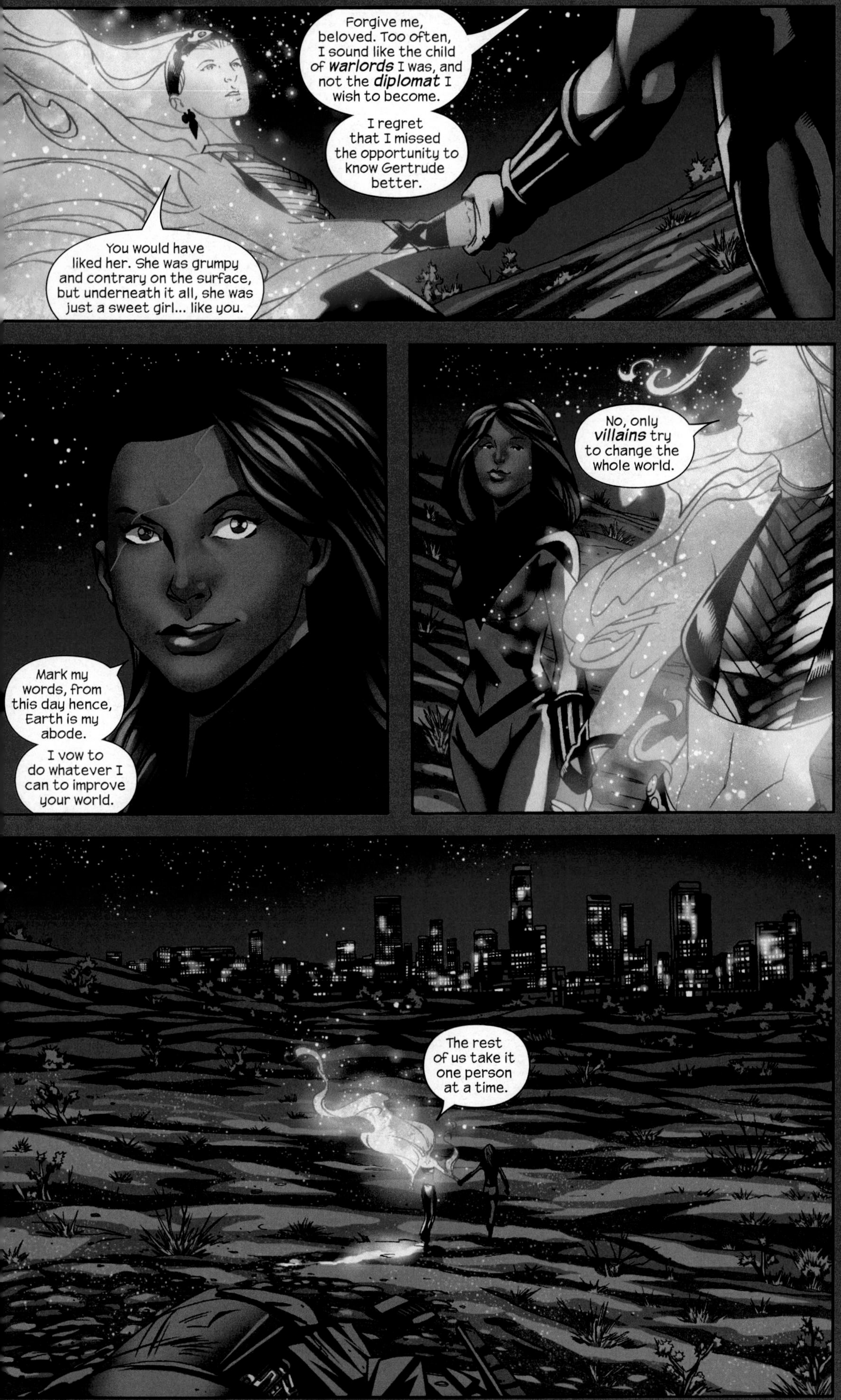

Forgive me, beloved. Too often, I sound like the child of *warlords* I was, and not the *diplomat* I wish to become.
I regret that I missed the opportunity to know Gertrude better.
You would have liked her. She was grumpy and contrary on the surface, but underneath it all, she was just a sweet girl... like you.
Mark my words, from this day hence, Earth is my abode.
I vow to do whatever I can to improve your world.
No, only *villains* try to change the whole world.
The rest of us take it one person at a time.

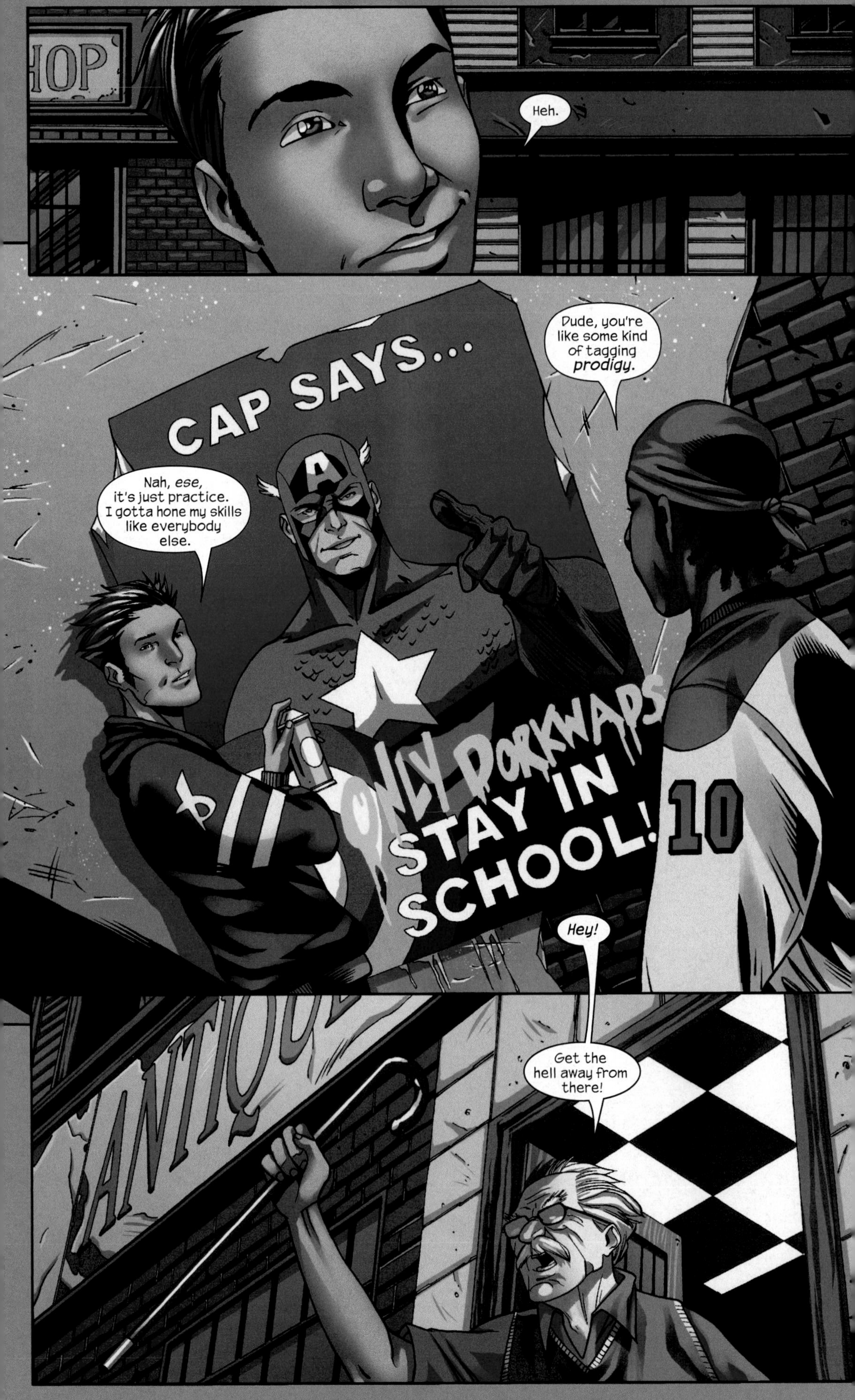
HOP
Heh.
CAP SAYS...
Dude, you're like some kind of tagging *prodigy*.
Nah, *ese*, it's just practice. I gotta hone my skills like everybody else.
ONLY DORKWADS
STAY IN SCHOOL!
10
Hey!
ANTIQUE
Get the hell away from there!

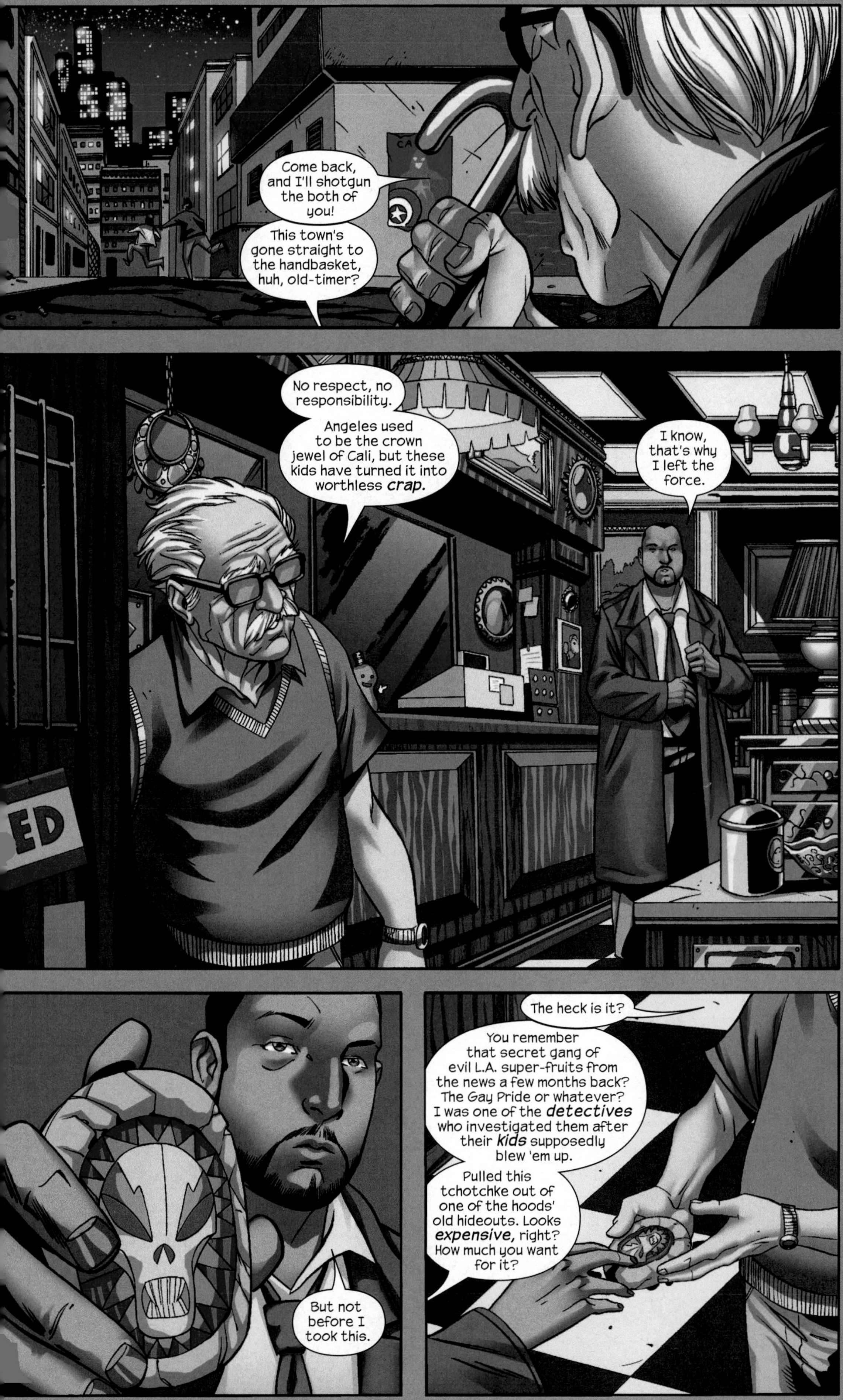
Come back, and I'll shotgun the both of you!
This town's gone straight to the handbasket, huh, old-timer?
No respect, no responsibility.
Angeles used to be the crown jewel of Cali, but these kids have turned it into worthless *crap.*
I know, that's why I left the force.
But not before I took this.
The heck is it?
You remember that secret gang of evil L.A. super-fruits from the news a few months back? The Gay Pride or whatever? I was one of the *detectives* who investigated them after their *kids* supposedly blew 'em up.
Pulled this tchotchke out of one of the hoods' old hideouts. Looks *expensive,* right? How much you want for it?

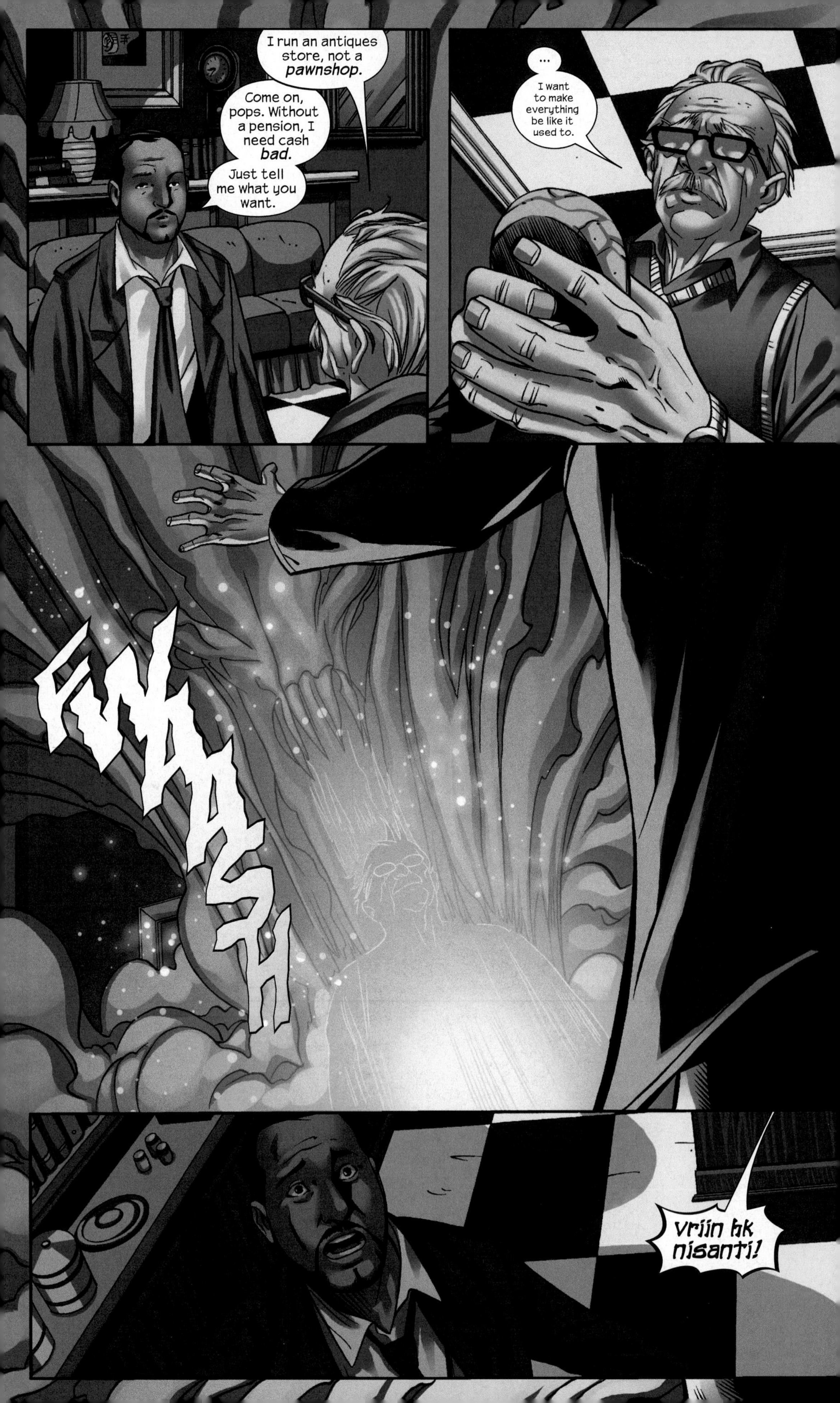
I run an antiques store, not a *pawnshop.*
Come on, pops. Without a pension, I need cash *bad.*
Just tell me what you want.
...
I want to make everything be like it used to.
FWASH
Vriin hk nisanti!

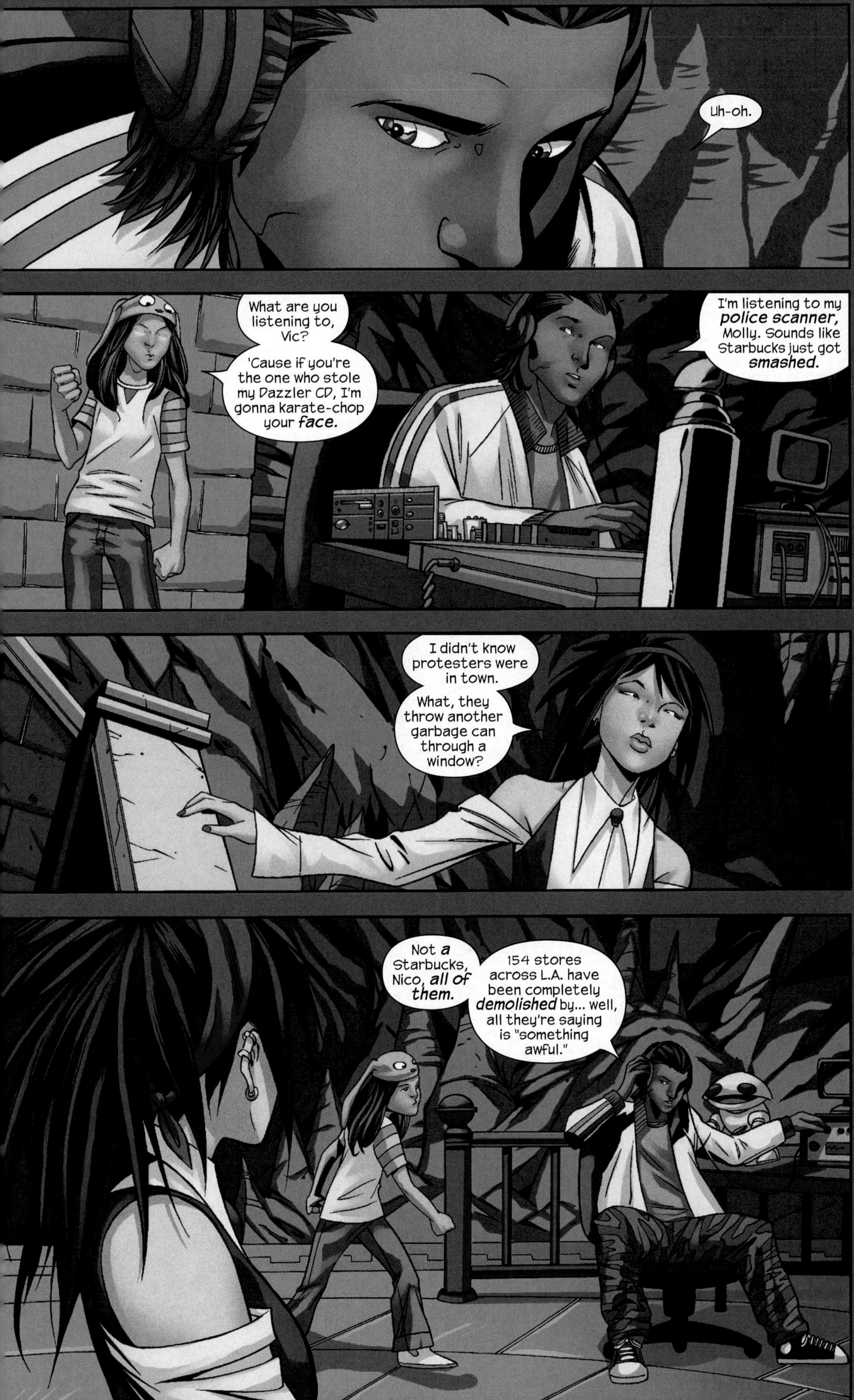
Uh-oh.
What are you listening to, Vic?
'Cause if you're the one who stole my Dazzler CD, I'm gonna karate-chop your *face.*
I'm listening to my *police scanner,* Molly. Sounds like Starbucks just got *smashed.*
I didn't know protesters were in town.
What, they throw another garbage can through a window?
Not *a* Starbucks, Nico, *all of them.*
154 stores across L.A. have been completely *demolished* by... well, all they're saying is "something awful."

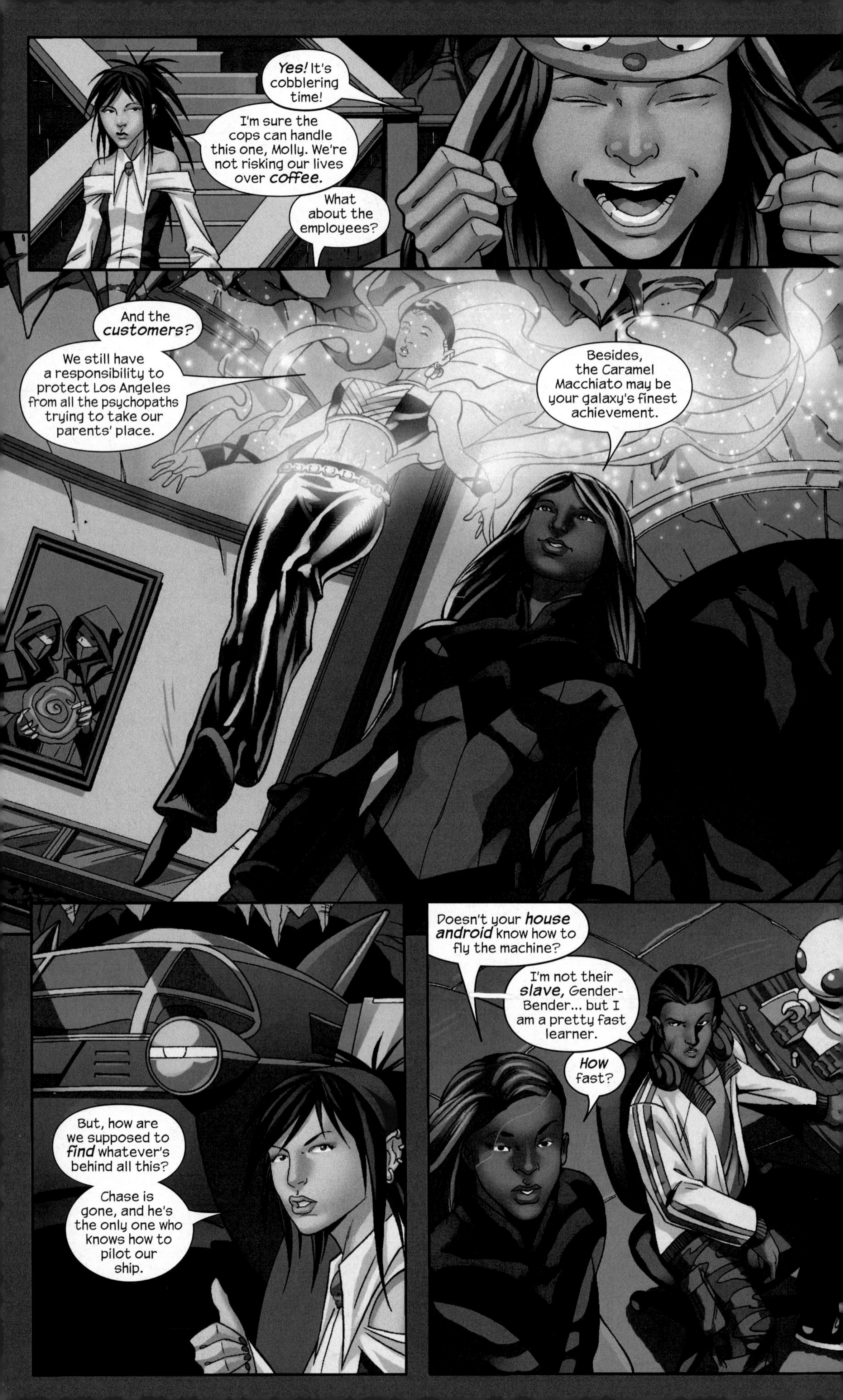
Yes! It's cobblering time!
I'm sure the cops can handle this one, Molly. We're not risking our lives over coffee.
What about the employees?
And the customers?
We still have a responsibility to protect Los Angeles from all the psychopaths trying to take our parents' place.
Besides, the Caramel Macchiato may be your galaxy's finest achievement.
But, how are we supposed to find whatever's behind all this?
Chase is gone, and he's the only one who knows how to pilot our ship.
Doesn't your house android know how to fly the machine?
I'm not their slave, Gender-Bender... but I am a pretty fast learner.
How fast?

AAAAHH!
SPRANG
AAAAHHH!
Sorry! Just a little turbulence, folks!
Um, do you know how to go *backwards,* Vic?
Not yet. Why, is that gonna be a problem?

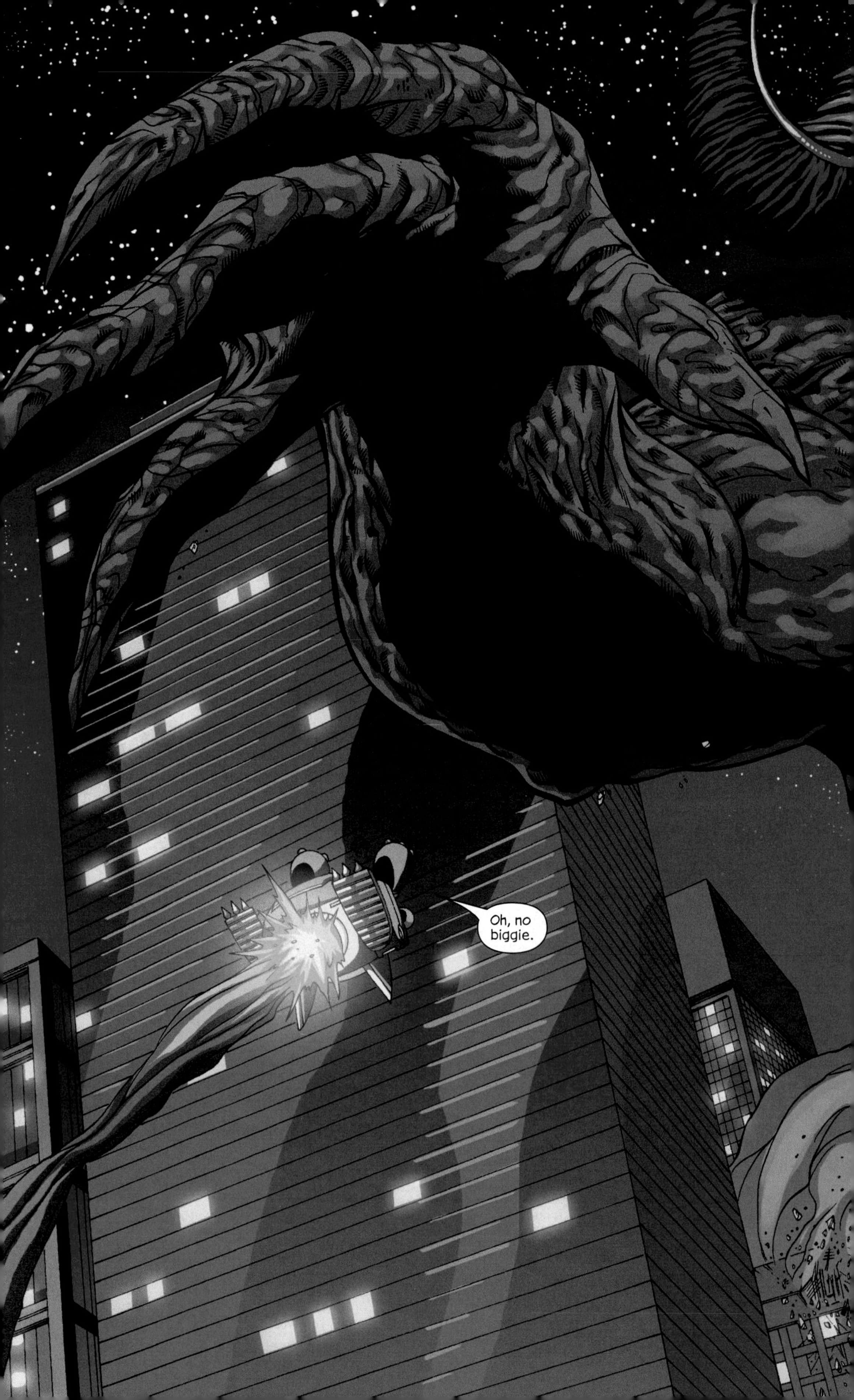
Oh, no biggie.

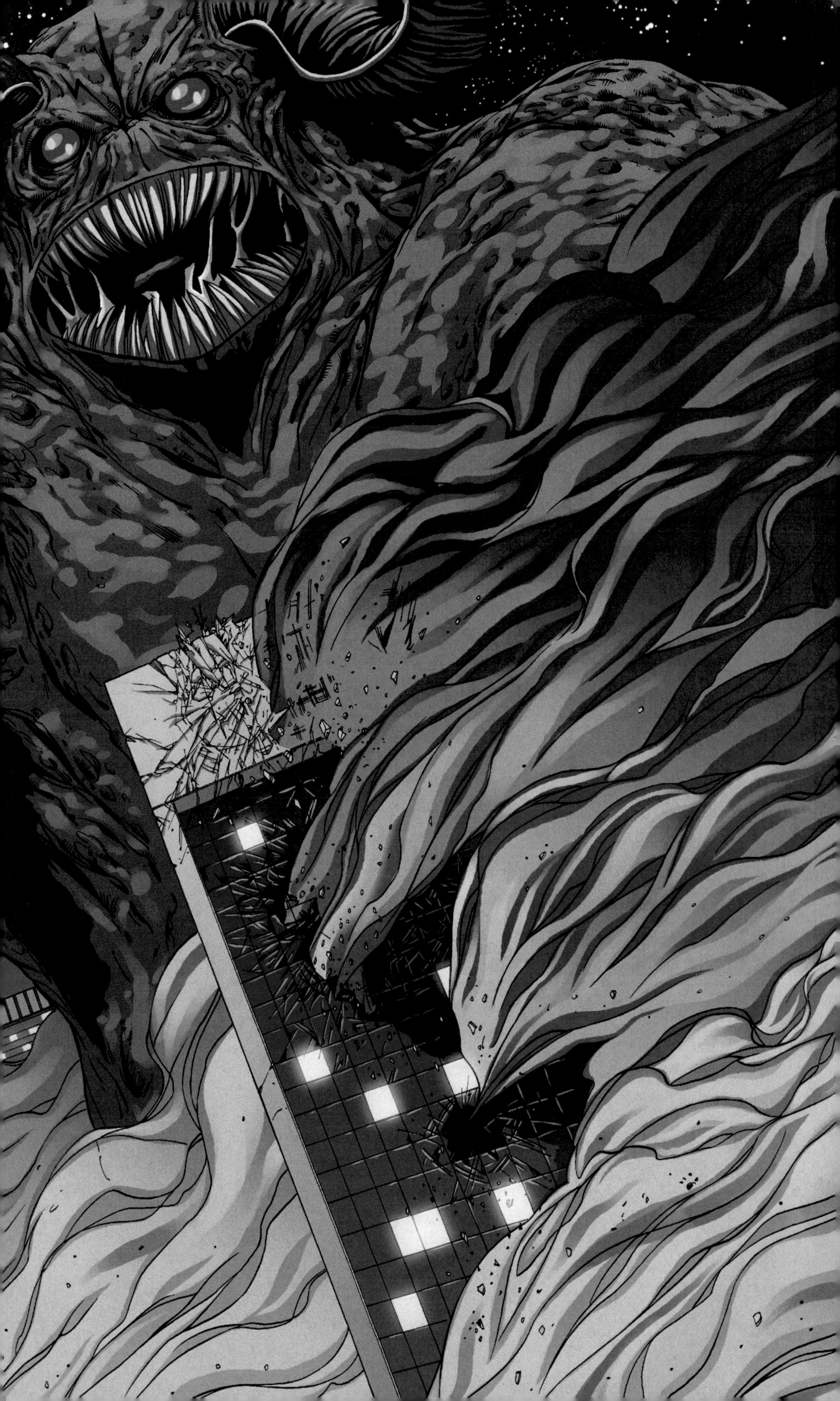

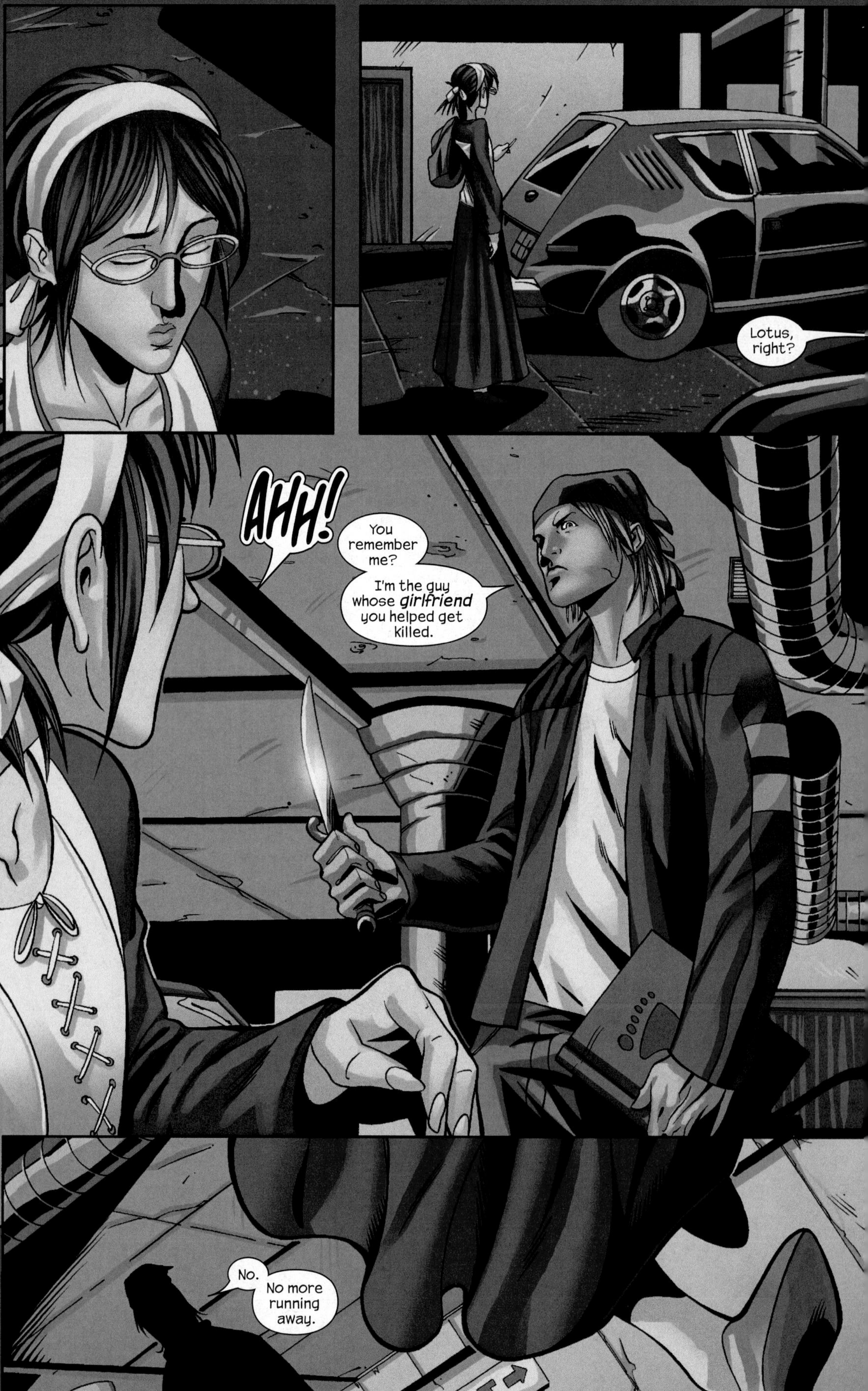
Lotus, right?
AHH!
You remember me?
I'm the guy whose *girlfriend* you helped get killed.
No.
No more running away.
EXIT

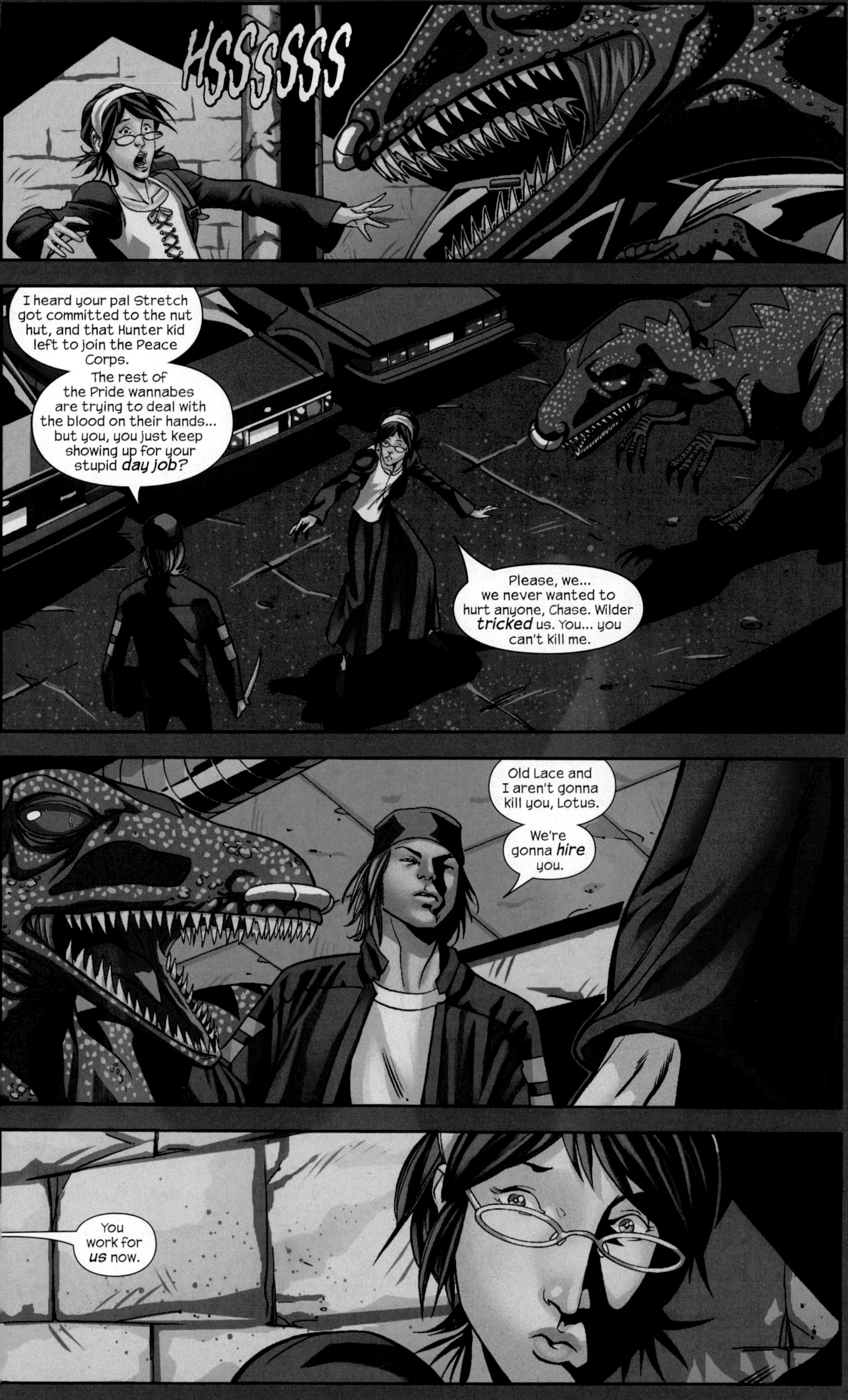
HSSSSSS
I heard your pal Stretch got committed to the nut hut, and that Hunter kid left to join the Peace Corps.
The rest of the Pride wannabes are trying to deal with the blood on their hands... but you, you just keep showing up for your stupid *day job?*
Please, we... we never wanted to hurt anyone, Chase. Wilder *tricked* us. You... you can't kill me.
Old Lace and I aren't gonna kill you, Lotus.
We're gonna *hire* you.
You work for *us* now.

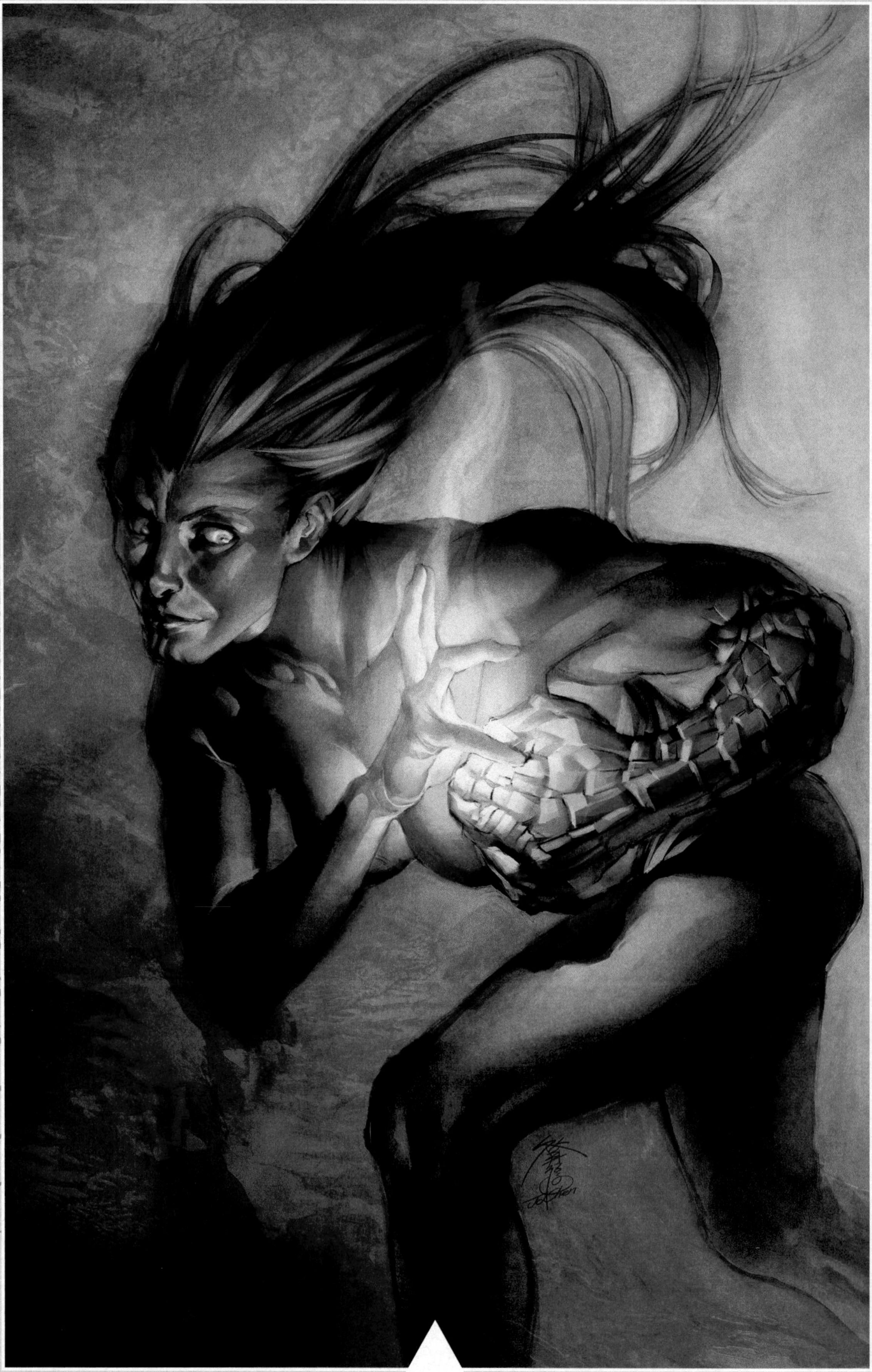

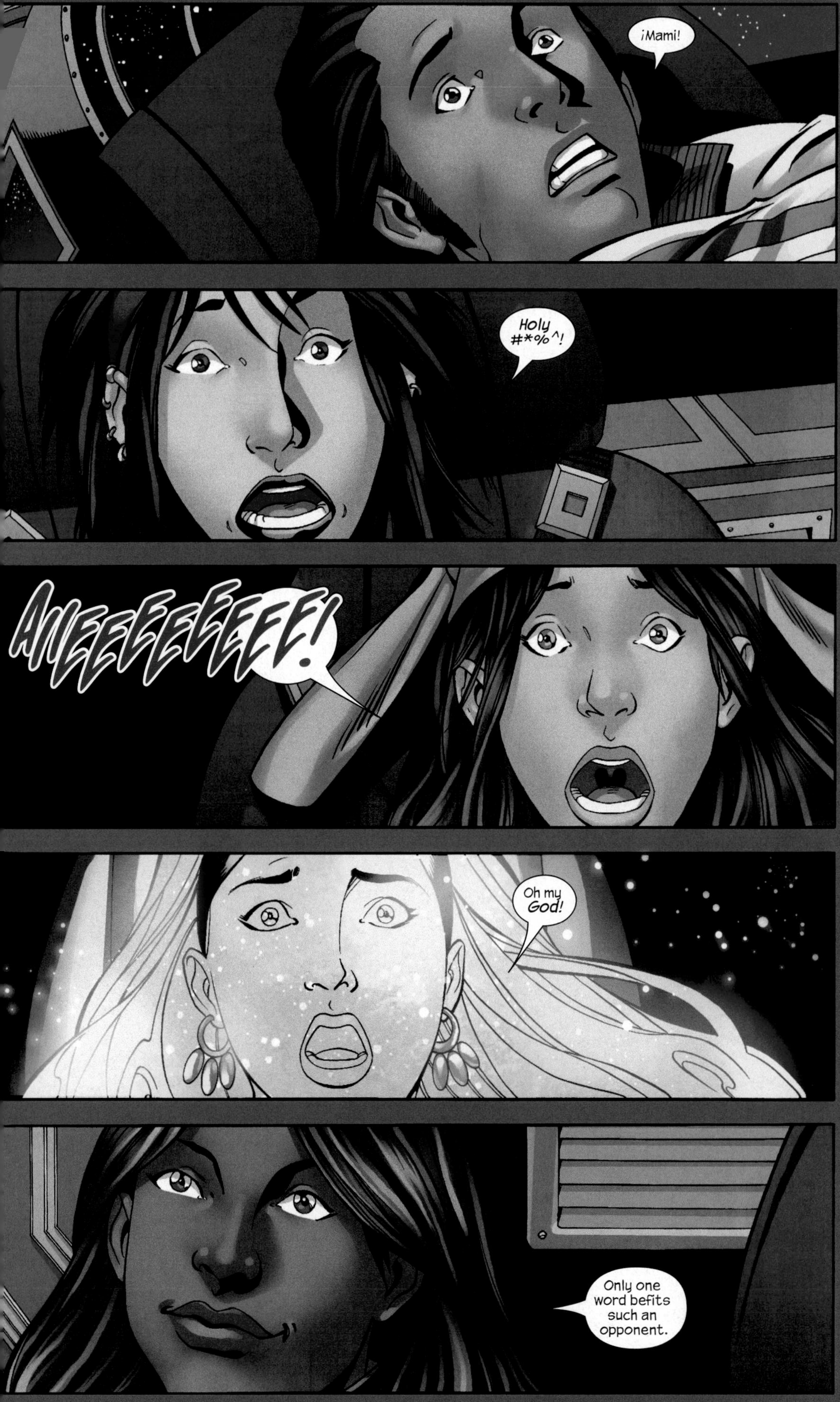
¡Mami!
Holy #*%^!
AIIEEEEEEEEE!
Oh my God!
Only one word befits such an opponent.

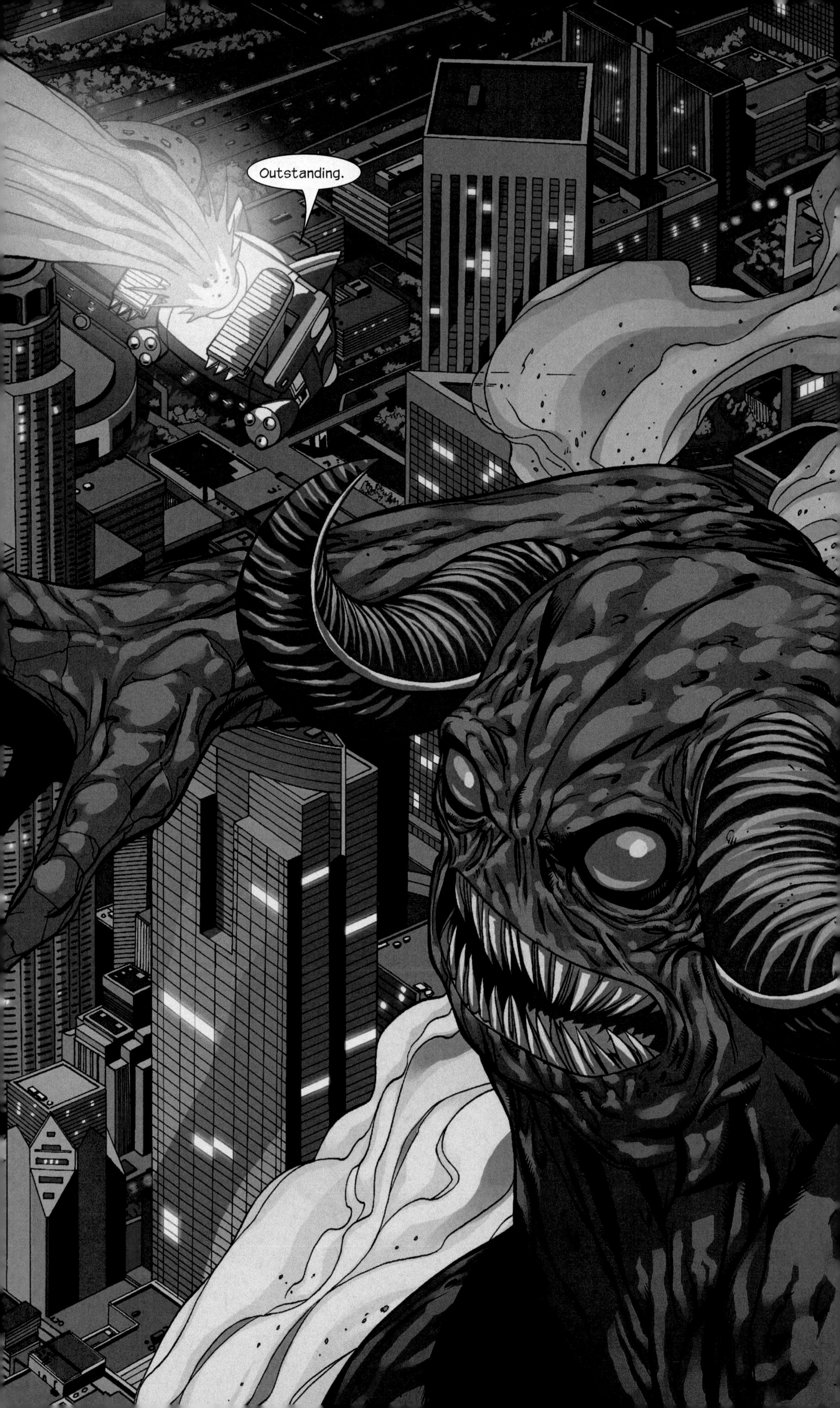
Outstanding.

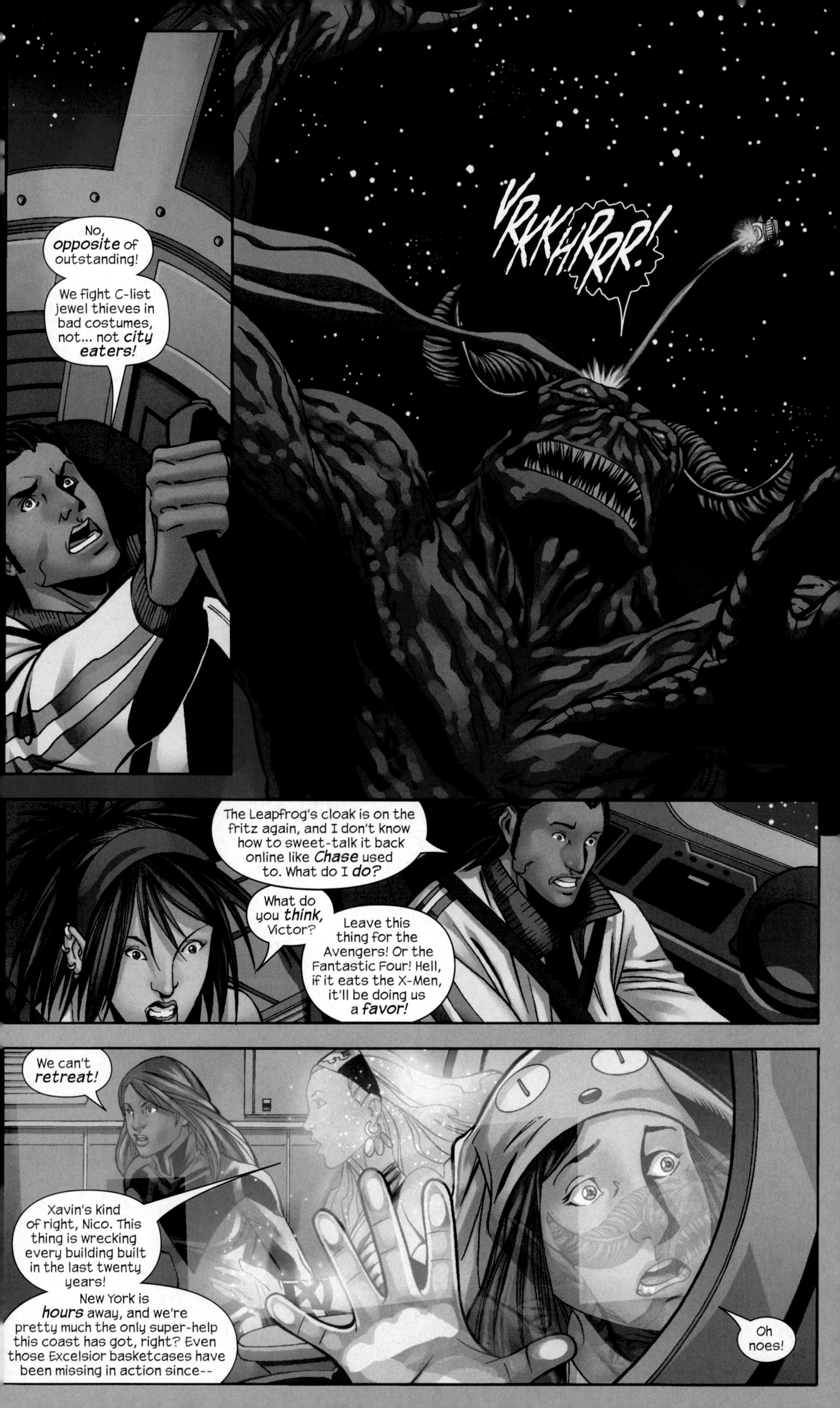

No, opposite of outstanding!
We fight C-list jewel thieves in bad costumes, not... not city eaters!
VRKKHRRR!
The Leapfrog's cloak is on the fritz again, and I don't know how to sweet-talk it back online like Chase used to. What do I do?
What do you think, Victor?
Leave this thing for the Avengers! Or the Fantastic Four! Hell, if it eats the X-Men, it'll be doing us a favor!
We can't retreat!
Xavin's kind of right, Nico. This thing is wrecking every building built in the last twenty years!
New York is hours away, and we're pretty much the only super-help this coast has got, right? Even those Excelsior basketcases have been missing in action since--
Oh noes!

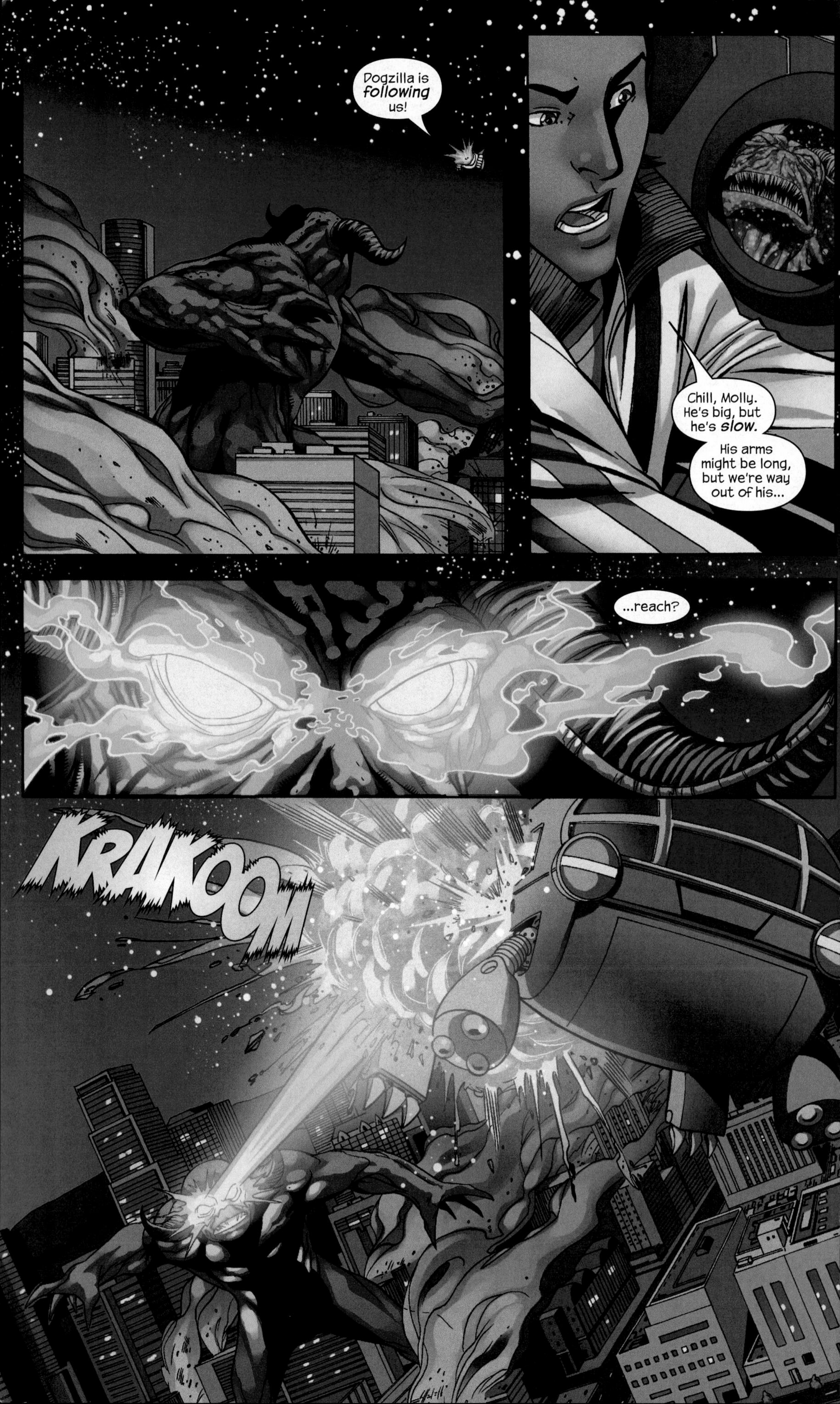
Dogzilla is following us!
Chill, Molly. He's big, but he's slow.
His arms might be long, but we're way out of his...
...reach?
KRAKOOM

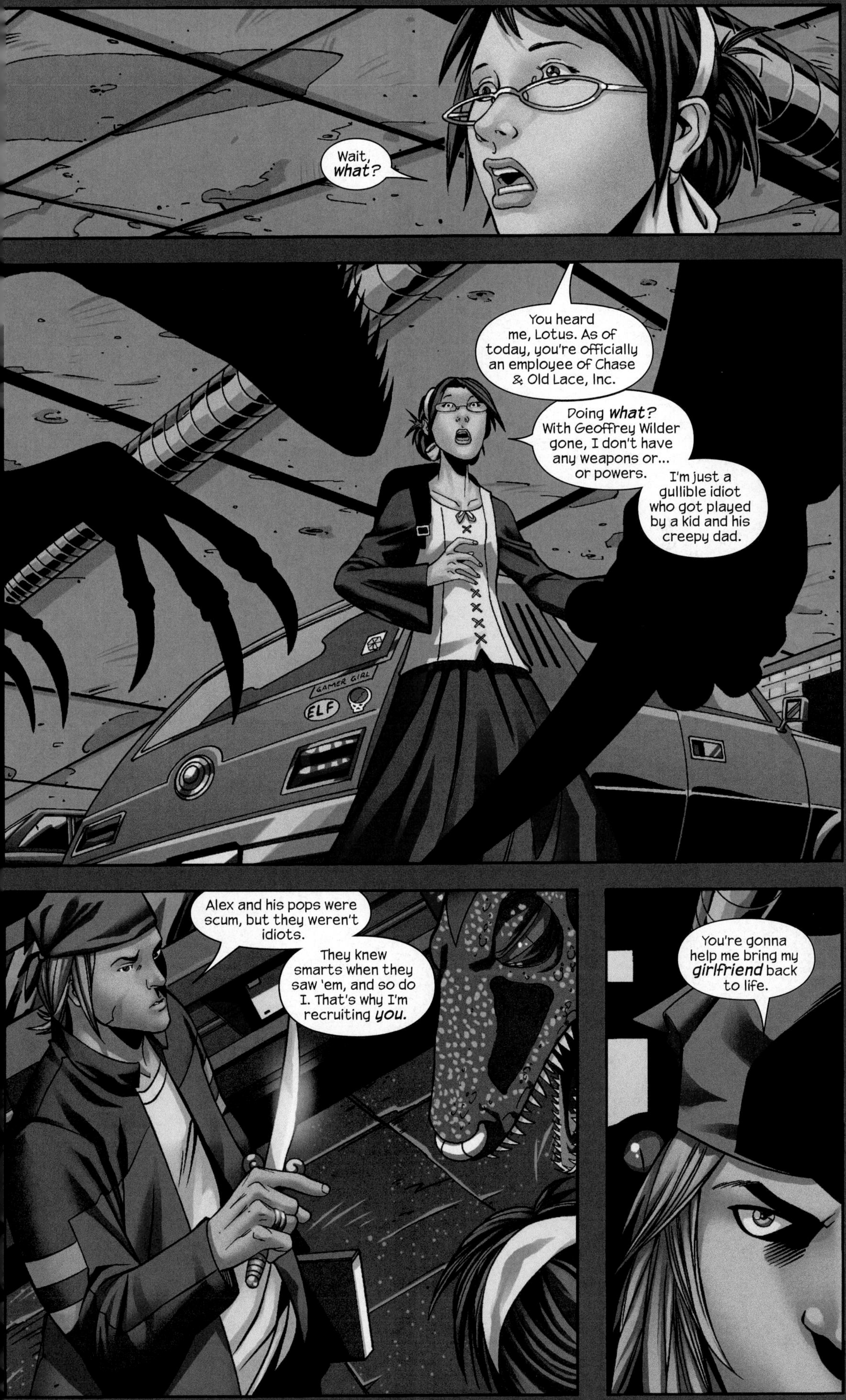

Wait, *what?*
You heard me, Lotus. As of today, you're officially an employee of Chase & Old Lace, Inc.
Doing *what?* With Geoffrey Wilder gone, I don't have any weapons or... or powers.
I'm just a gullible idiot who got played by a kid and his creepy dad.
GAMER GIRL
ELF
Alex and his pops were scum, but they weren't idiots.
They knew smarts when they saw 'em, and so do I. That's why I'm recruiting *you.*
You're gonna help me bring my *girlfriend* back to life.

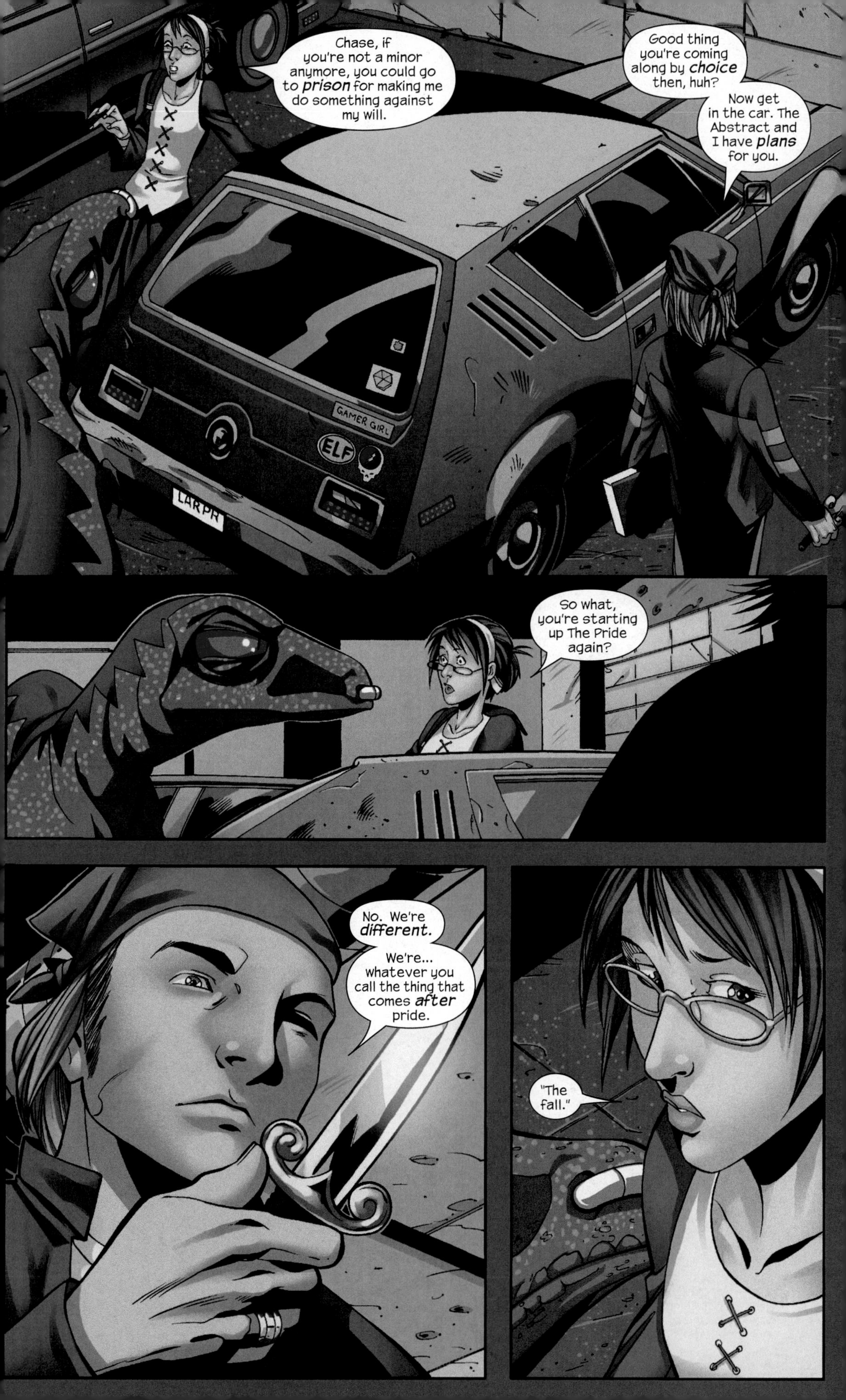
Chase, if you're not a minor anymore, you could go to *prison* for making me do something against my will.
Good thing you're coming along by *choice* then, huh?
Now get in the car. The Abstract and I have *plans* for you.
GAMER GIRL
ELF
LARPR
So what, you're starting up The Pride again?
No. We're *different*.
We're... whatever you call the thing that comes *after* pride.
"The fall."

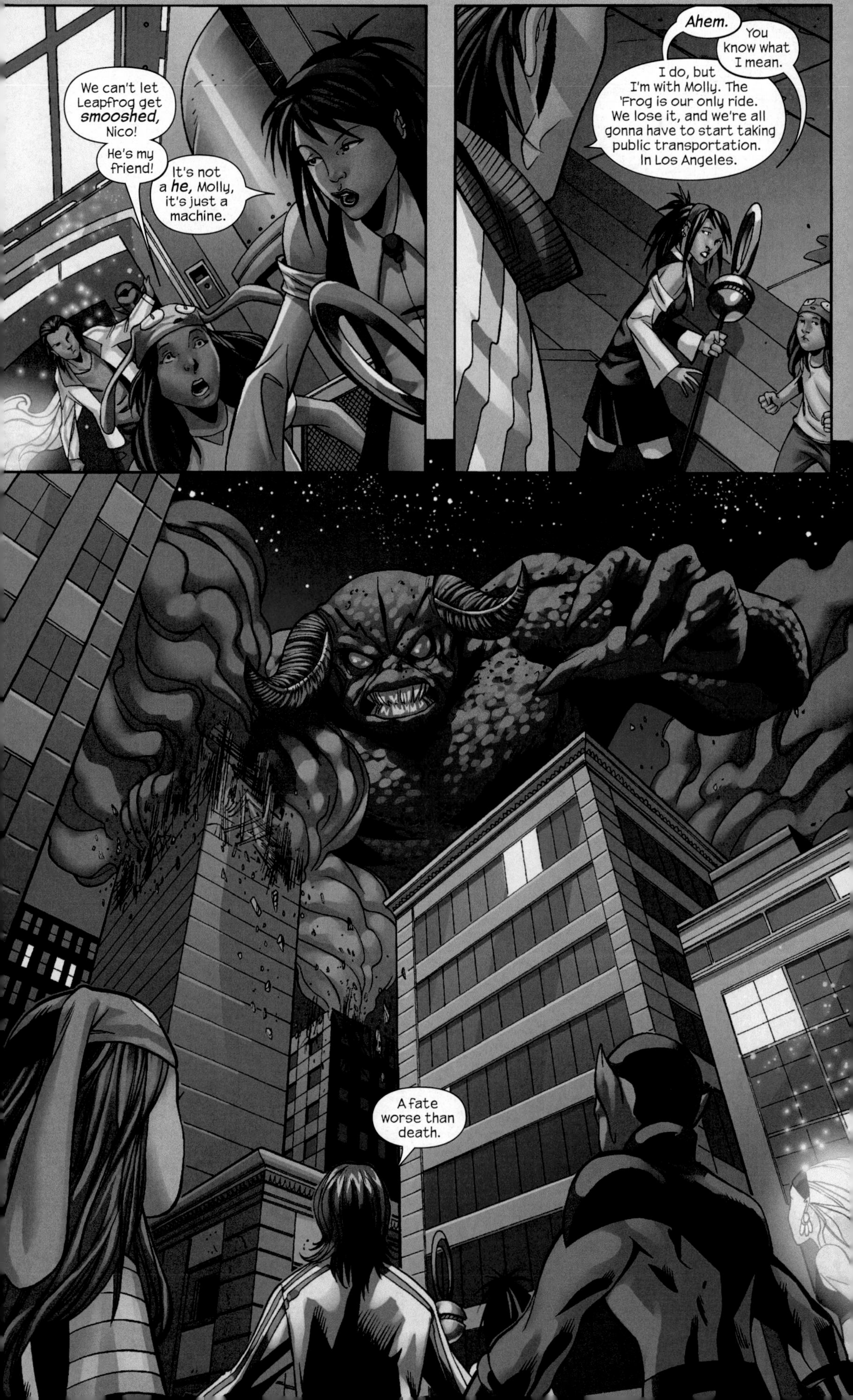
We can't let Leapfrog get *smooshed,* Nico!
He's my friend!
It's not a *he,* Molly, it's just a machine.
I do, but I'm with Molly. The 'Frog is our only ride. We lose it, and we're all gonna have to start taking public transportation. In Los Angeles.
Ahem.
You know what I mean.
A fate worse than death.

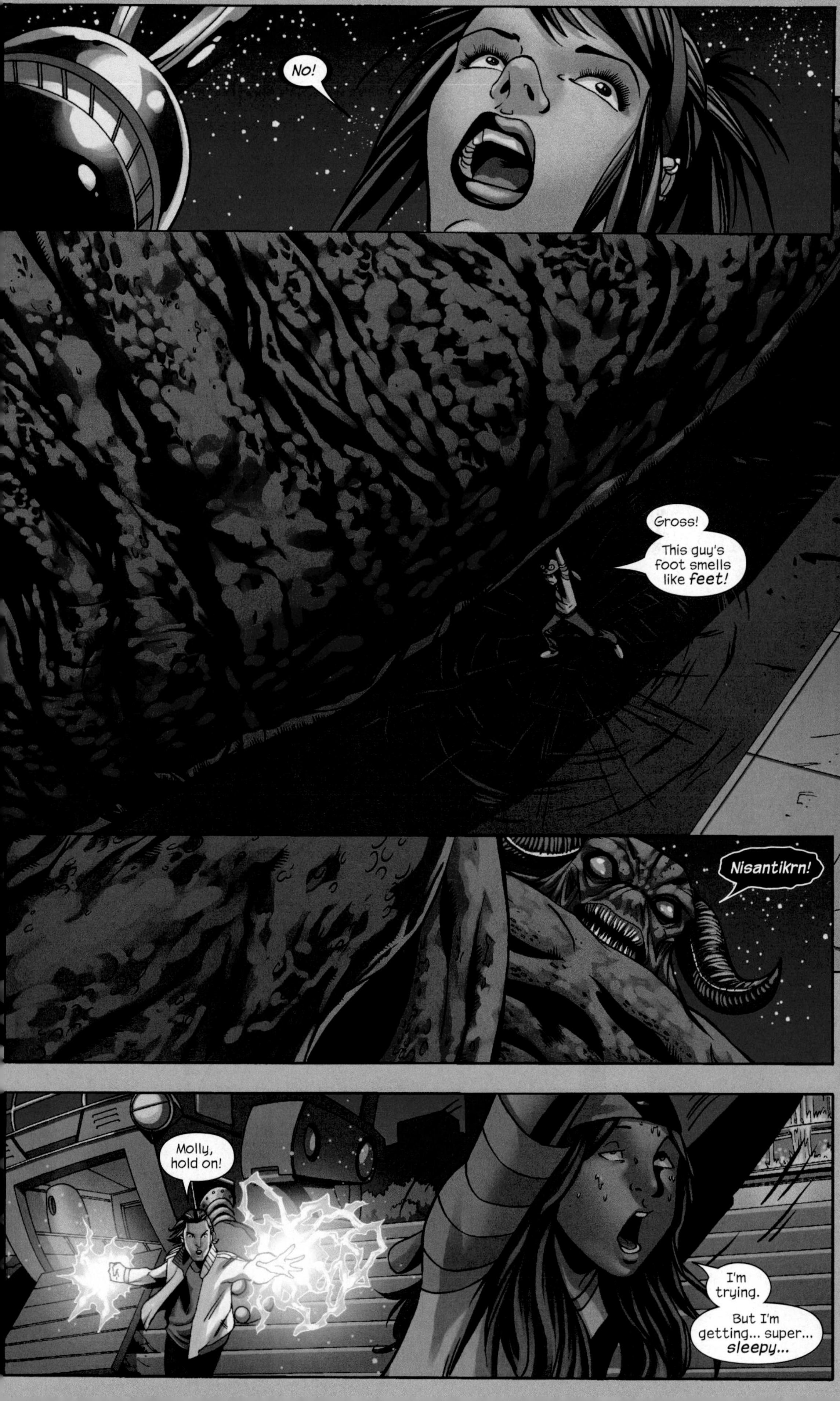
No!
Gross!
This guy's foot smells like *feet!*
Nisantikrn!
Molly, hold on!
I'm trying.
But I'm getting... super... *sleepy...*

I'm on it.

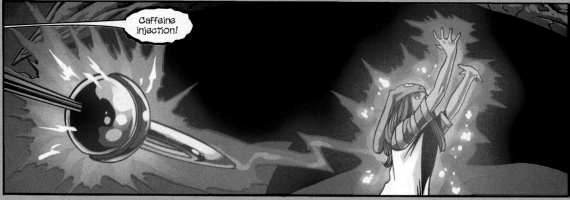

Caffeine injection!

Heh.

It's like my heart is having a pizza party.

YA HHOOOOOO!

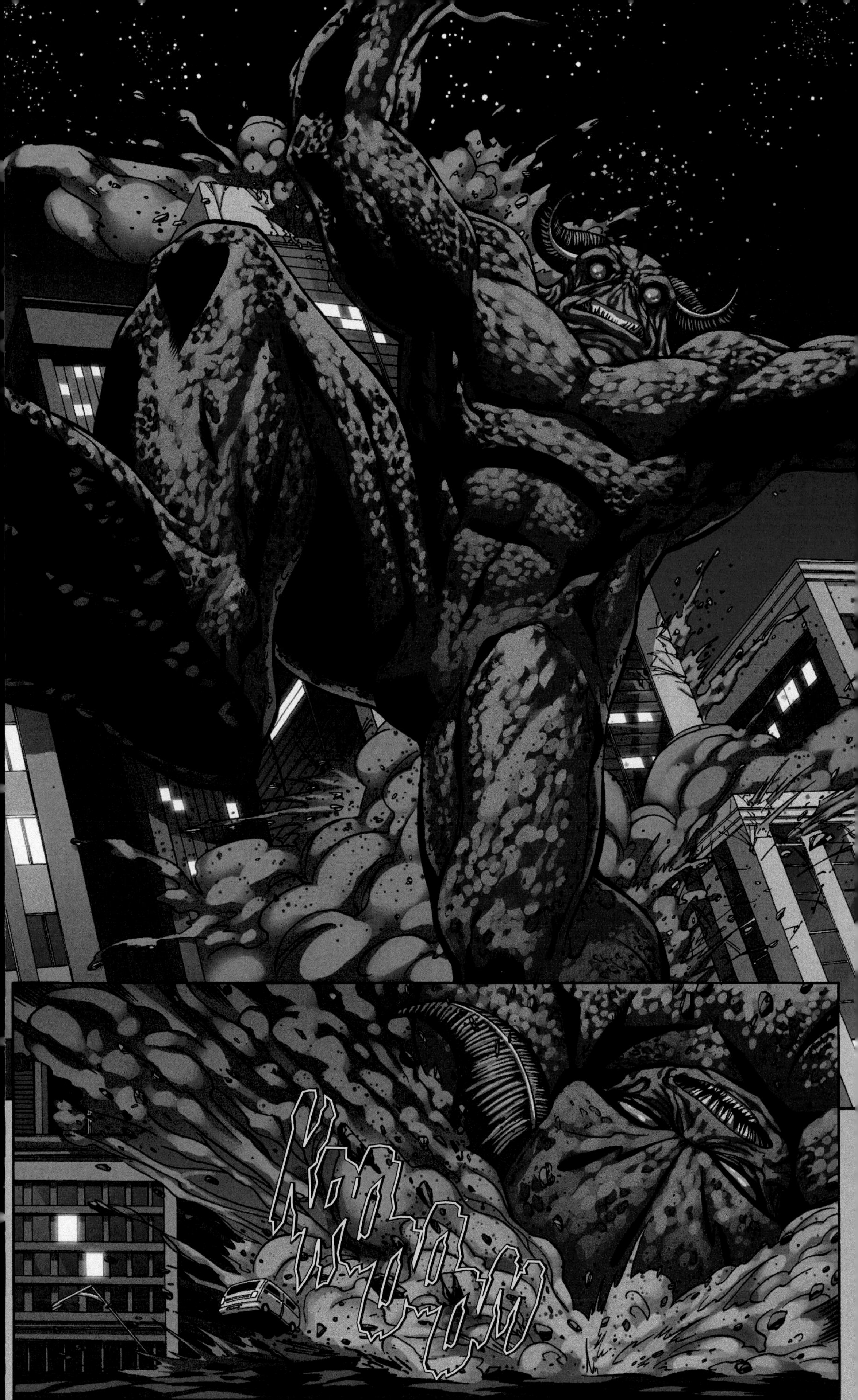

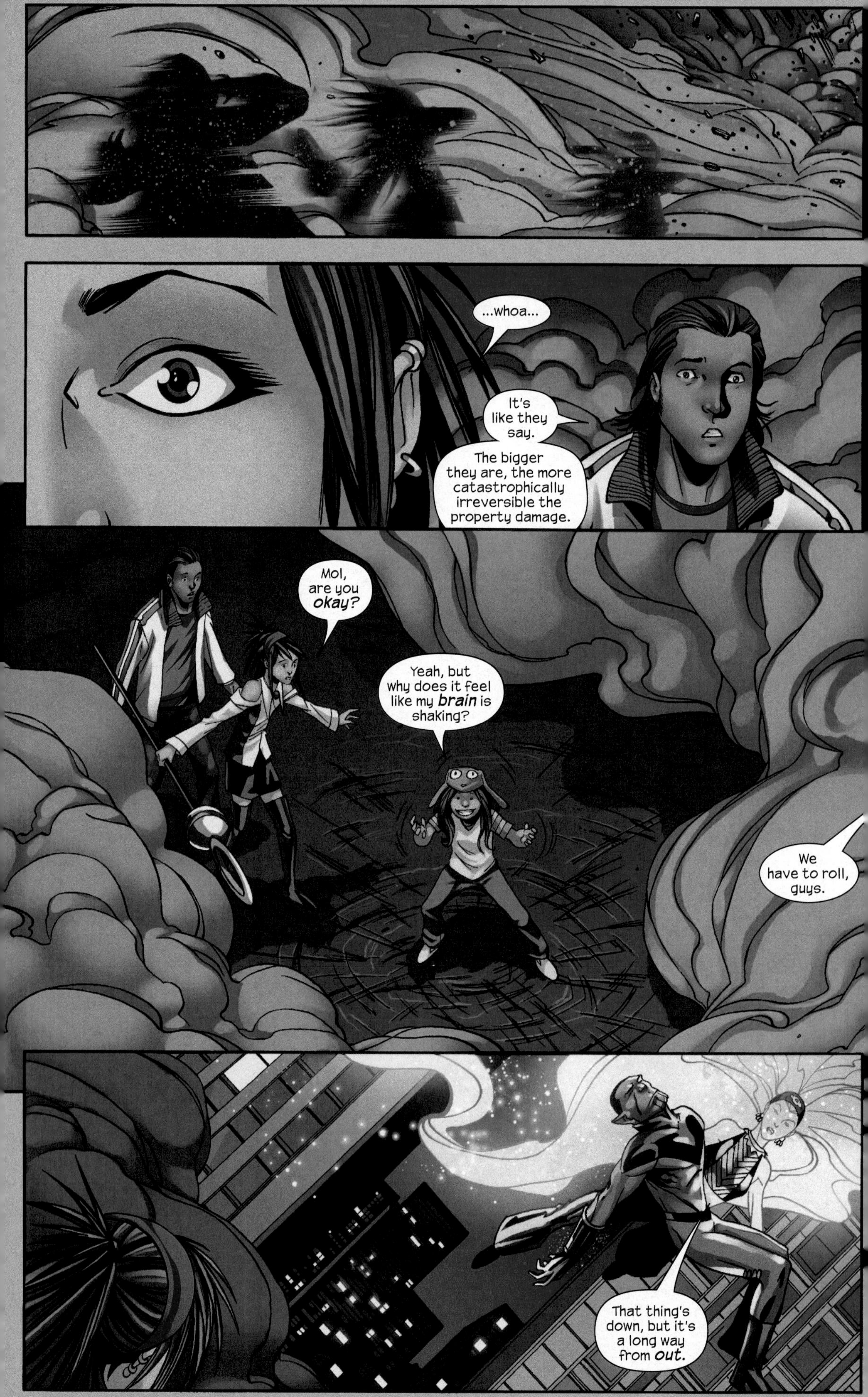
...whoa...
It's like they say.
The bigger they are, the more catastrophically irreversible the property damage.
Mol, are you *okay*?
Yeah, but why does it feel like my *brain* is shaking?
We have to roll, guys.
That thing's down, but it's a long way from *out.*

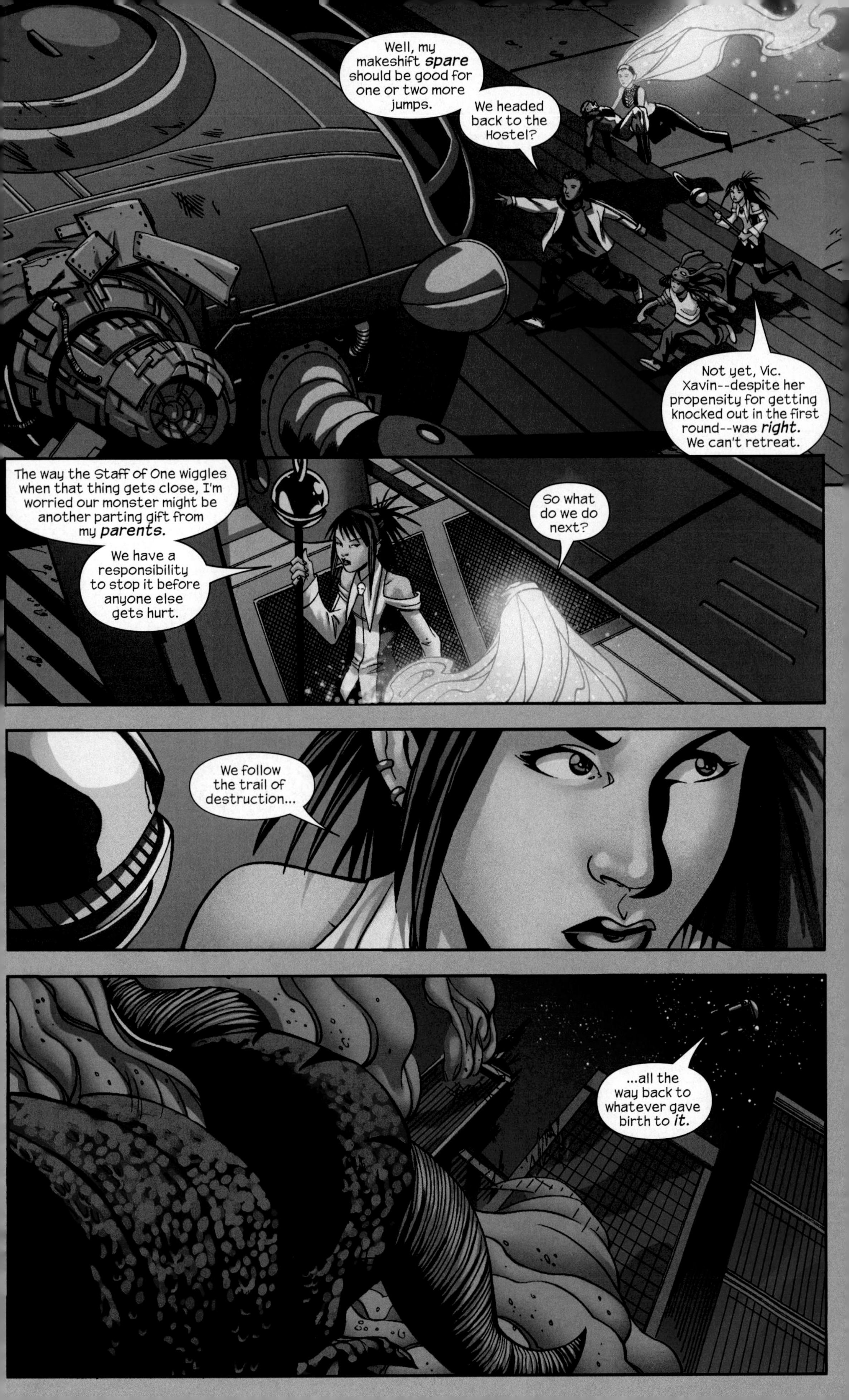
Well, my makeshift *spare* should be good for one or two more jumps.
We headed back to the Hostel?
Not yet, Vic. Xavin--despite her propensity for getting knocked out in the first round--was *right.* We can't retreat.
The way the Staff of One wiggles when that thing gets close, I'm worried our monster might be another parting gift from my *parents.*
We have a responsibility to stop it before anyone else gets hurt.
So what do we do next?
We follow the trail of destruction...
...all the way back to whatever gave birth to *it.*

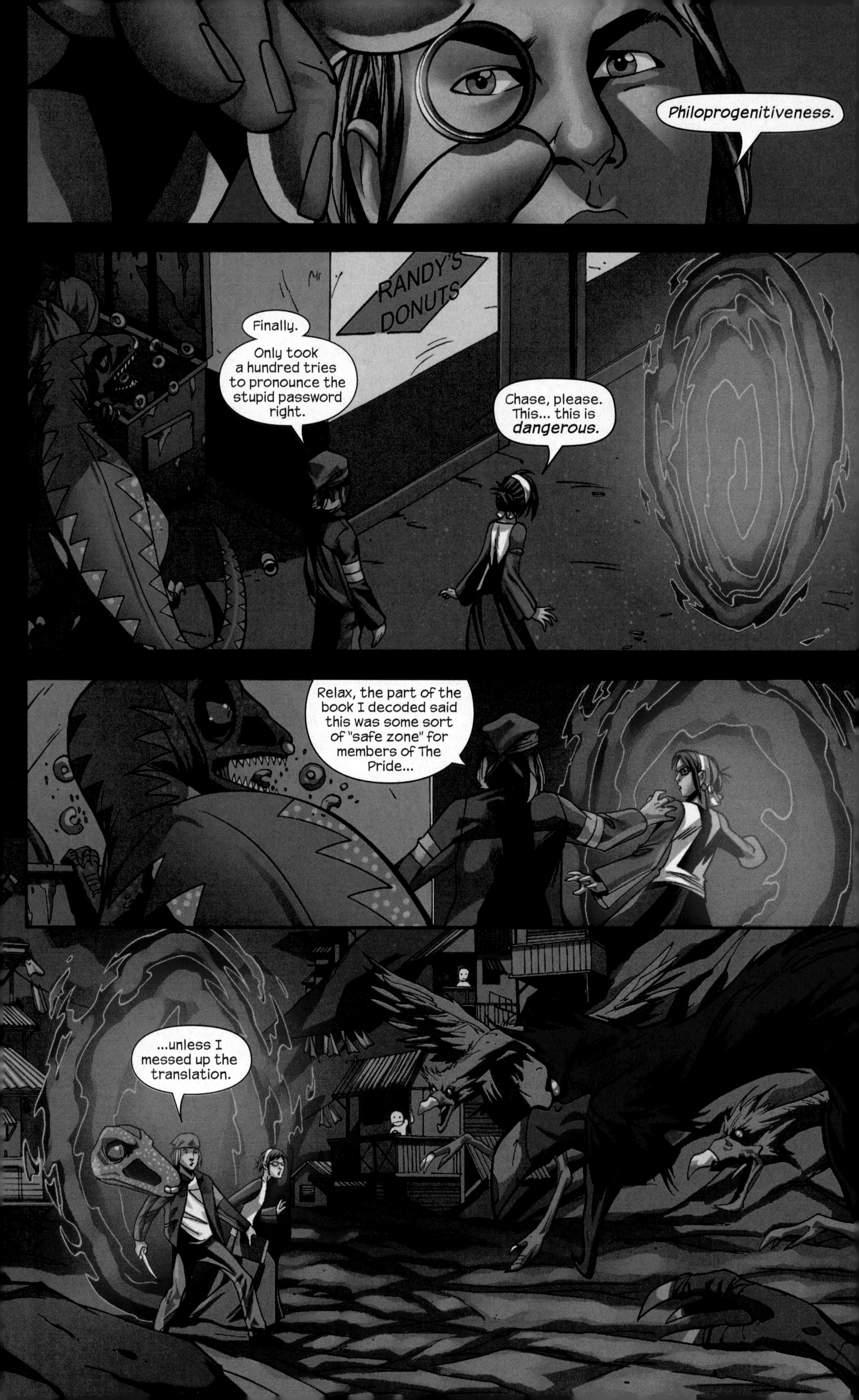
Philoprogenitiveness.
RANDY'S DONUTS
Finally.
Only took a hundred tries to pronounce the stupid password right.
Chase, please. This... this is dangerous.
Relax, the part of the book I decoded said this was some sort of "safe zone" for members of The Pride...
...unless I messed up the translation.

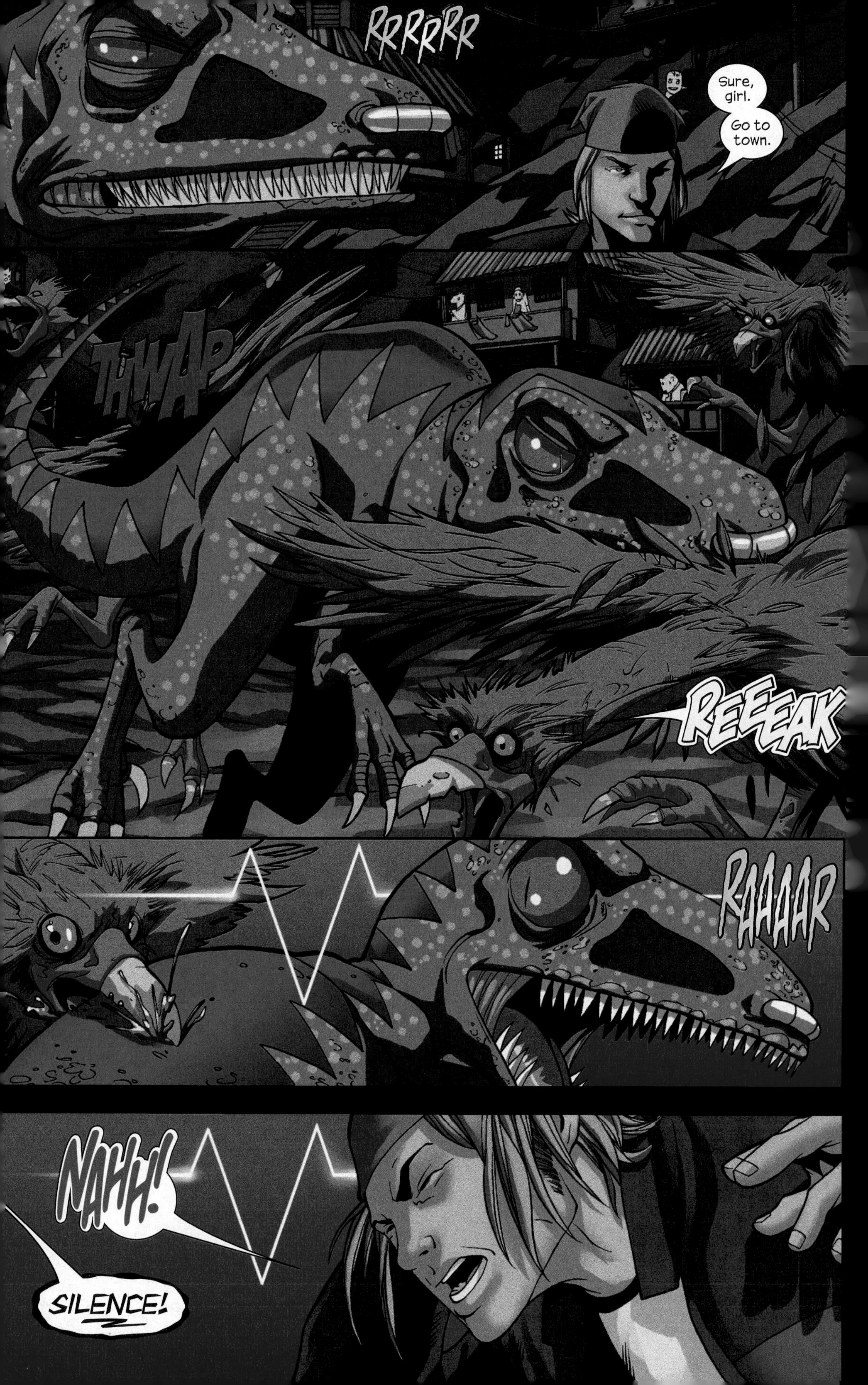
RRRRRR
Sure, girl.
Go to town.
THWAP
REEEAK
RAAAAR
NAHH!
SILENCE!

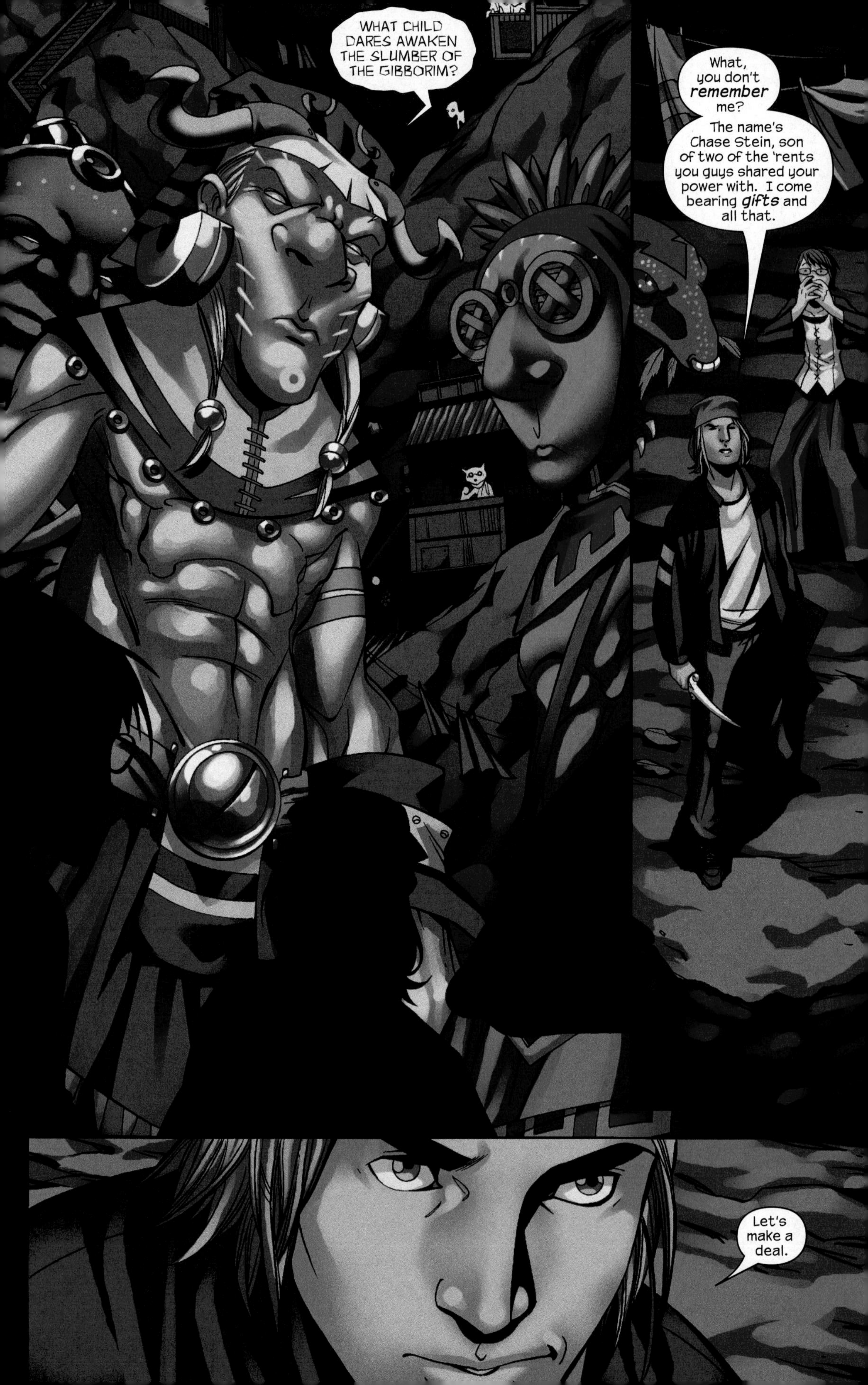
WHAT CHILD DARES AWAKEN THE SLUMBER OF THE GIBBORIM?
What, you don't remember me?
The name's Chase Stein, son of two of the 'rents you guys shared your power with. I come bearing gifts and all that.
Let's make a deal.

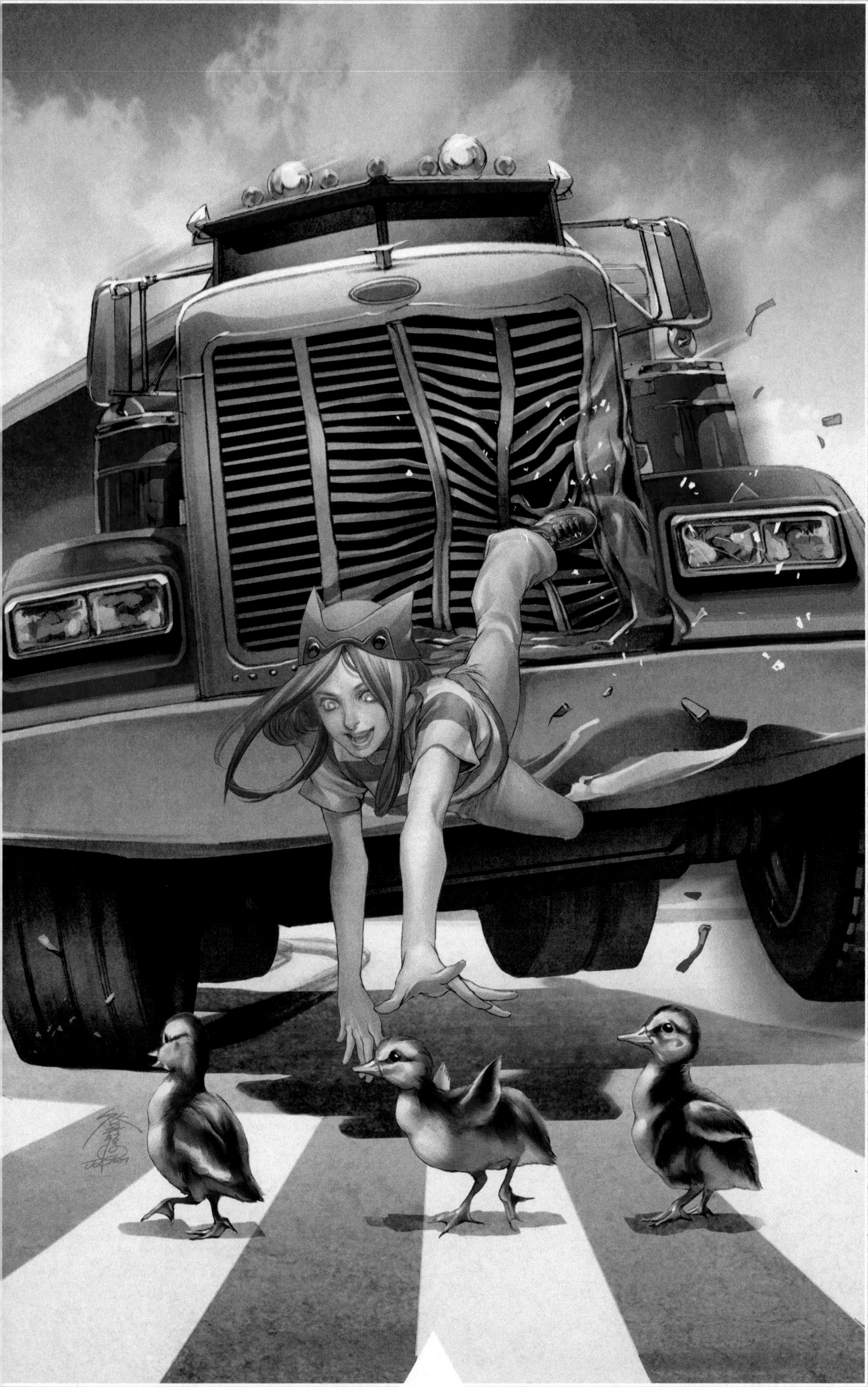

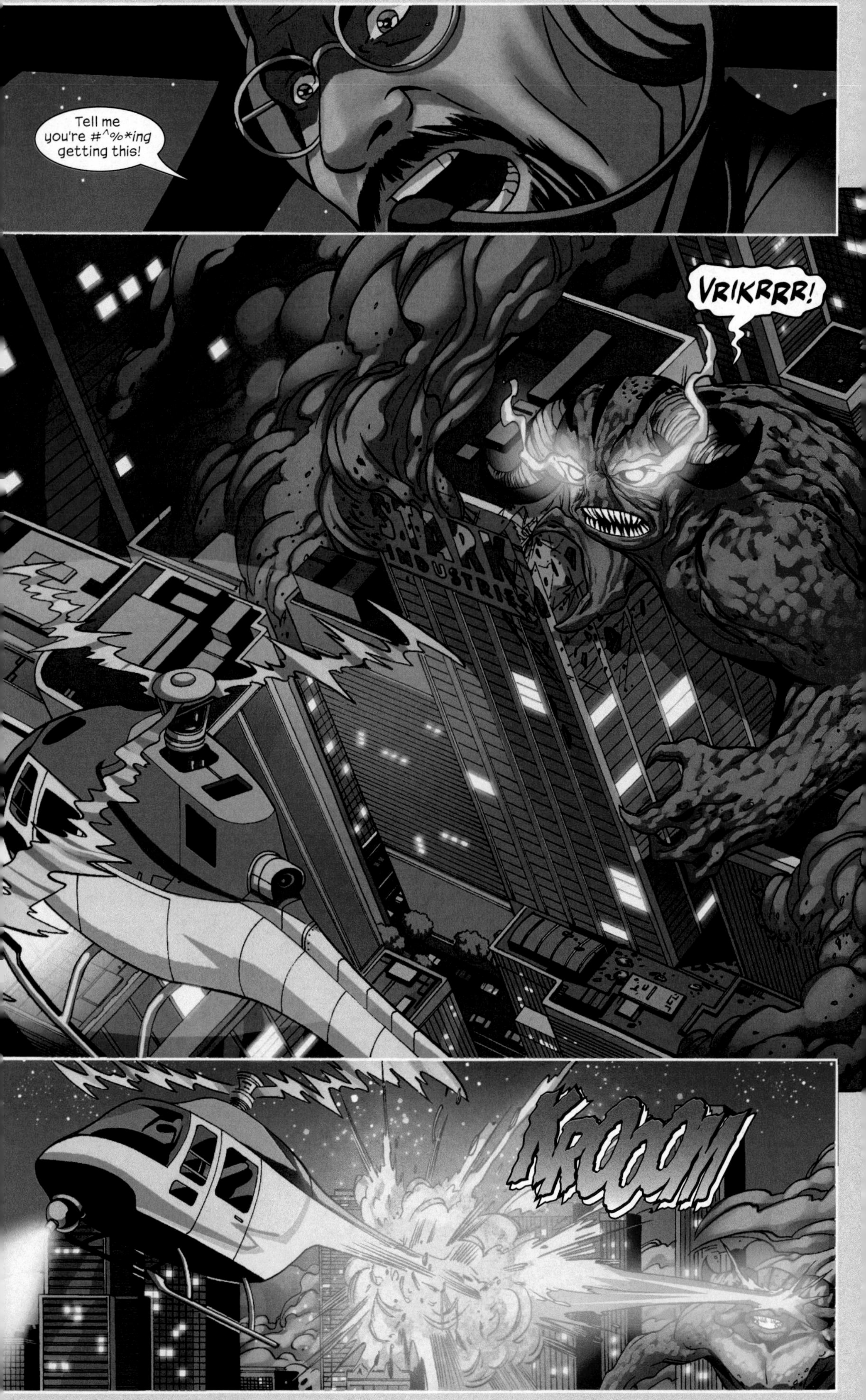
Tell me you're #^%*ing getting this!
VRIKRRR!
KROOOM

AHHH!

Cadie, are you...?

Chester, I'm not sure if we're still broadcasting, but our helicopter is... is *losing altitude.*

If this gets out, remind the heroes of this country that we need them!

It's time for them to stop acting like *children* and get back to--

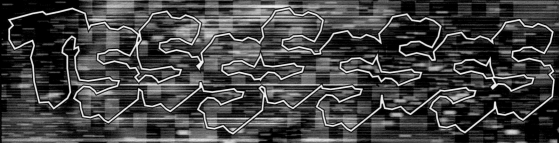

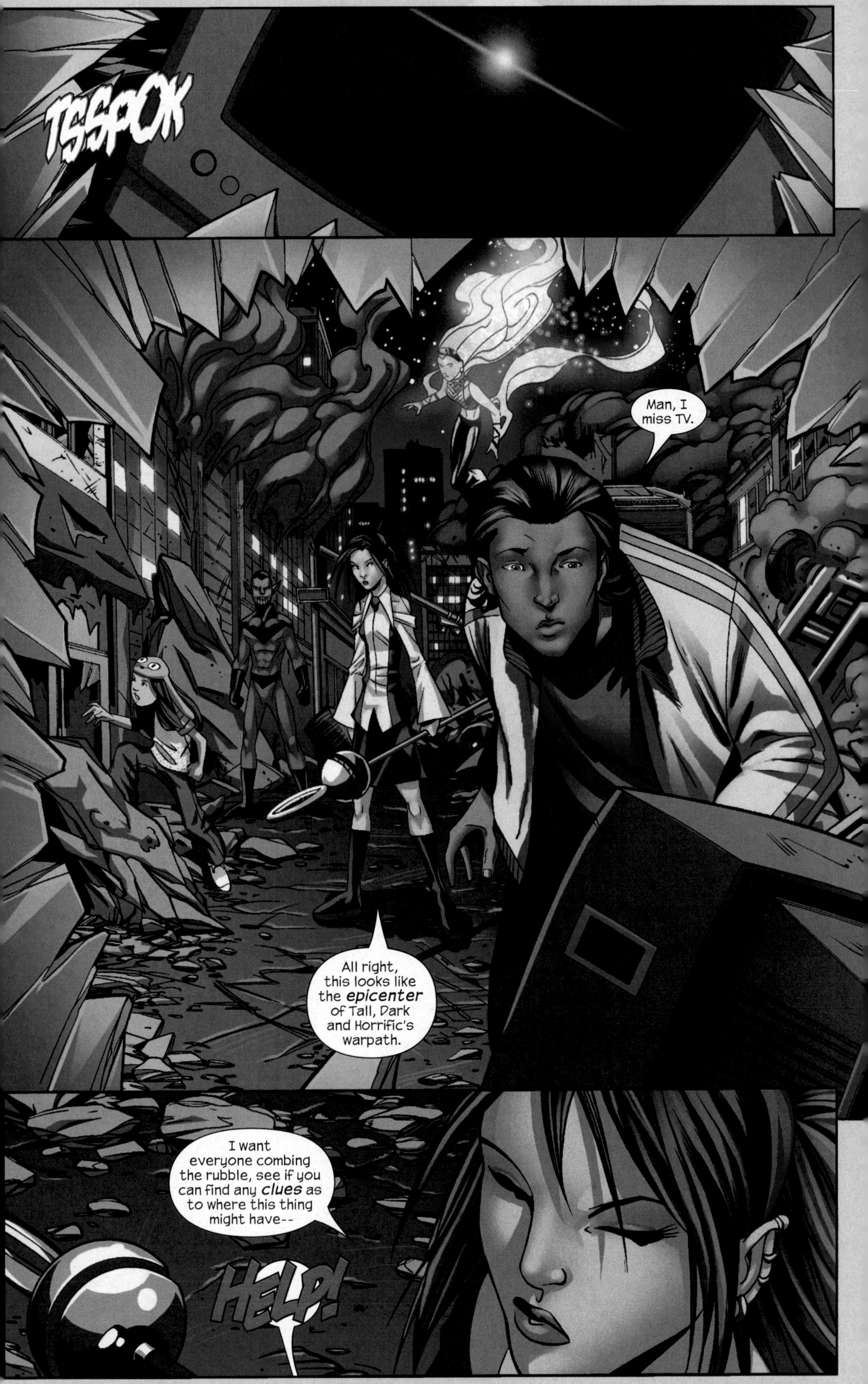
TSSPOK
Man, I miss TV.
All right, this looks like the *epicenter* of Tall, Dark and Horrific's warpath.
I want everyone combing the rubble, see if you can find any *clues* as to where this thing might have--
HELP!

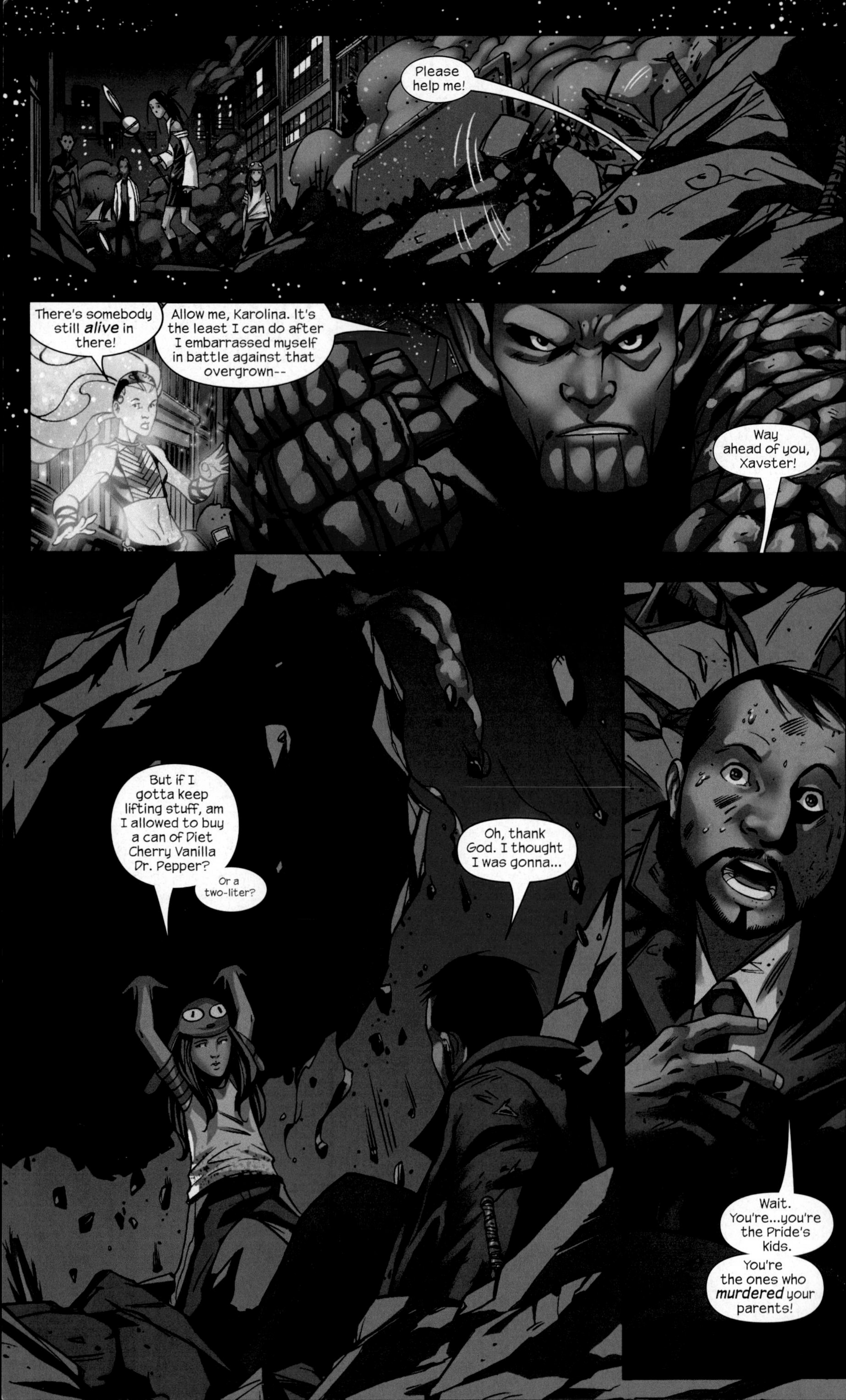
Please help me!
There's somebody still *alive* in there!
Allow me, Karolina. It's the least I can do after I embarrassed myself in battle against that overgrown--
Way ahead of you, Xavster!
But if I gotta keep lifting stuff, am I allowed to buy a can of Diet Cherry Vanilla Dr. Pepper?
Or a two-liter?
Oh, thank God. I thought I was gonna...
Wait. You're...you're the Pride's kids.
You're the ones who *murdered* your parents!

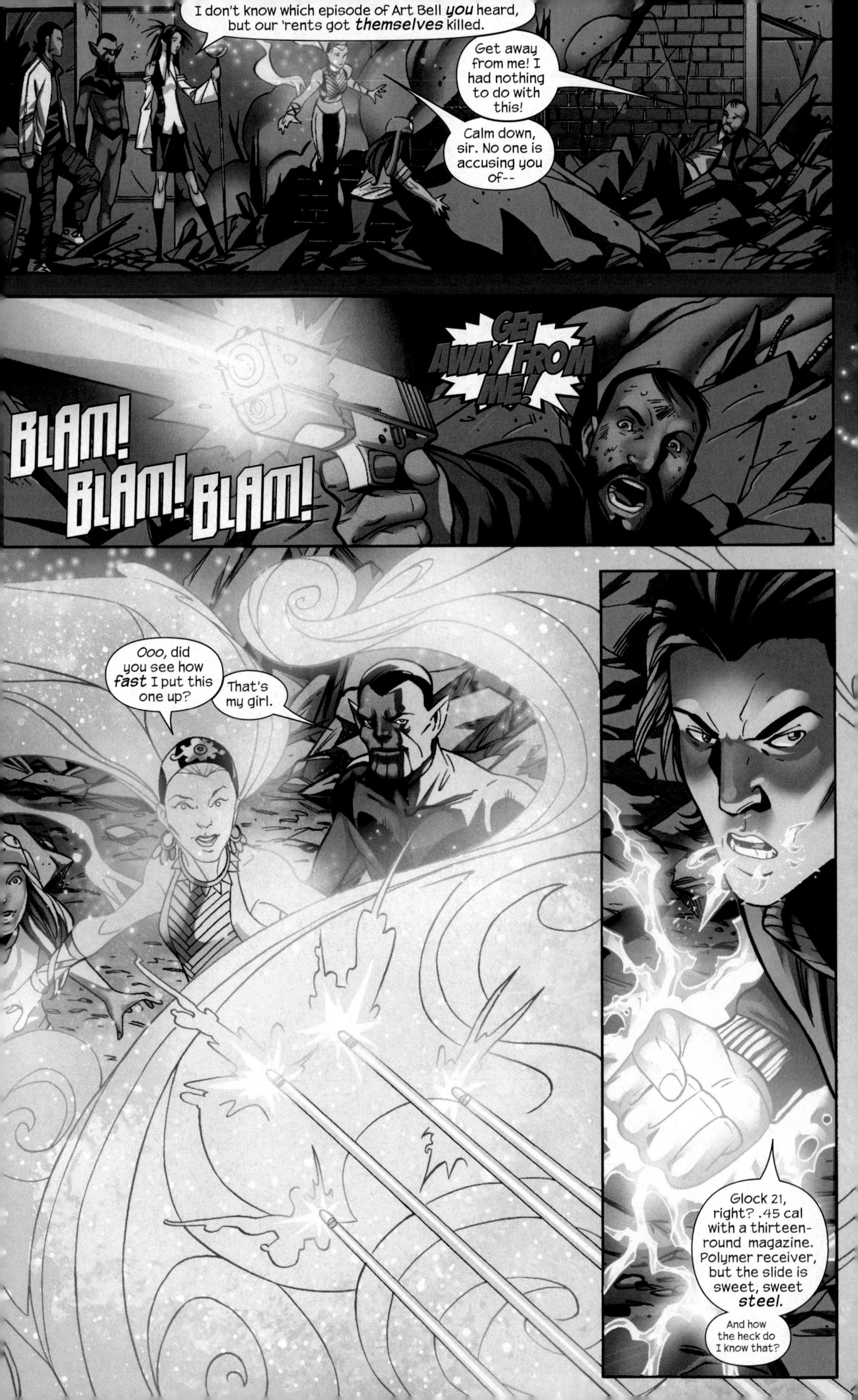

I don't know which episode of Art Bell *you* heard, but our 'rents got *themselves* killed.
Get away from me! I had nothing to do with this!
Calm down, sir. No one is accusing you of--
GET AWAY FROM ME!
BLAM! BLAM! BLAM!
Ooo, did you see how *fast* I put this one up?
That's my girl.
Glock 21, right? .45 cal with a thirteen-round magazine. Polymer receiver, but the slide is sweet, sweet *steel.*
And how the heck do I know that?

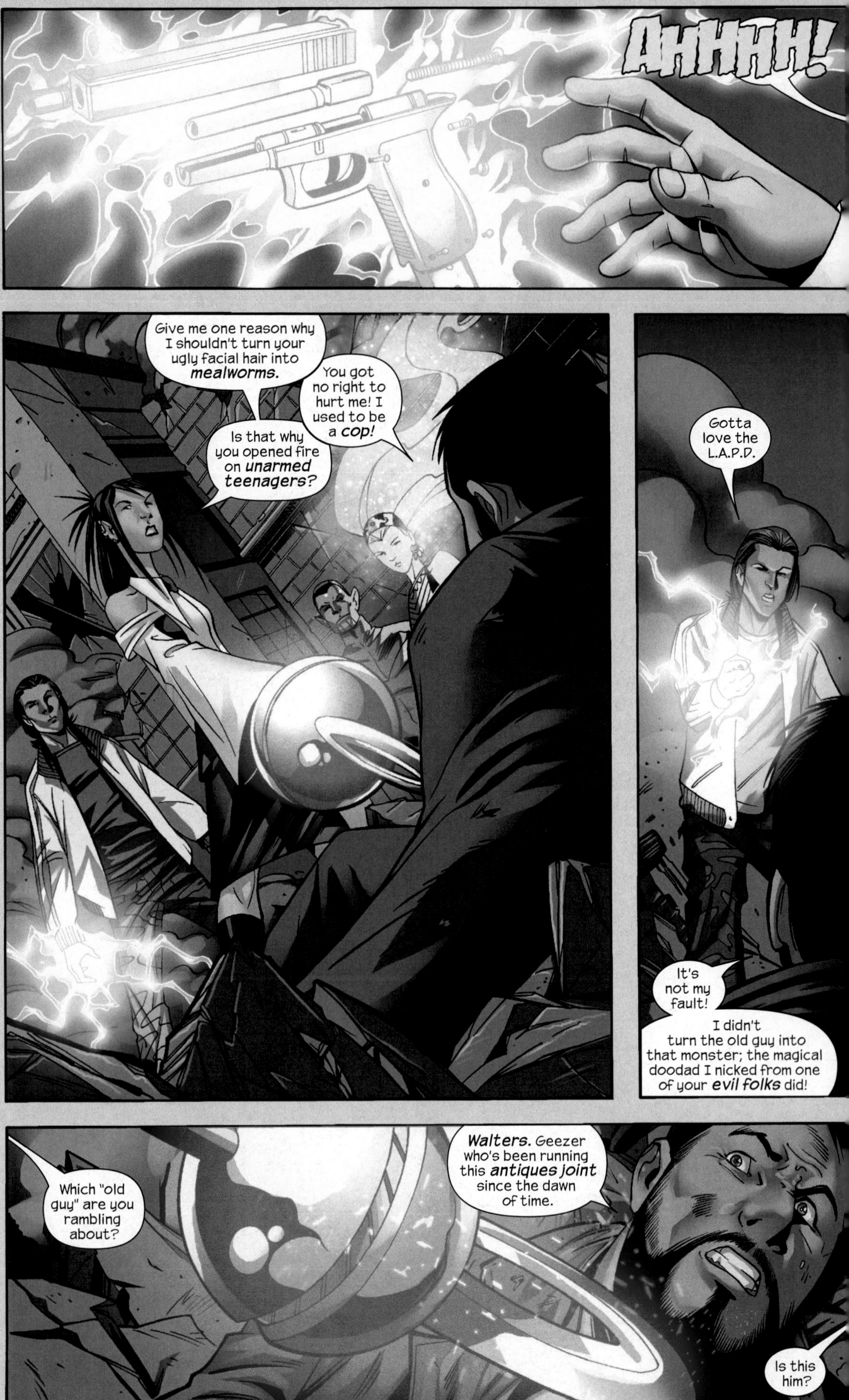
AHHHH!
Give me one reason why I shouldn't turn your ugly facial hair into mealworms.
You got no right to hurt me! I used to be a cop!
Is that why you opened fire on unarmed teenagers?
Gotta love the L.A.P.D.
It's not my fault!
I didn't turn the old guy into that monster; the magical doodad I nicked from one of your evil folks did!
Which "old guy" are you rambling about?
Walters. Geezer who's been running this antiques joint since the dawn of time.
Is this him?

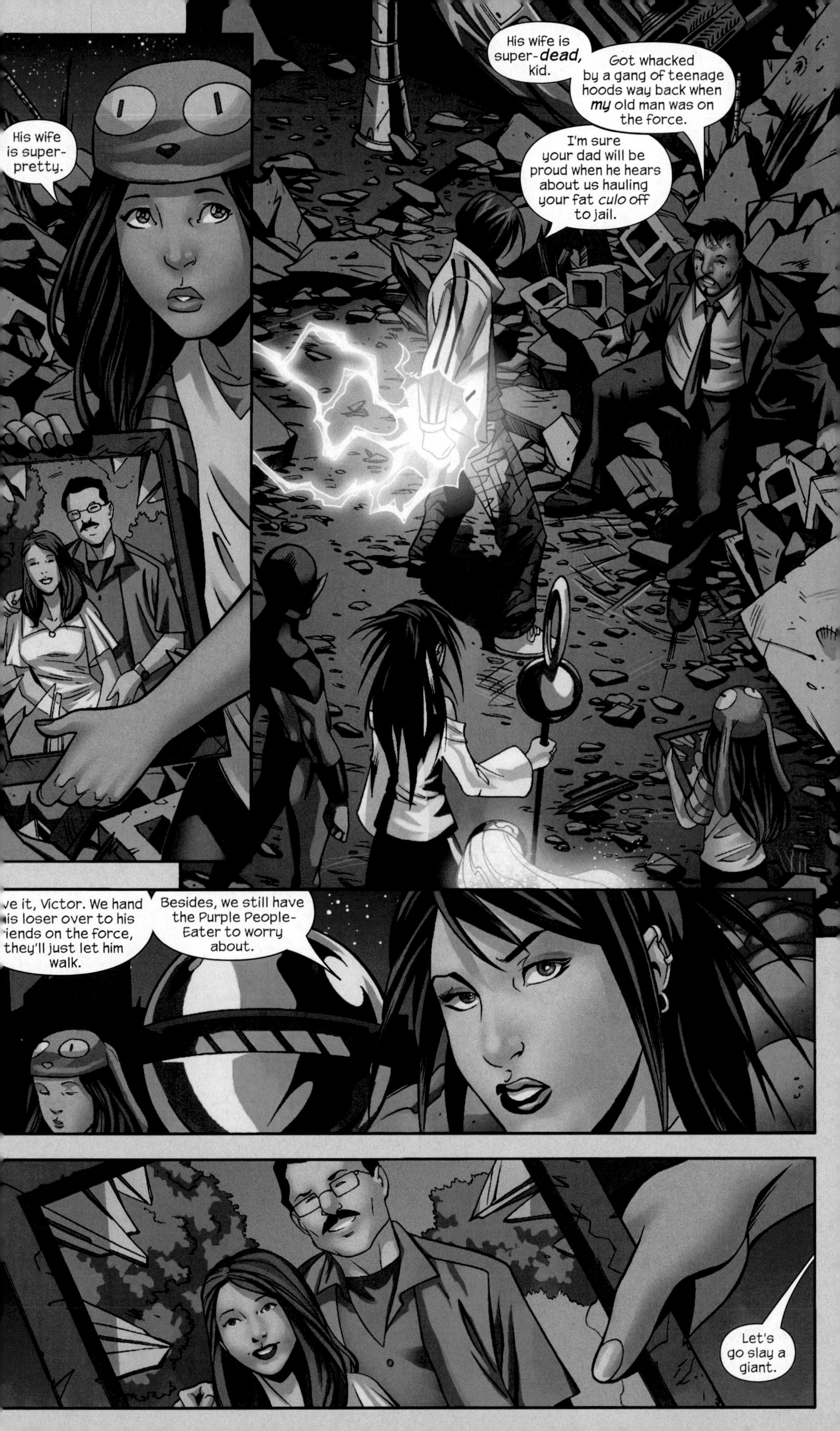

His wife is super-pretty.
His wife is super-**dead,** kid.
Got whacked by a gang of teenage hoods way back when ***my*** old man was on the force.
I'm sure your dad will be proud when he hears about us hauling your fat *culo* off to jail.
ve it, Victor. We hand is loser over to his iends on the force, they'll just let him walk.
Besides, we still have the Purple People-Eater to worry about.
Let's go slay a giant.

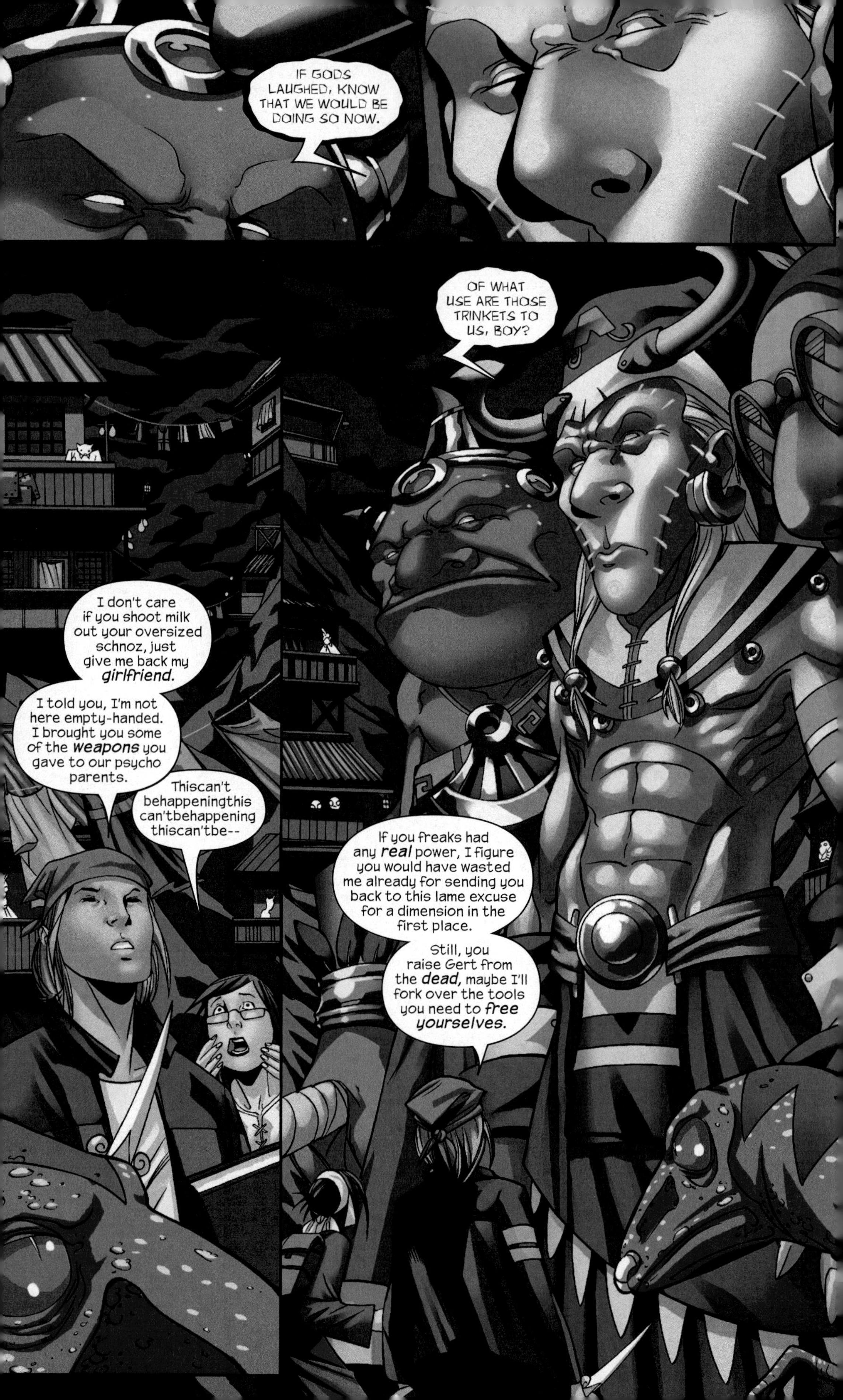
IF GODS LAUGHED, KNOW THAT WE WOULD BE DOING SO NOW.
OF WHAT USE ARE THOSE TRINKETS TO US, BOY?
I don't care if you shoot milk out your oversized schnoz, just give me back my *girlfriend.*
I told you, I'm not here empty-handed. I brought you some of the *weapons* you gave to our psycho parents.
Thiscan't behappeningthis can'tbehappening thiscan'tbe--
If you freaks had any *real* power, I figure you would have wasted me already for sending you back to this lame excuse for a dimension in the first place.
Still, you raise Gert from the *dead,* maybe I'll fork over the tools you need to *free yourselves.*

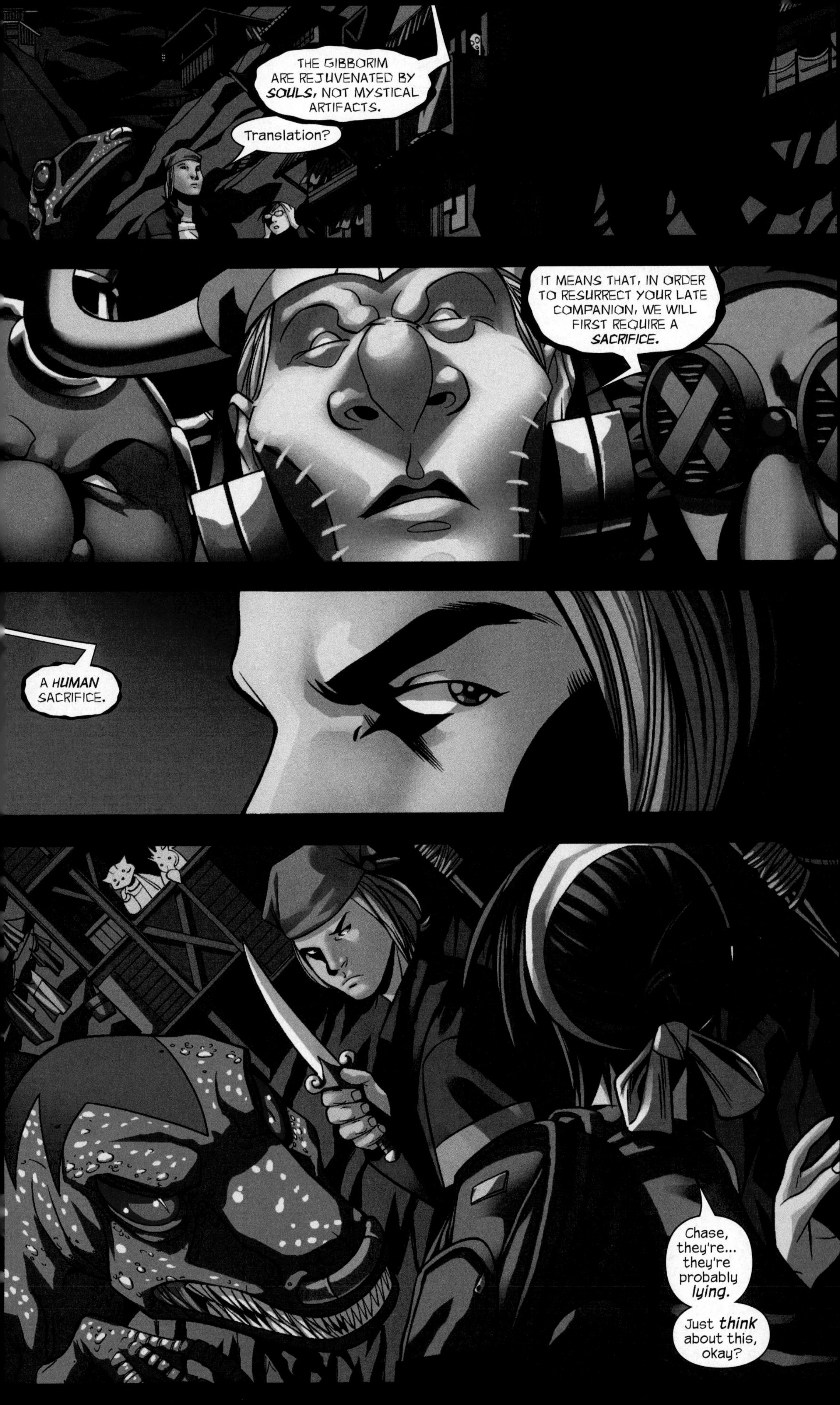
THE GIBBORIM ARE REJUVENATED BY SOULS, NOT MYSTICAL ARTIFACTS.
Translation?
IT MEANS THAT, IN ORDER TO RESURRECT YOUR LATE COMPANION, WE WILL FIRST REQUIRE A SACRIFICE.
A HUMAN SACRIFICE.
Chase, they're... they're probably lying.
Just think about this, okay?

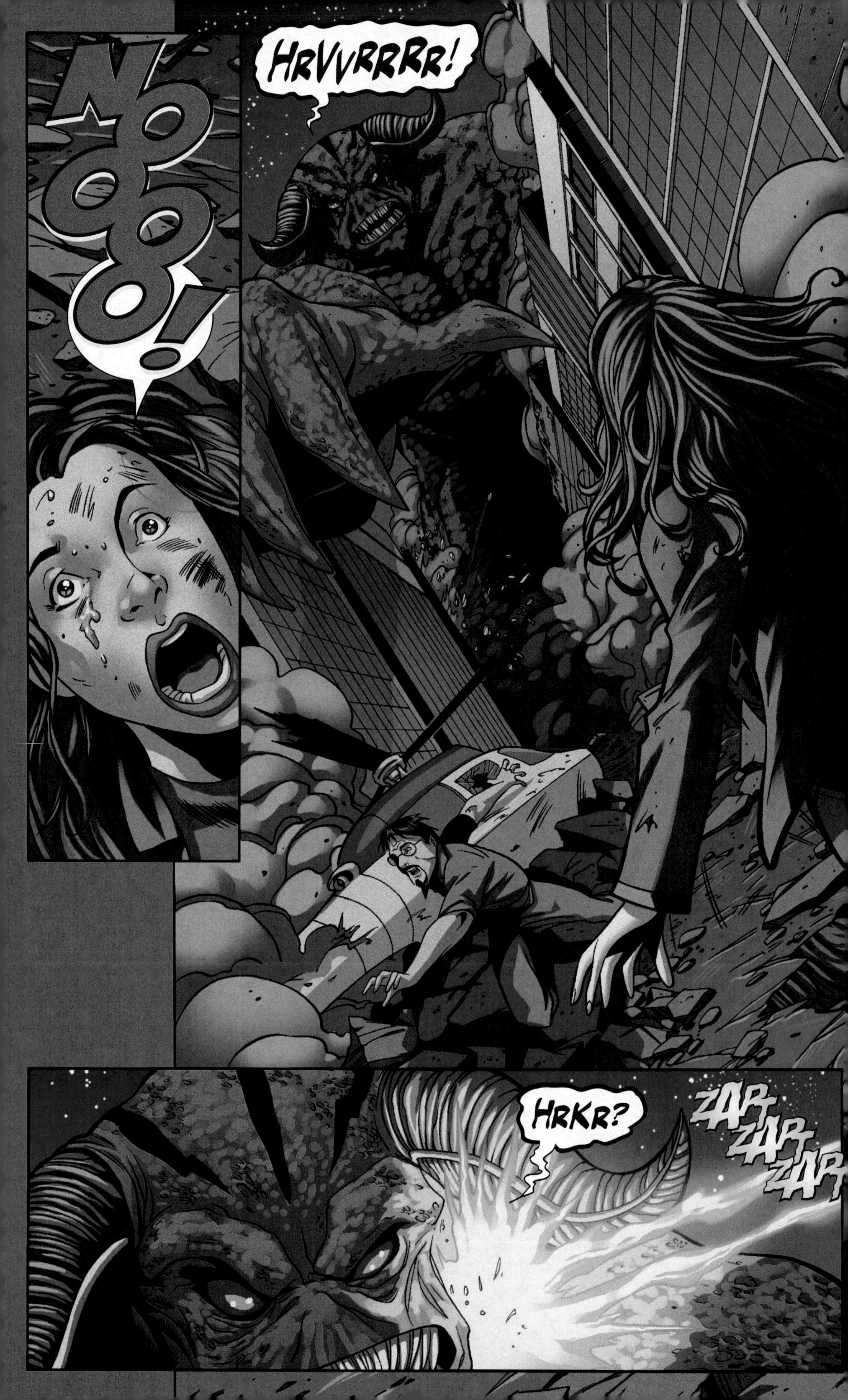
NOOO!
HRVVRRRR!
HRKR?
ZAP ZAP ZAP

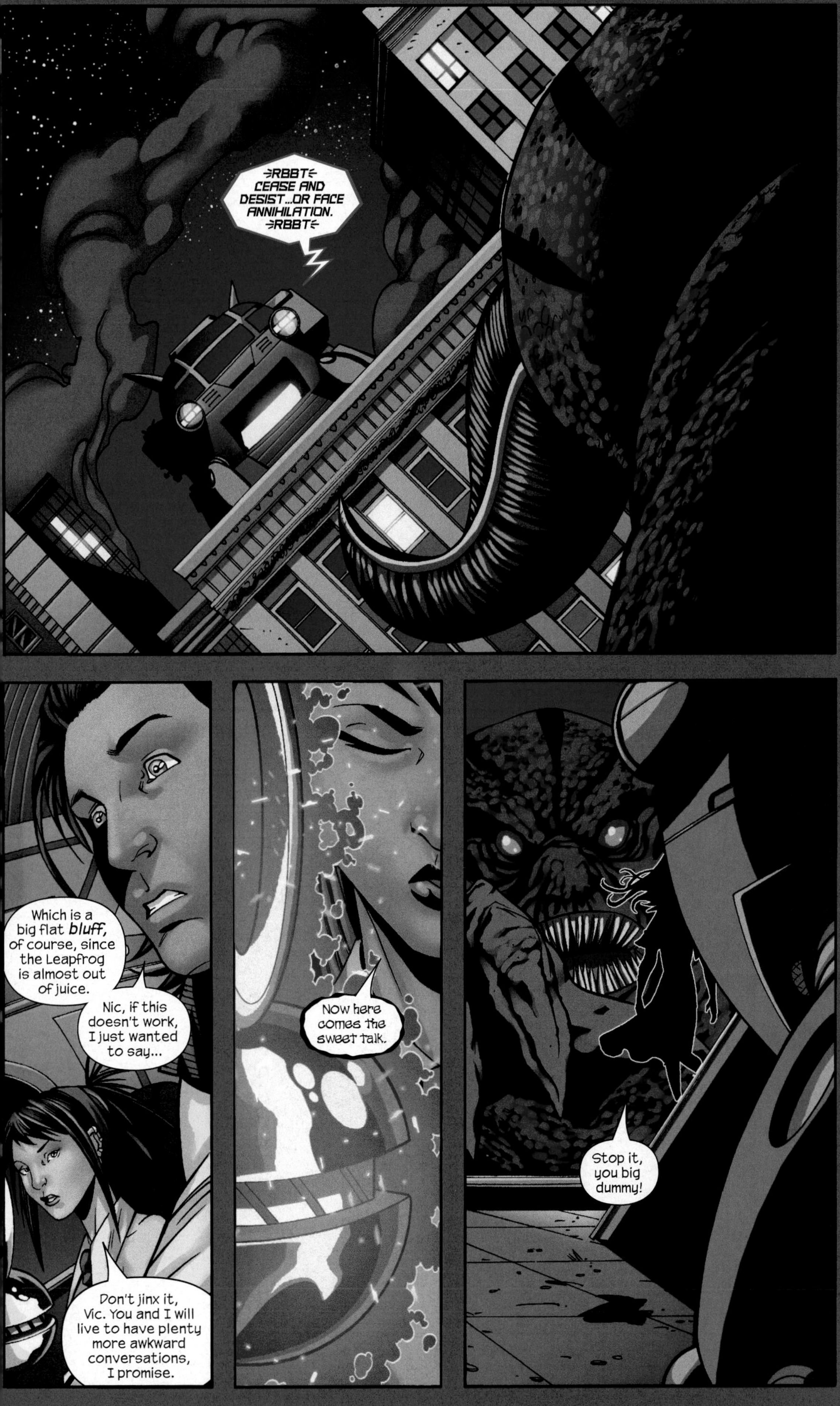

≠RBBT≠ CEASE AND DESIST...OR FACE ANNIHILATION. ≠RBBT≠
Which is a big flat *bluff*, of course, since the Leapfrog is almost out of juice.
Nic, if this doesn't work, I just wanted to say...
Don't jinx it, Vic. You and I will live to have plenty more awkward conversations, I promise.
Now here comes the sweet talk.
Stop it, you big dummy!

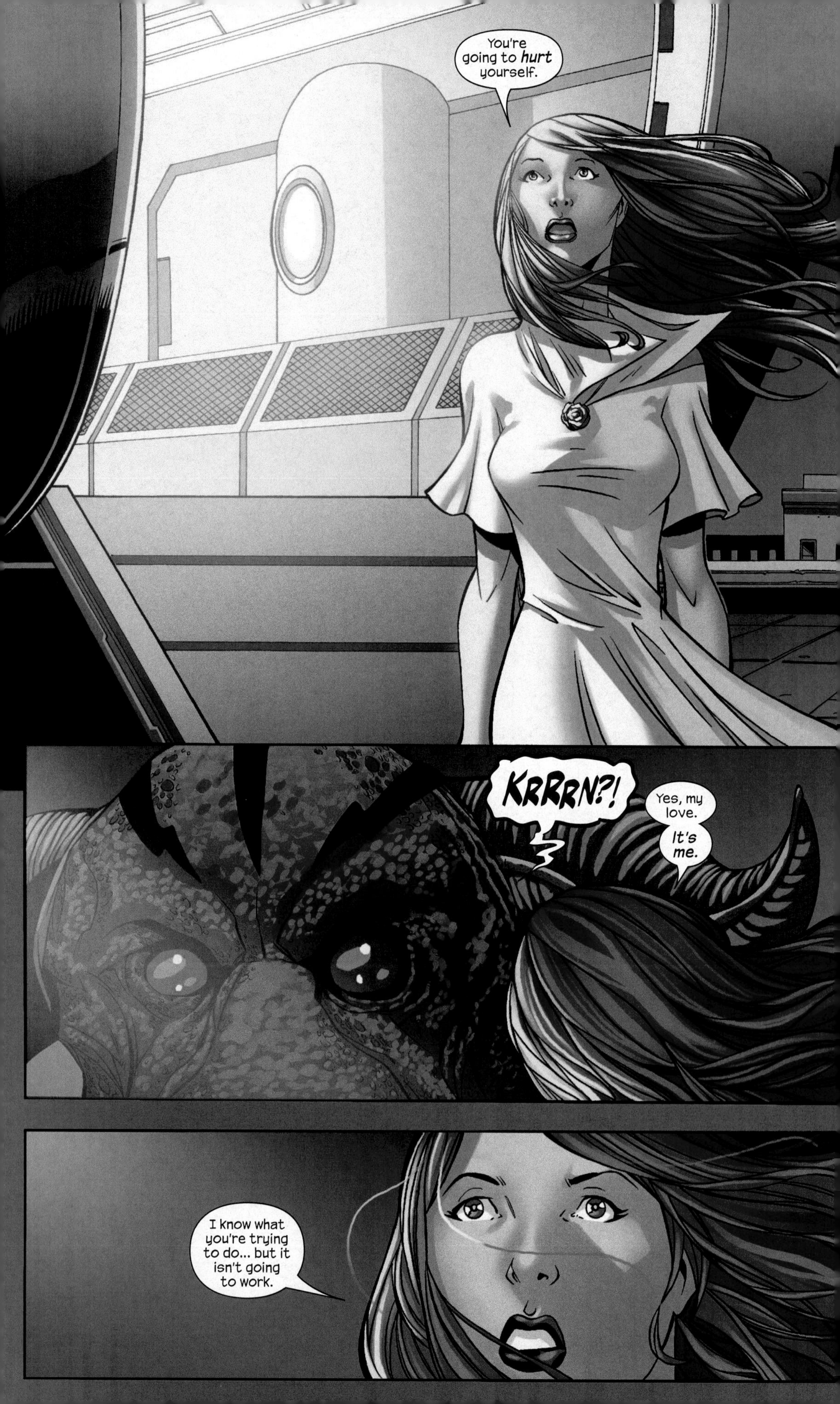
You're going to *hurt* yourself.
KRRRN?!
Yes, my love.
It's me.
I know what you're trying to do... but it isn't going to work.

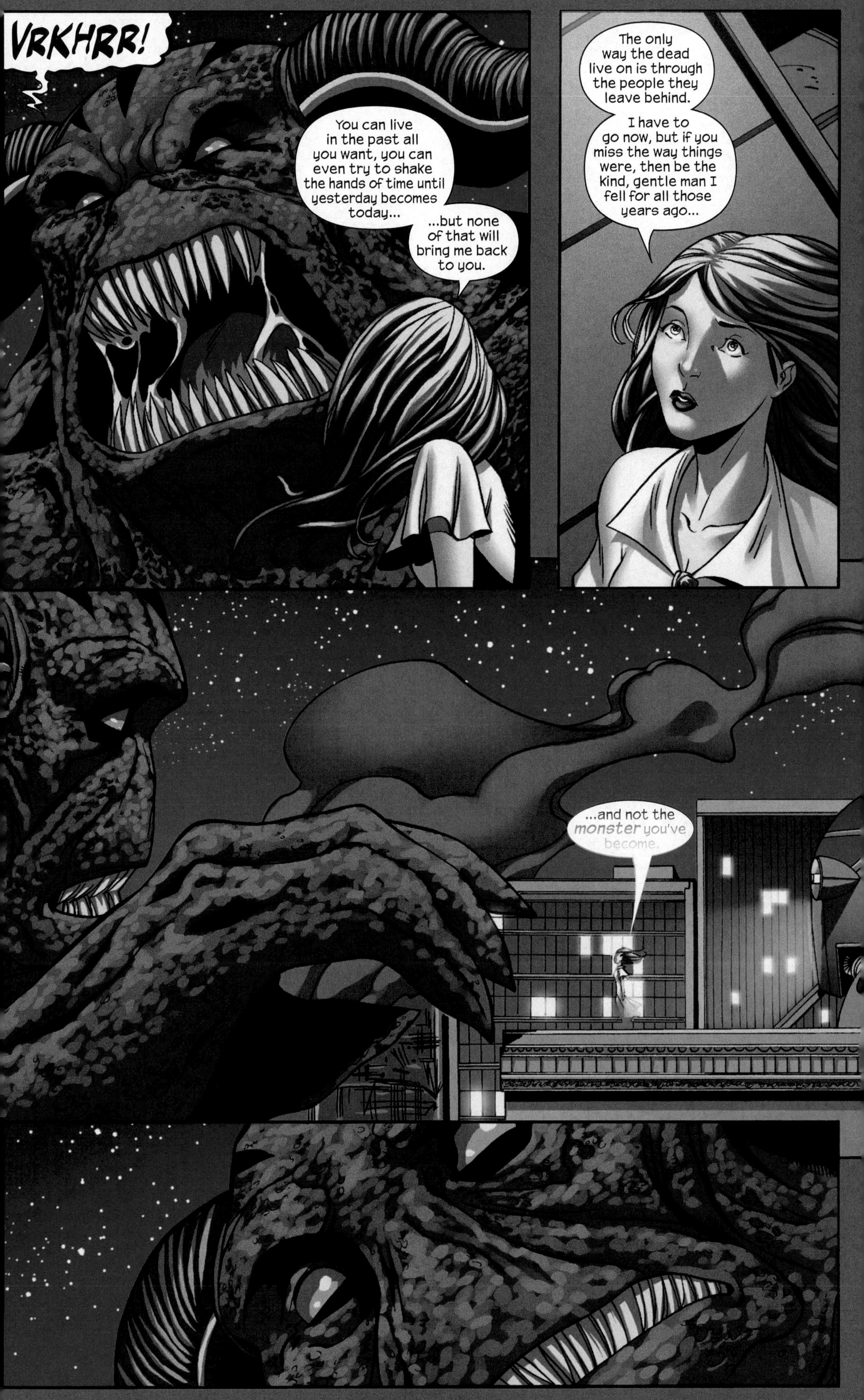
VRKHRR!
You can live in the past all you want, you can even try to shake the hands of time until yesterday becomes today...
...but none of that will bring me back to you.
The only way the dead live on is through the people they leave behind.
I have to go now, but if you miss the way things were, then be the kind, gentle man I fell for all those years ago...
...and not the monster you've become.

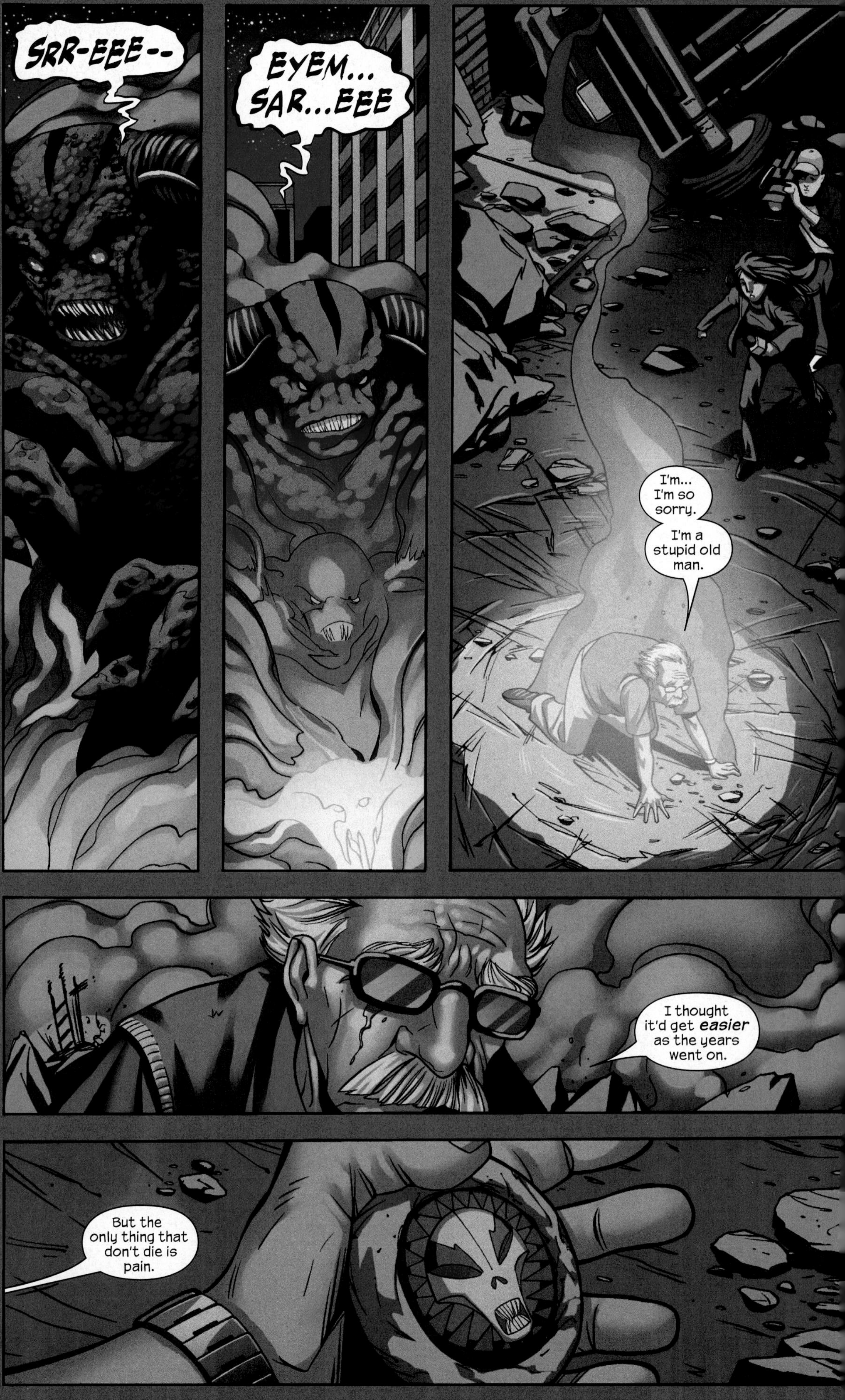

SRR-EEE--
EYEM... SAR...EEE
I'm... I'm so sorry.
I'm a stupid old man.
I thought it'd get easier as the years went on.
But the only thing that don't die is pain.

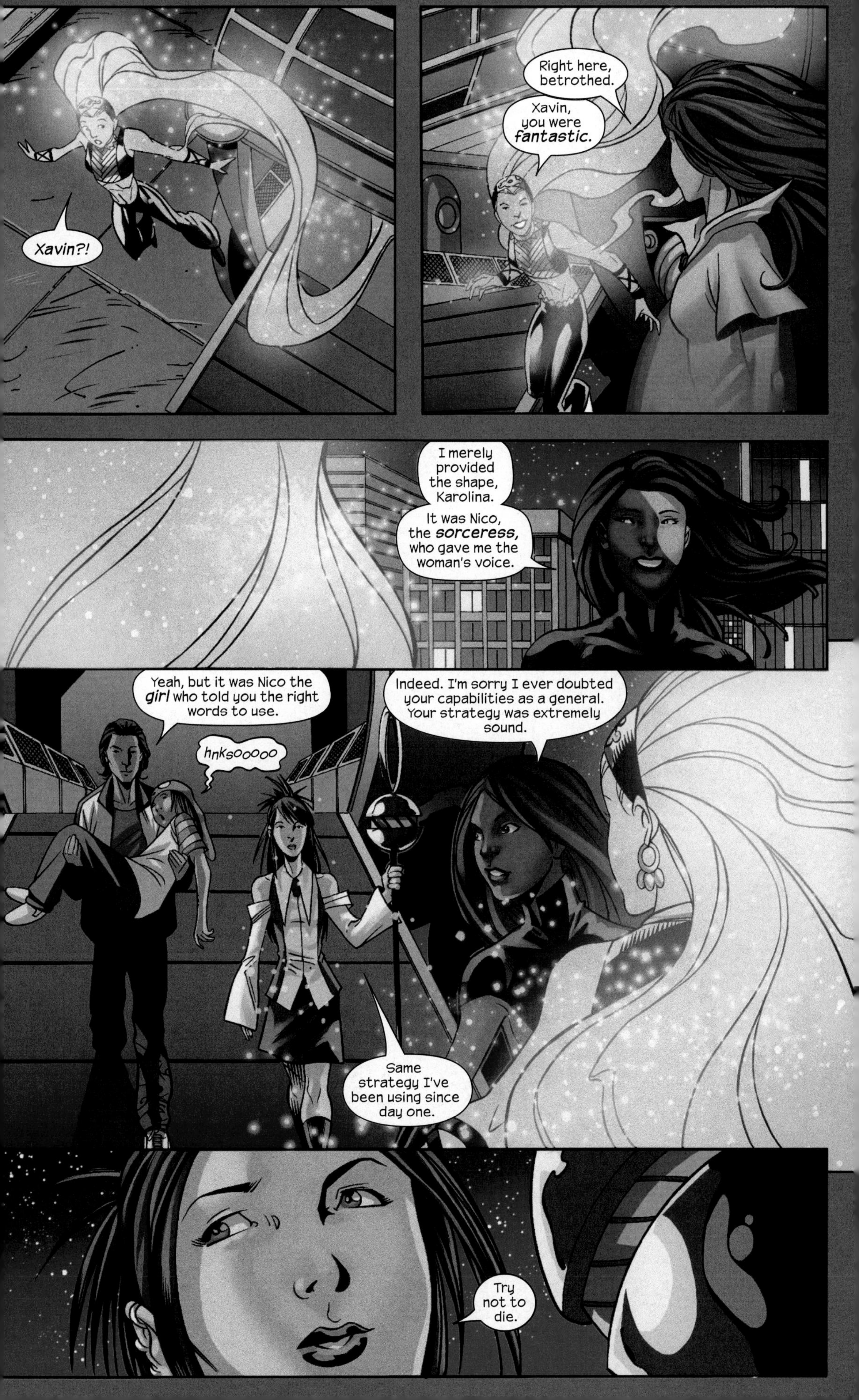
Xavin?!
Right here, betrothed.
Xavin, you were *fantastic*.
I merely provided the shape, Karolina.
It was Nico, the ***sorceress,*** who gave me the woman's voice.
Yeah, but it was Nico the ***girl*** who told you the right words to use.
hnksooooo
Indeed. I'm sorry I ever doubted your capabilities as a general. Your strategy was extremely sound.
Same strategy I've been using since day one.
Try not to die.

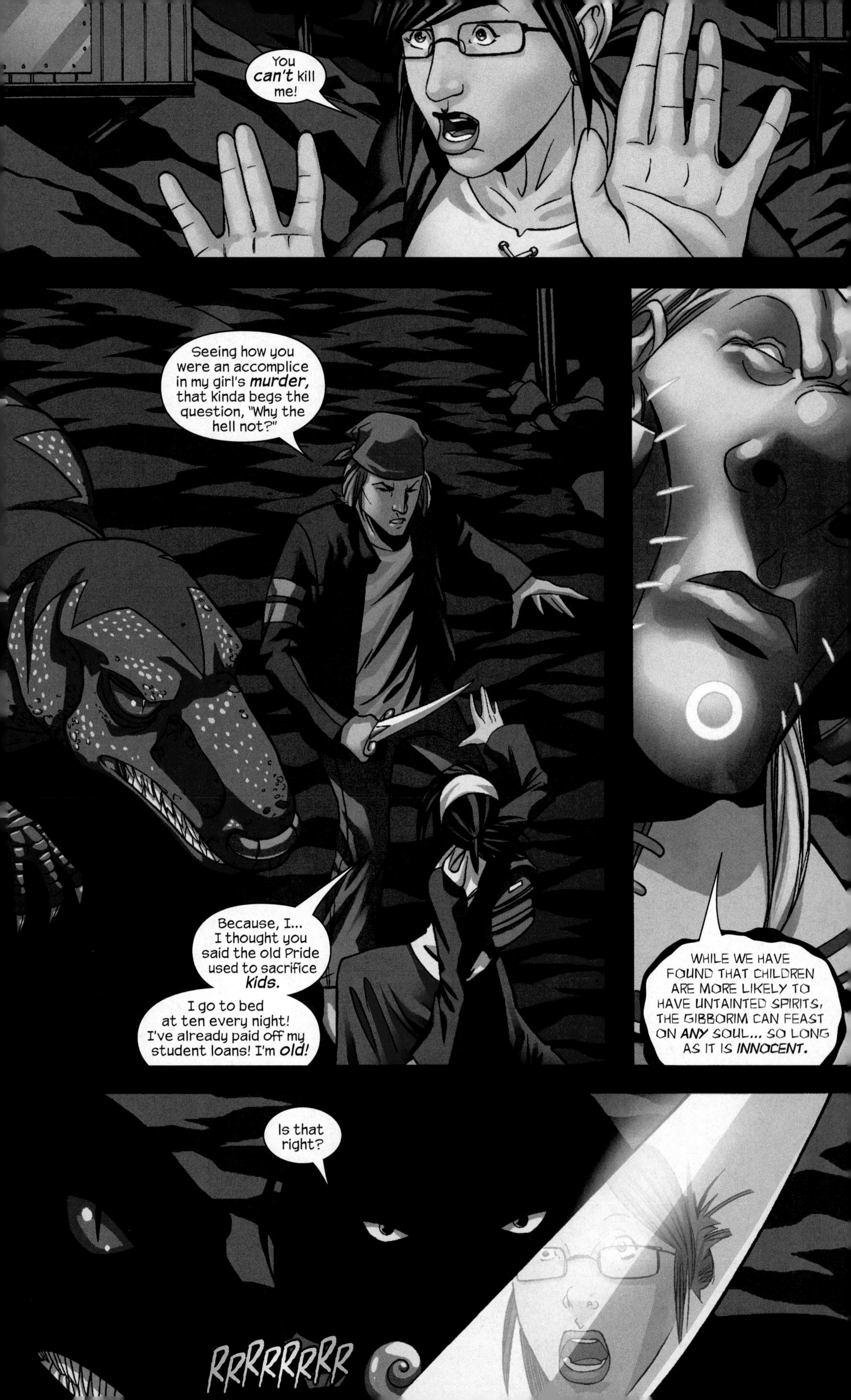
You can't kill me!
Seeing how you were an accomplice in my girl's murder, that kinda begs the question, "Why the hell not?"
Because, I... I thought you said the old Pride used to sacrifice kids.
I go to bed at ten every night! I've already paid off my student loans! I'm old!
WHILE WE HAVE FOUND THAT CHILDREN ARE MORE LIKELY TO HAVE UNTAINTED SPIRITS, THE GIBBORIM CAN FEAST ON ANY SOUL... SO LONG AS IT IS INNOCENT.
Is that right?
RRRRRRRR

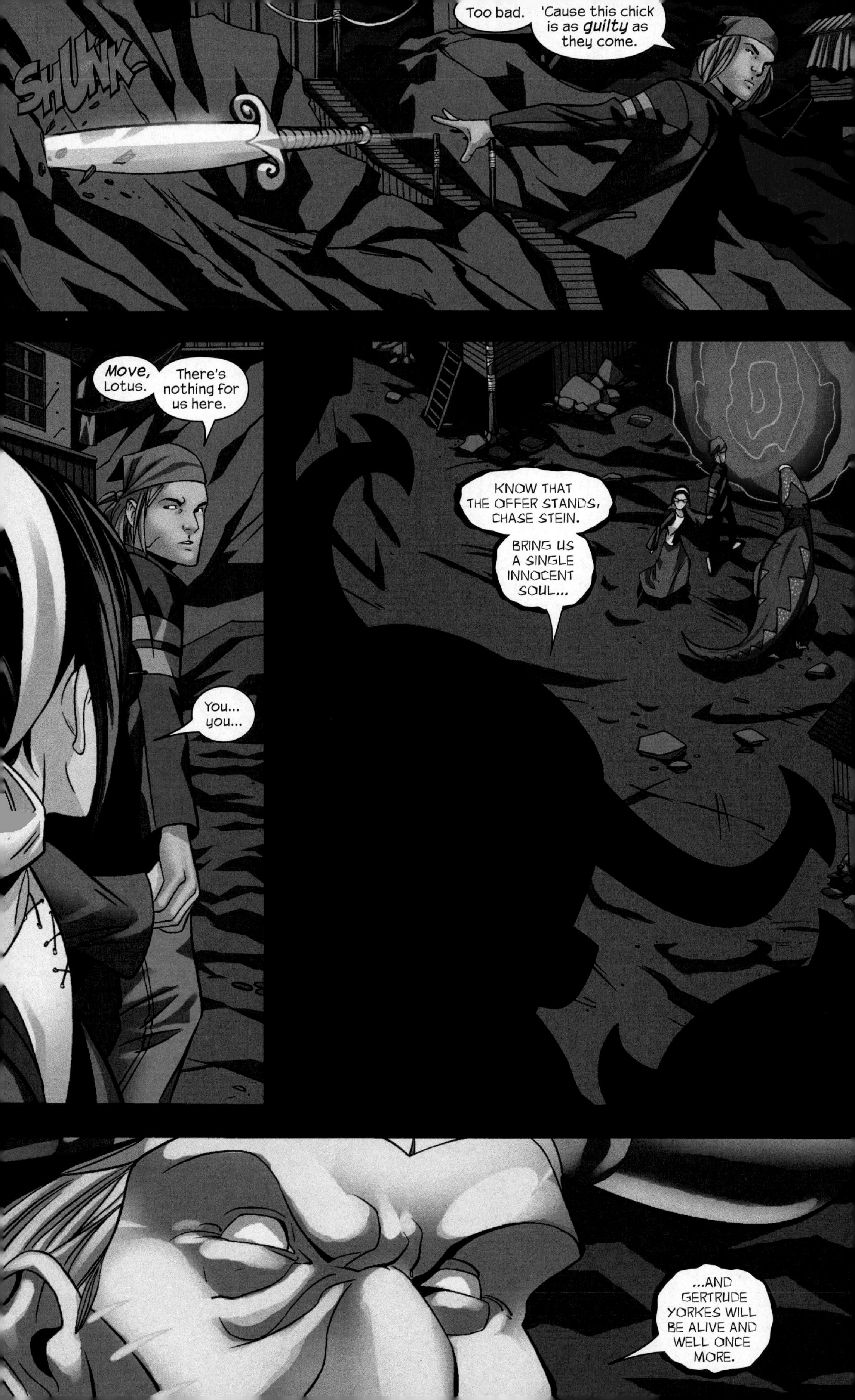
SHUNK
Too bad.
'Cause this chick is as *guilty* as they come.
Move, Lotus.
There's nothing for us here.
You... you...
KNOW THAT THE OFFER STANDS, CHASE STEIN.
BRING US A SINGLE INNOCENT SOUL...
...AND GERTRUDE YORKES WILL BE ALIVE AND WELL ONCE MORE.

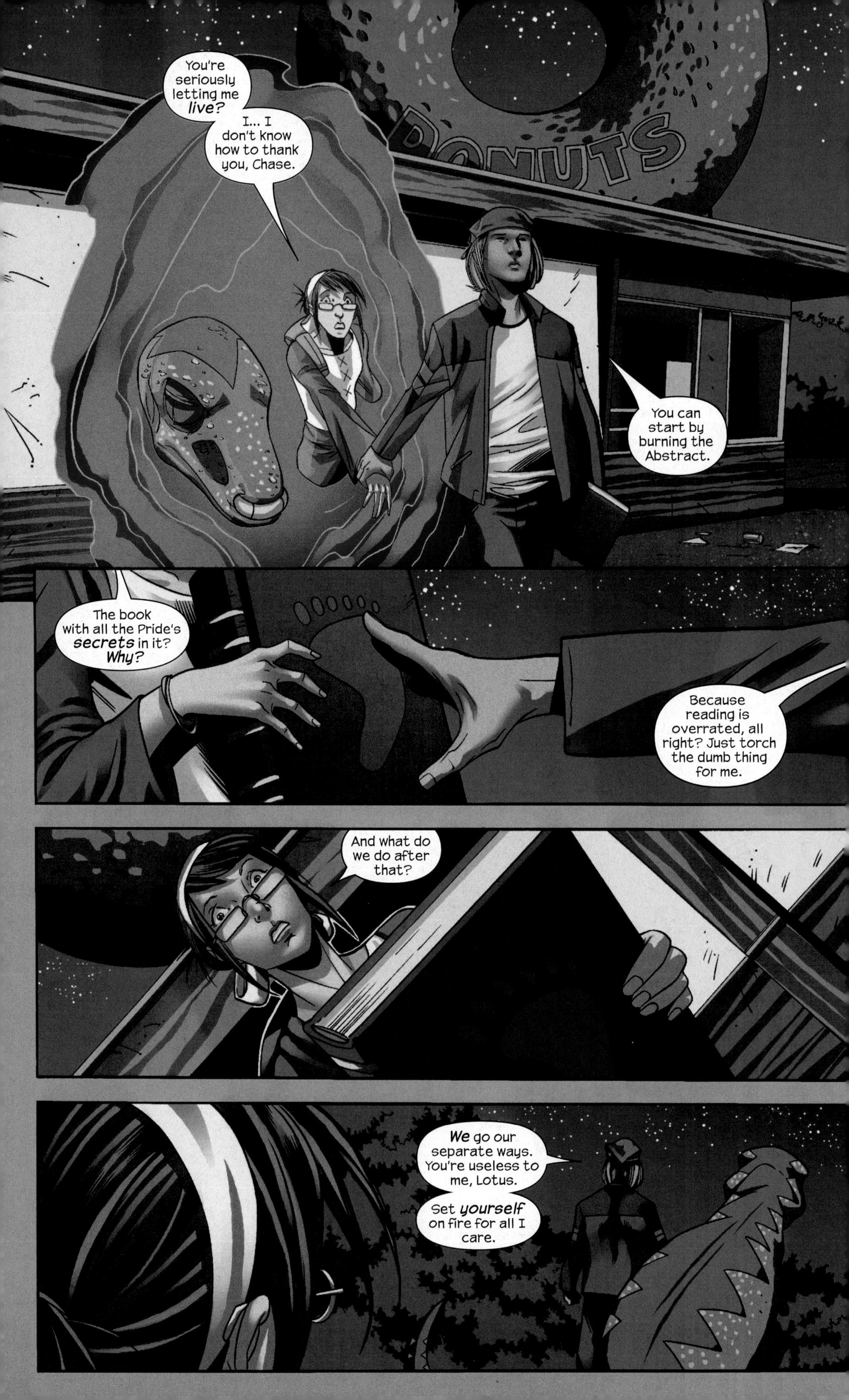

DONUTS
You're seriously letting me *live?*
I... I don't know how to thank you, Chase.
You can start by burning the Abstract.
The book with all the Pride's *secrets* in it? *Why?*
Because reading is overrated, all right? Just torch the dumb thing for me.
And what do we do after that?
We go our separate ways. You're useless to me, Lotus.
Set *yourself* on fire for all I care.

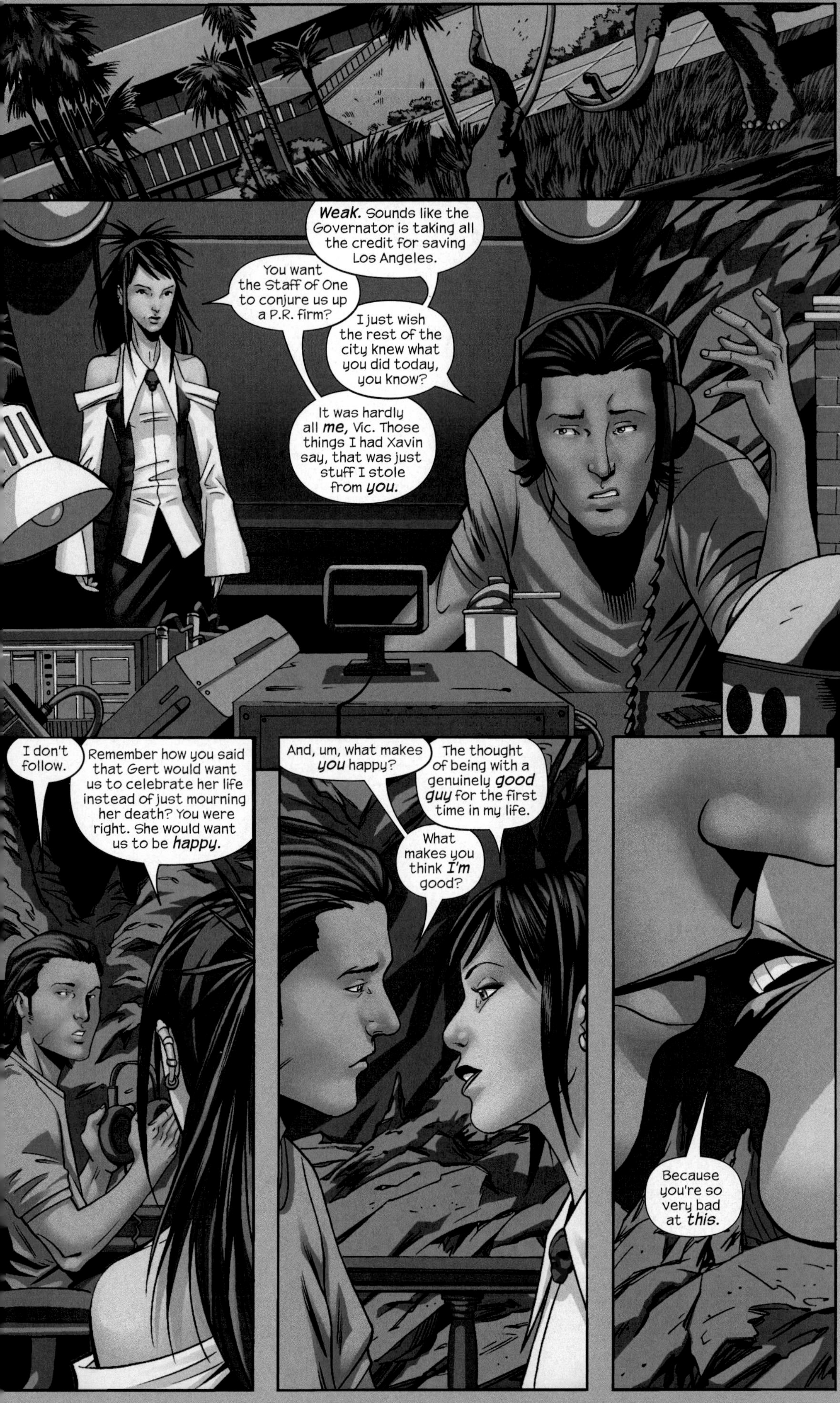

Weak. Sounds like the Governator is taking all the credit for saving Los Angeles.
You want the Staff of One to conjure us up a P.R. firm?
I just wish the rest of the city knew what you did today, you know?
It was hardly all me, Vic. Those things I had Xavin say, that was just stuff I stole from you.
I don't follow.
Remember how you said that Gert would want us to celebrate her life instead of just mourning her death? You were right. She would want us to be happy.
And, um, what makes you happy?
The thought of being with a genuinely good guy for the first time in my life.
What makes you think I'm good?
Because you're so very bad at this.

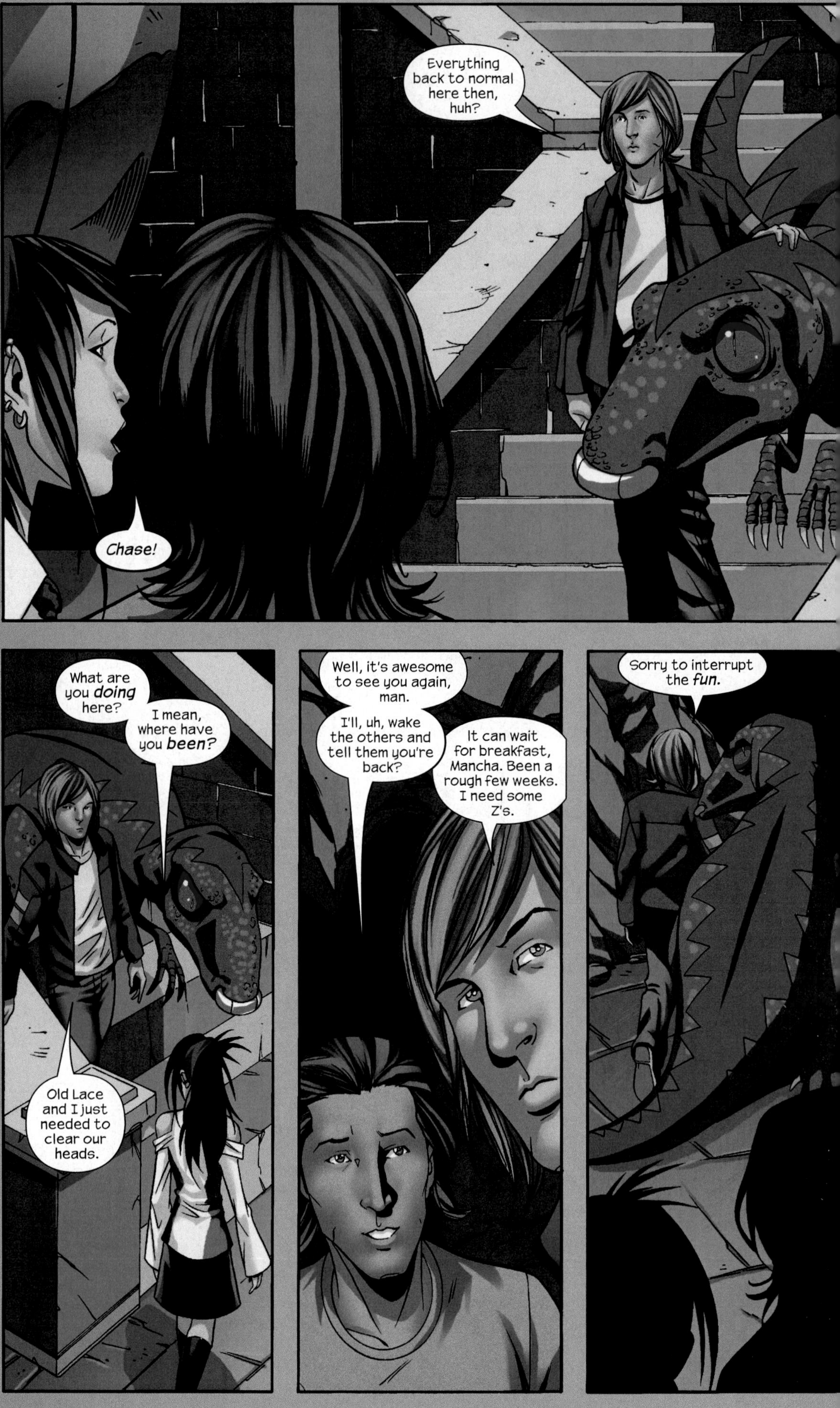
Everything back to normal here then, huh?
Chase!
What are you doing here?
I mean, where have you been?
Old Lace and I just needed to clear our heads.
Well, it's awesome to see you again, man.
I'll, uh, wake the others and tell them you're back?
It can wait for breakfast, Mancha. Been a rough few weeks. I need some Z's.
Sorry to interrupt the fun.

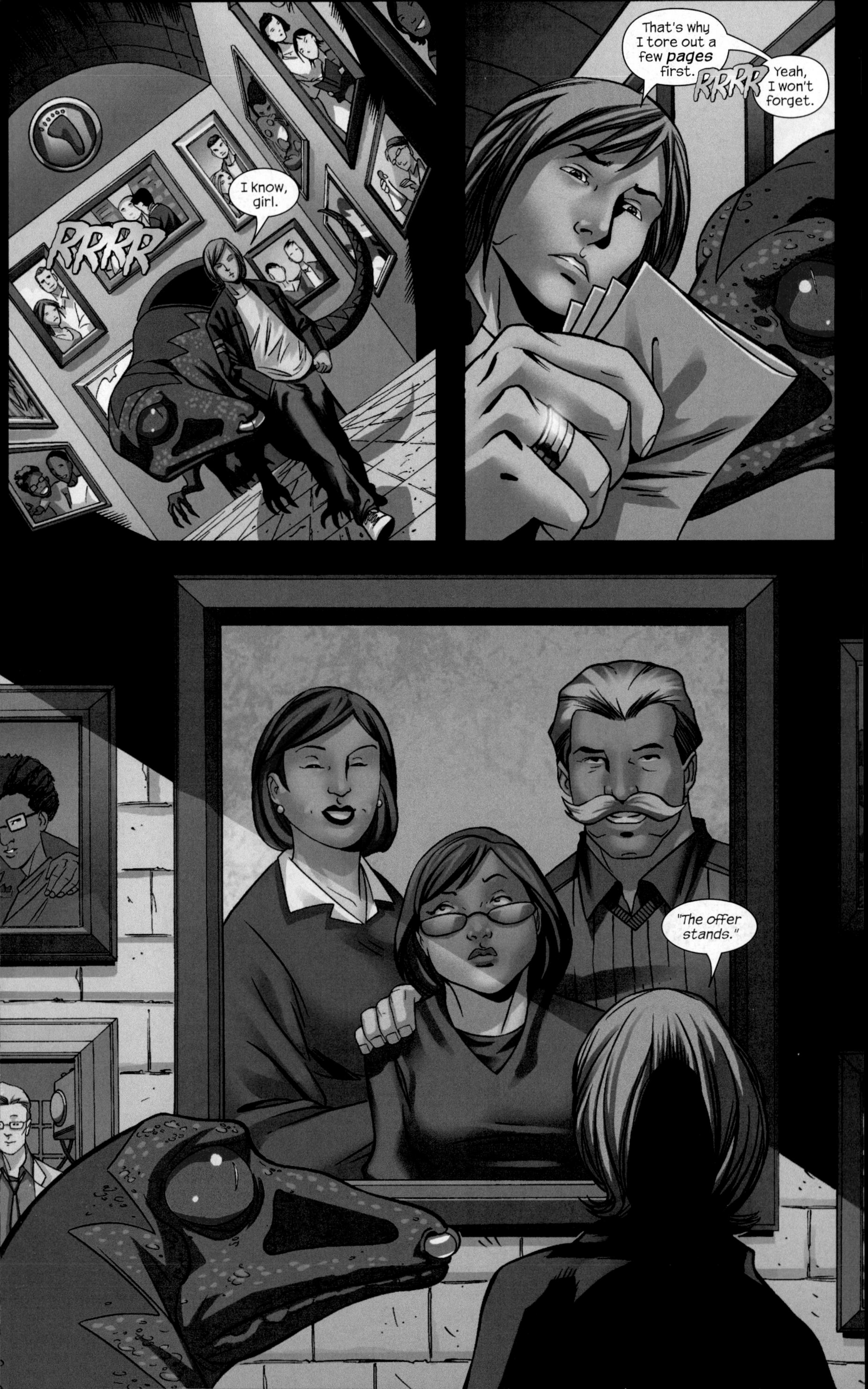
RRRR
I know, girl.
That's why I tore out a few *pages* first.
RRRR
Yeah, I won't forget.
"The offer stands."

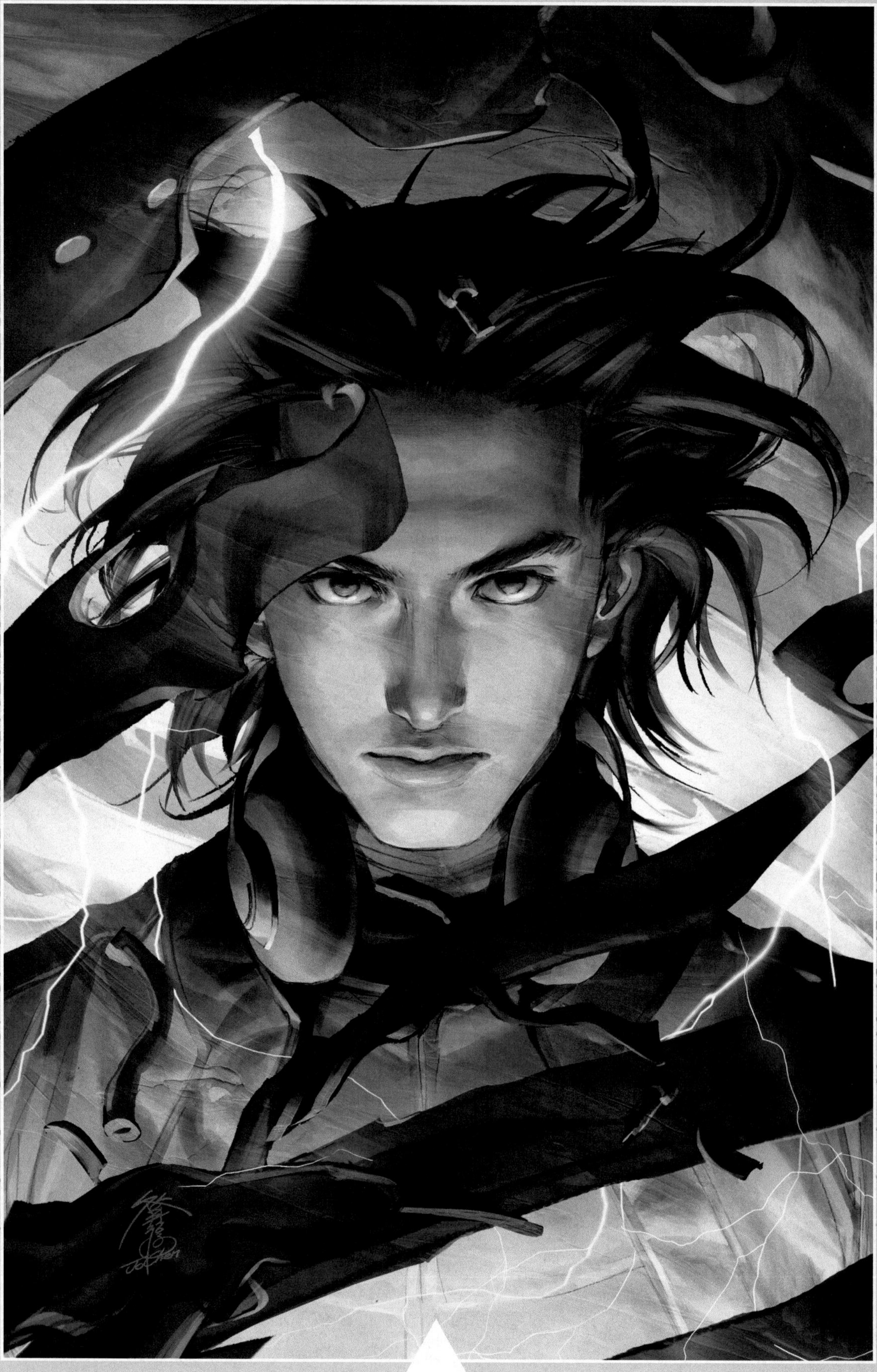

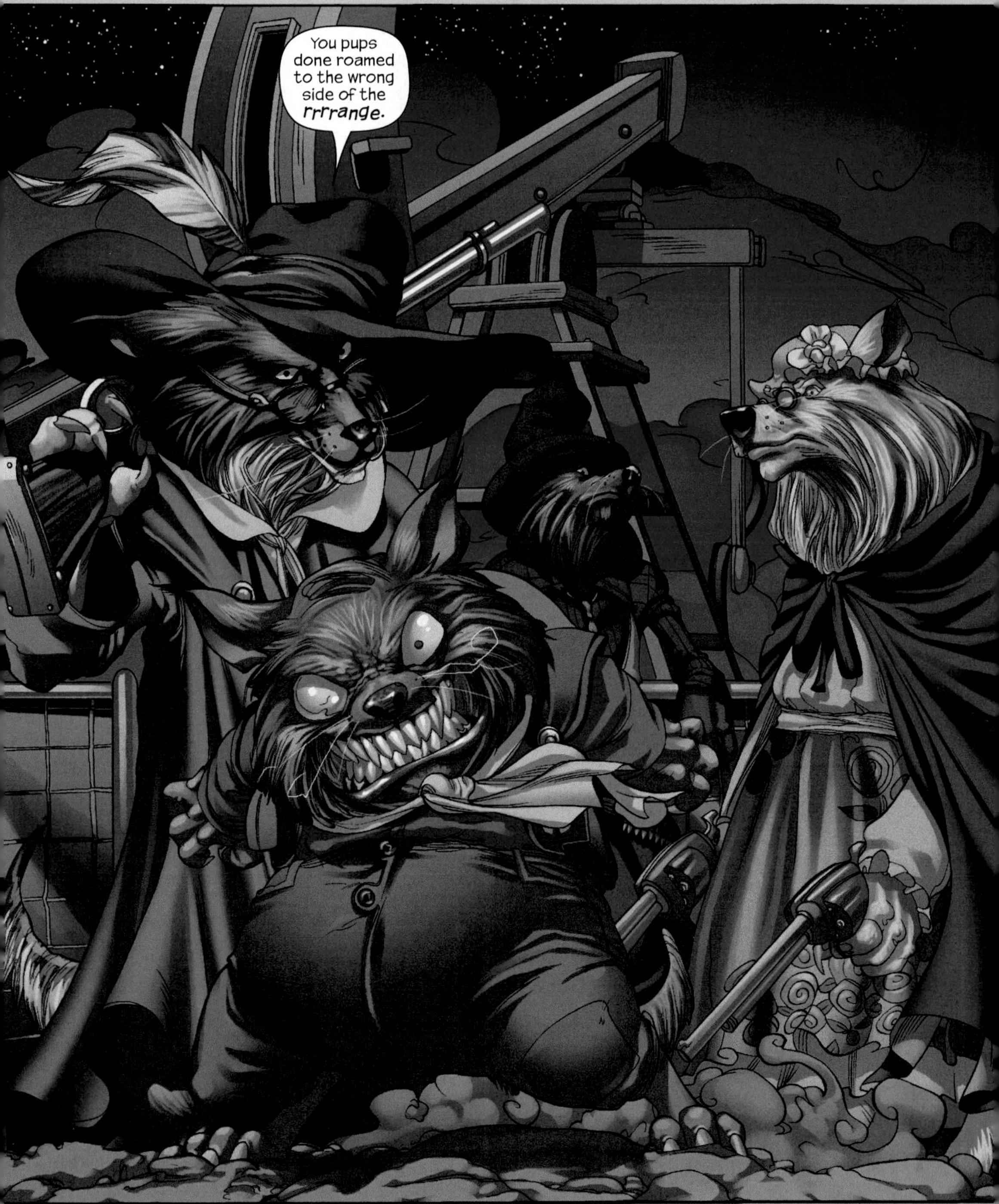
You pups done roamed to the wrong side of the rrrrange.

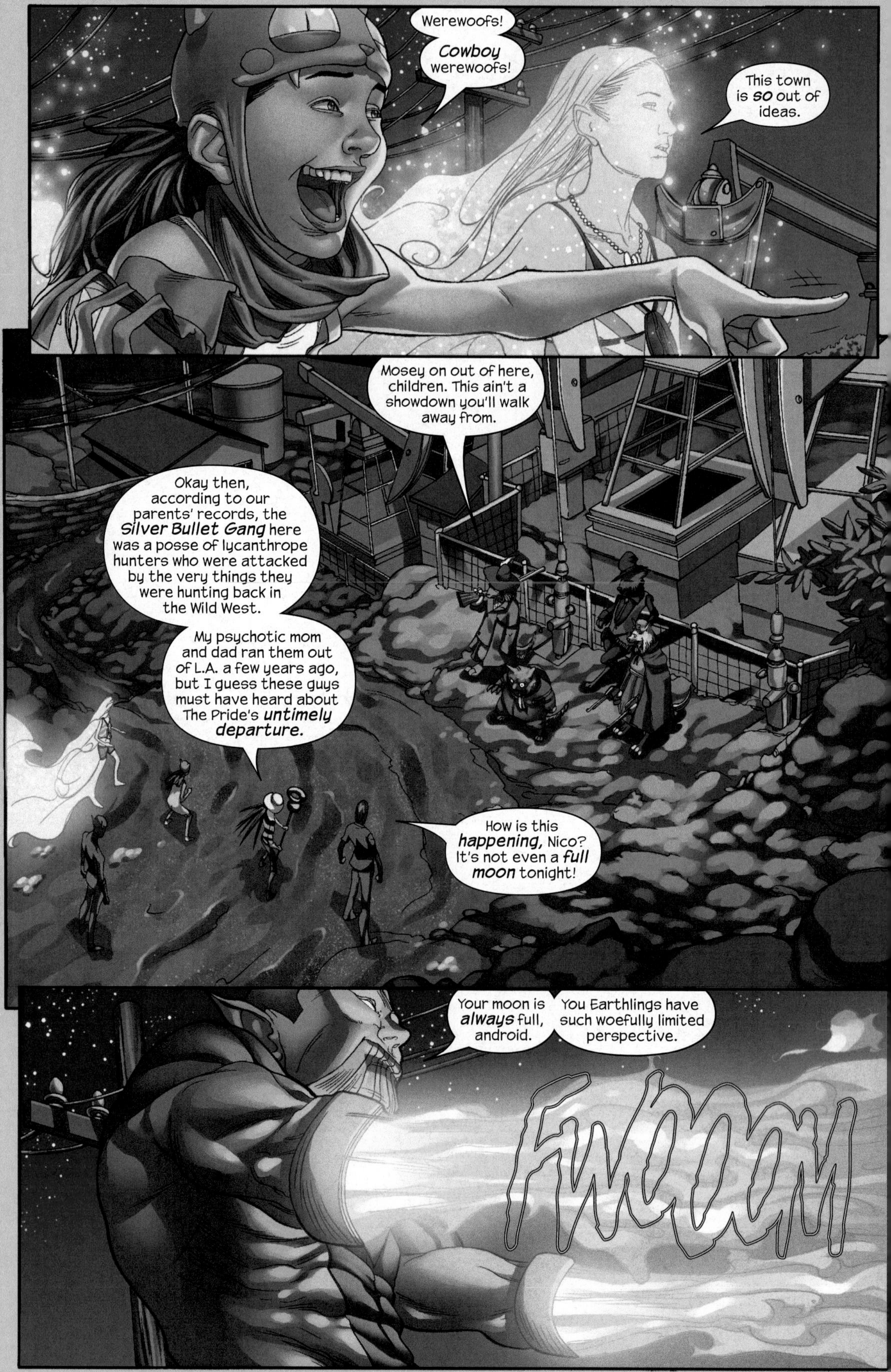
Werewoofs!
Cowboy werewoofs!
This town is *so* out of ideas.
Mosey on out of here, children. This ain't a showdown you'll walk away from.
Okay then, according to our parents' records, the *Silver Bullet Gang* here was a posse of lycanthrope hunters who were attacked by the very things they were hunting back in the Wild West.
My psychotic mom and dad ran them out of L.A. a few years ago, but I guess these guys must have heard about The Pride's *untimely departure.*
How is this *happening,* Nico? It's not even a *full moon* tonight!
Your moon is *always* full, android.
You Earthlings have such woefully limited perspective.
FWOOOM

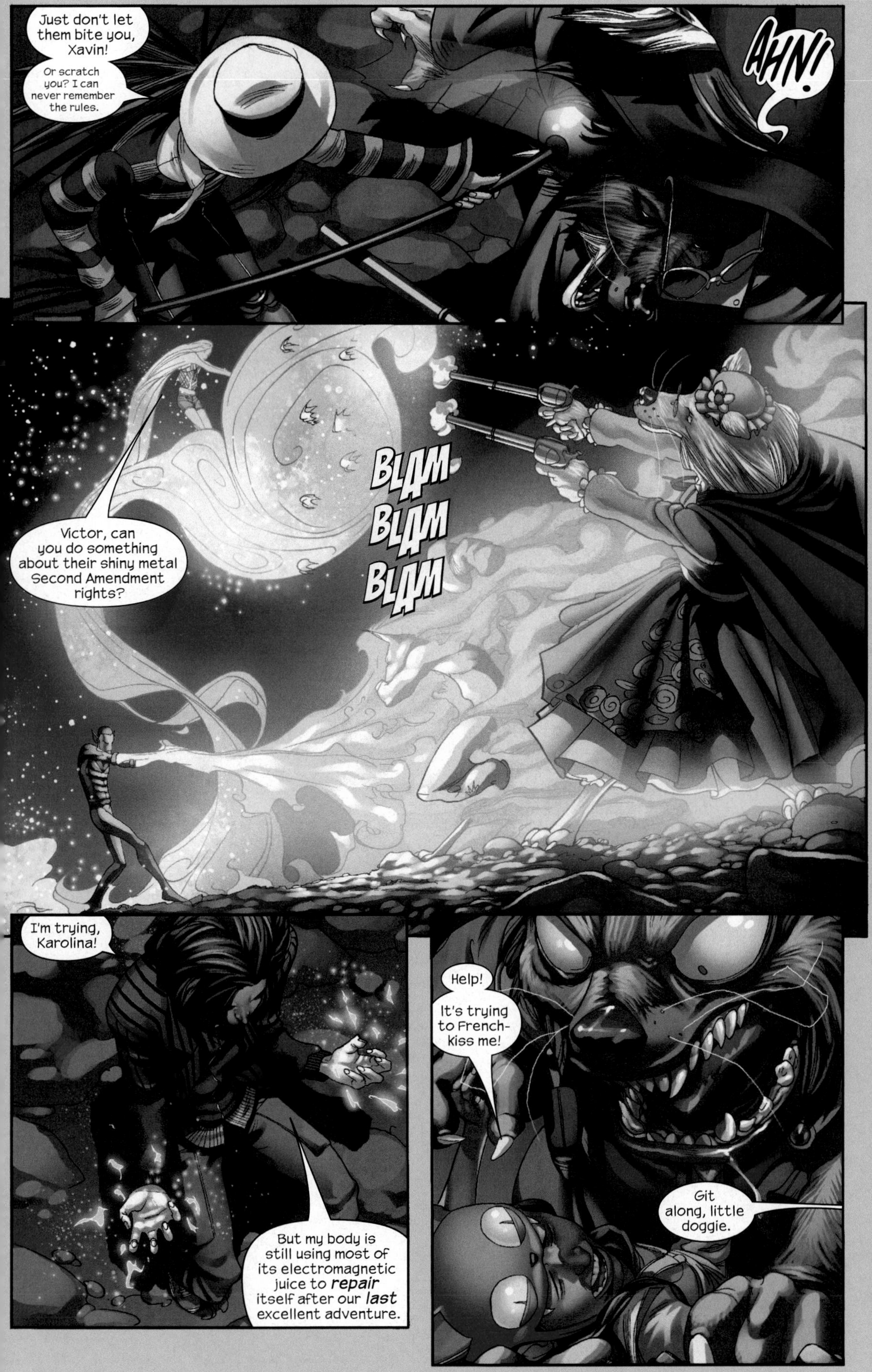
Just don't let them bite you, Xavin!
Or scratch you? I can never remember the rules.
AHN!
BLAM
BLAM
BLAM
Victor, can you do something about their shiny metal Second Amendment rights?
I'm trying, Karolina!
But my body is still using most of its electromagnetic juice to *repair* itself after our *last* excellent adventure.
Help!
It's trying to French-kiss me!
Git along, little doggie.

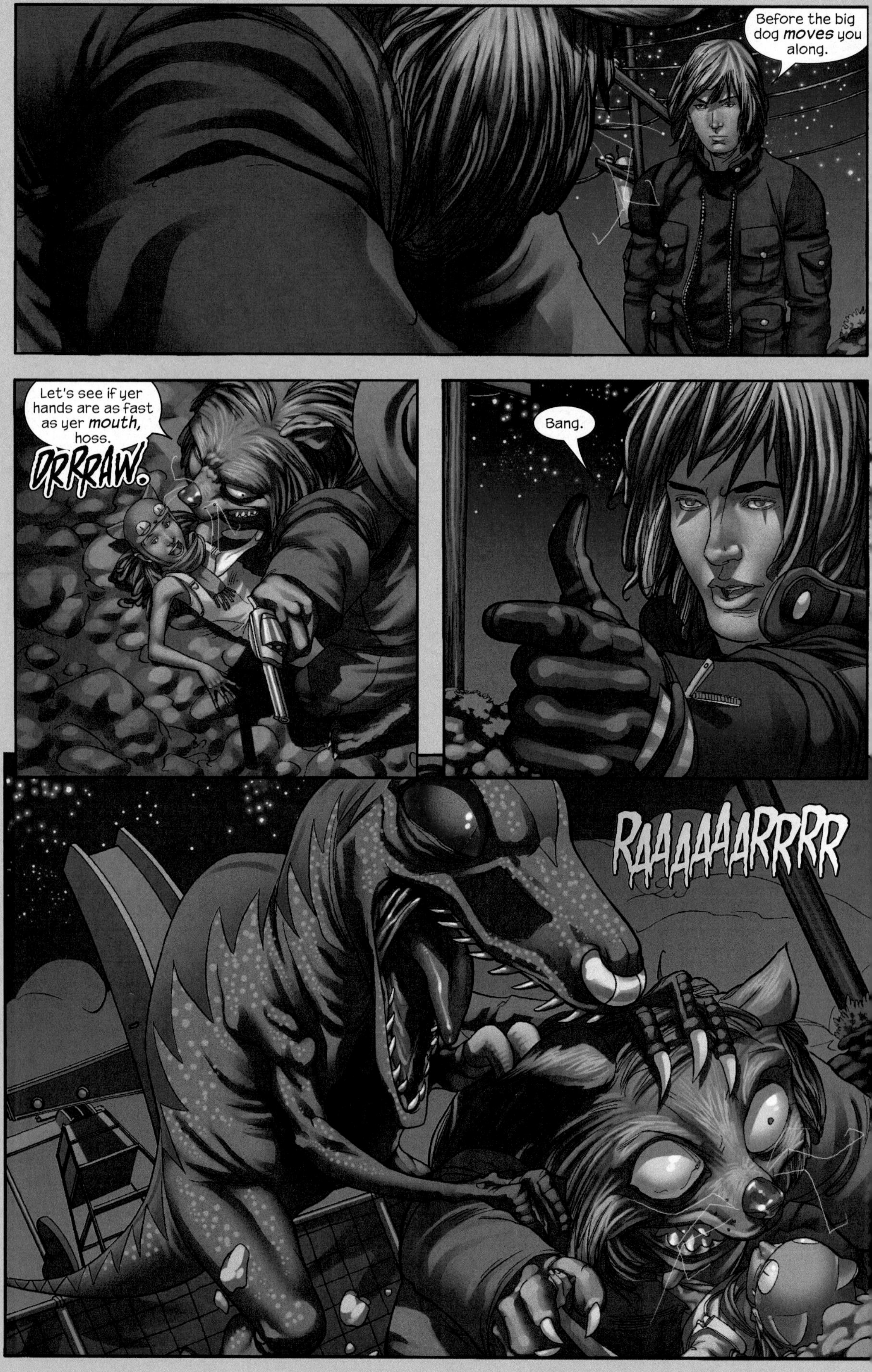
Before the big dog *moves* you along.
Let's see if yer hands are as fast as yer *mouth,* hoss.
DRRRAW.
Bang.
RAAAAARRRR

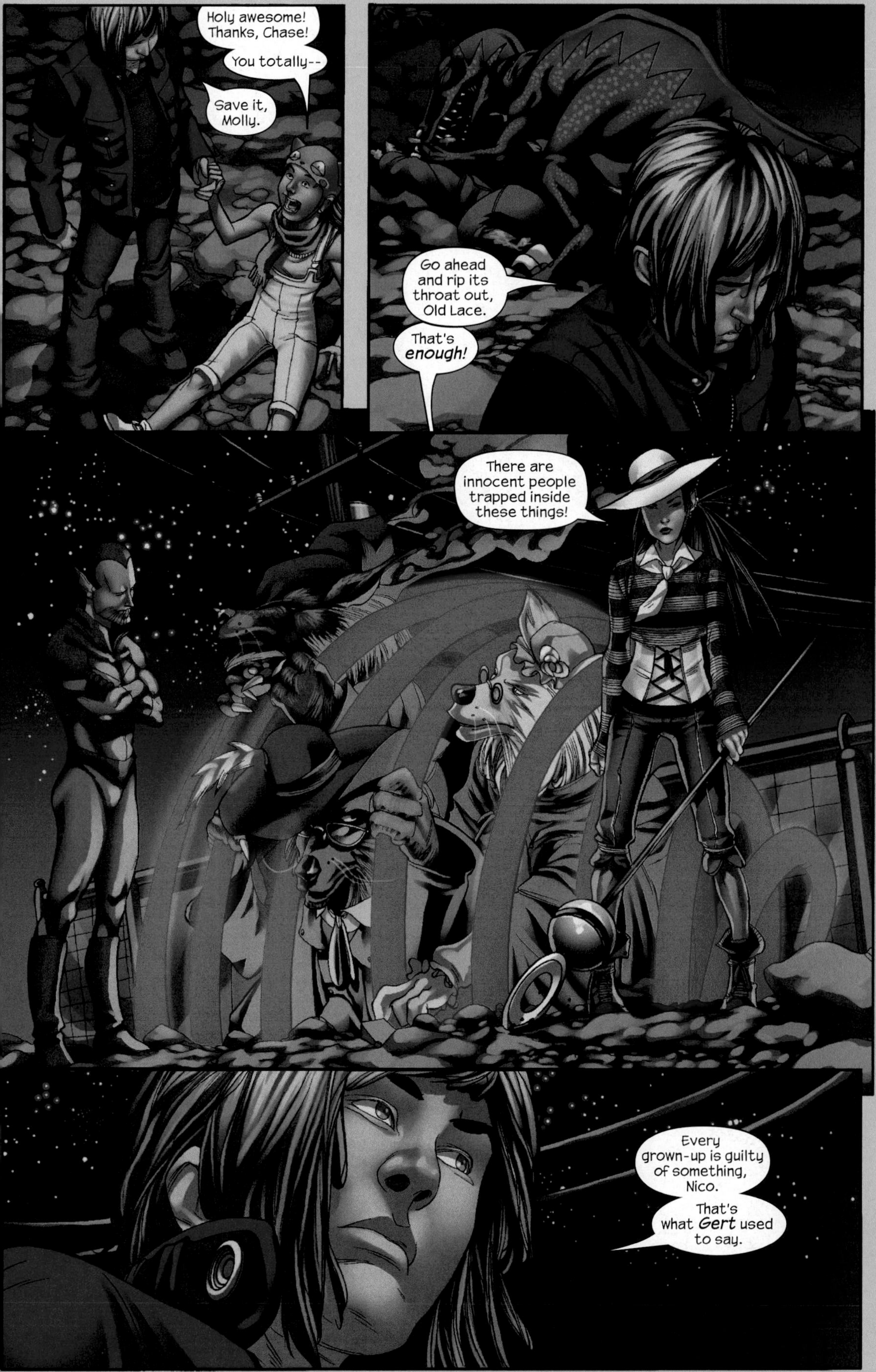
Holy awesome! Thanks, Chase!
You totally--
Save it, Molly.
Go ahead and rip its throat out, Old Lace.
That's *enough!*
There are innocent people trapped inside these things!
Every grown-up is guilty of something, Nico.
That's what *Gert* used to say.

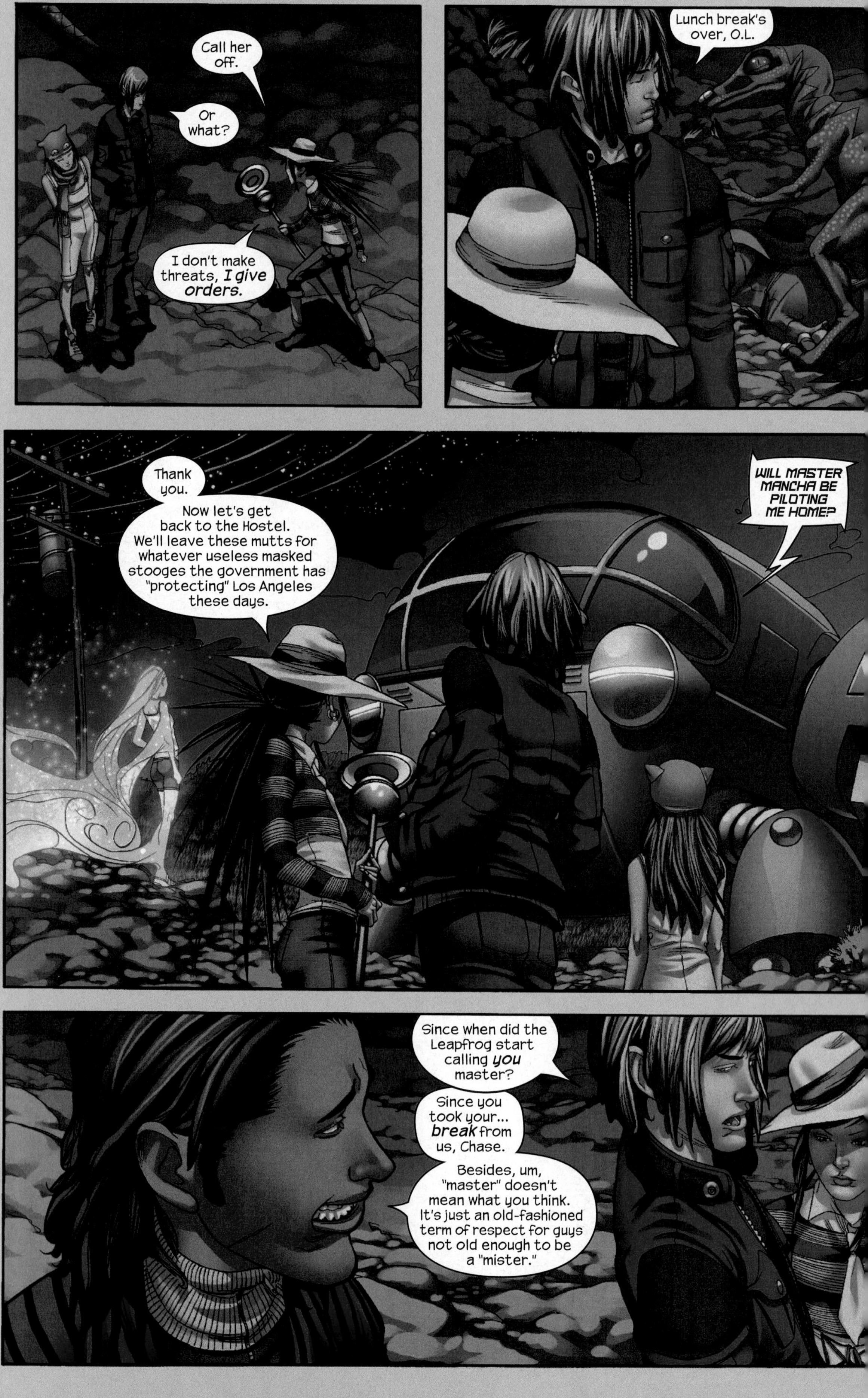
Call her off.
Or what?
I don't make threats, *I give orders.*
Lunch break's over, O.L.
Thank you.
Now let's get back to the Hostel. We'll leave these mutts for whatever useless masked stooges the government has "protecting" Los Angeles these days.
WILL MASTER MANCHA BE PILOTING ME HOME?
Since when did the Leapfrog start calling *you* master?
Since you took your... *break* from us, Chase.
Besides, um, "master" doesn't mean what you think. It's just an old-fashioned term of respect for guys not old enough to be a "mister."

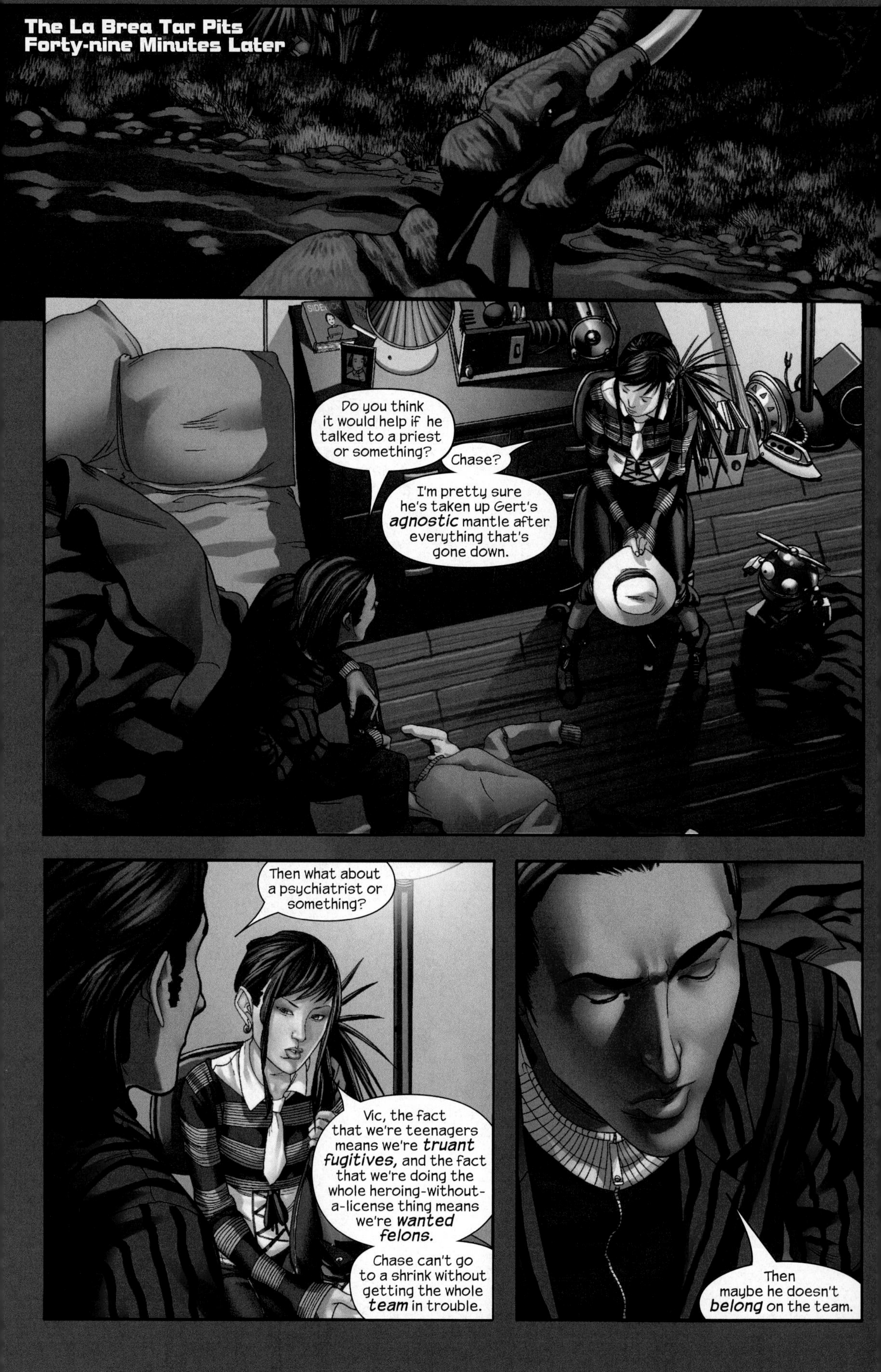

The La Brea Tar Pits
Forty-nine Minutes Later
Do you think it would help if he talked to a priest or something?
Chase?
I'm pretty sure he's taken up Gert's *agnostic* mantle after everything that's gone down.
Then what about a psychiatrist or something?
Vic, the fact that we're teenagers means we're *truant fugitives,* and the fact that we're doing the whole heroing-without-a-license thing means we're *wanted felons.*
Chase can't go to a shrink without getting the whole *team* in trouble.
Then maybe he doesn't *belong* on the team.

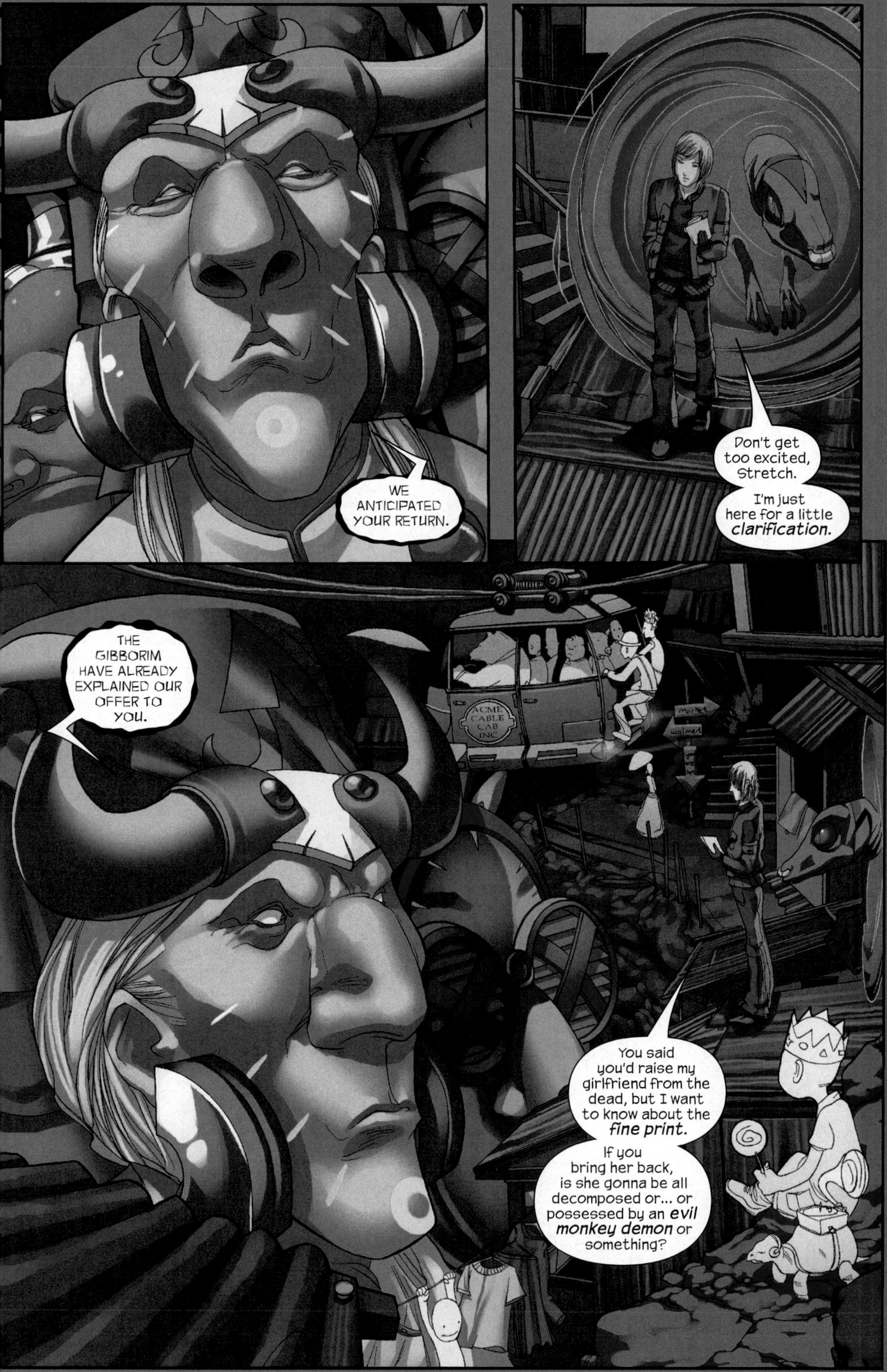
WE ANTICIPATED YOUR RETURN.
Don't get too excited, Stretch.
I'm just here for a little *clarification.*
THE GIBBORIM HAVE ALREADY EXPLAINED OUR OFFER TO YOU.
ACME CABLE CAB INC
You said you'd raise my girlfriend from the dead, but I want to know about the *fine print.*
If you bring her back, is she gonna be all decomposed or... or possessed by an *evil monkey demon* or something?

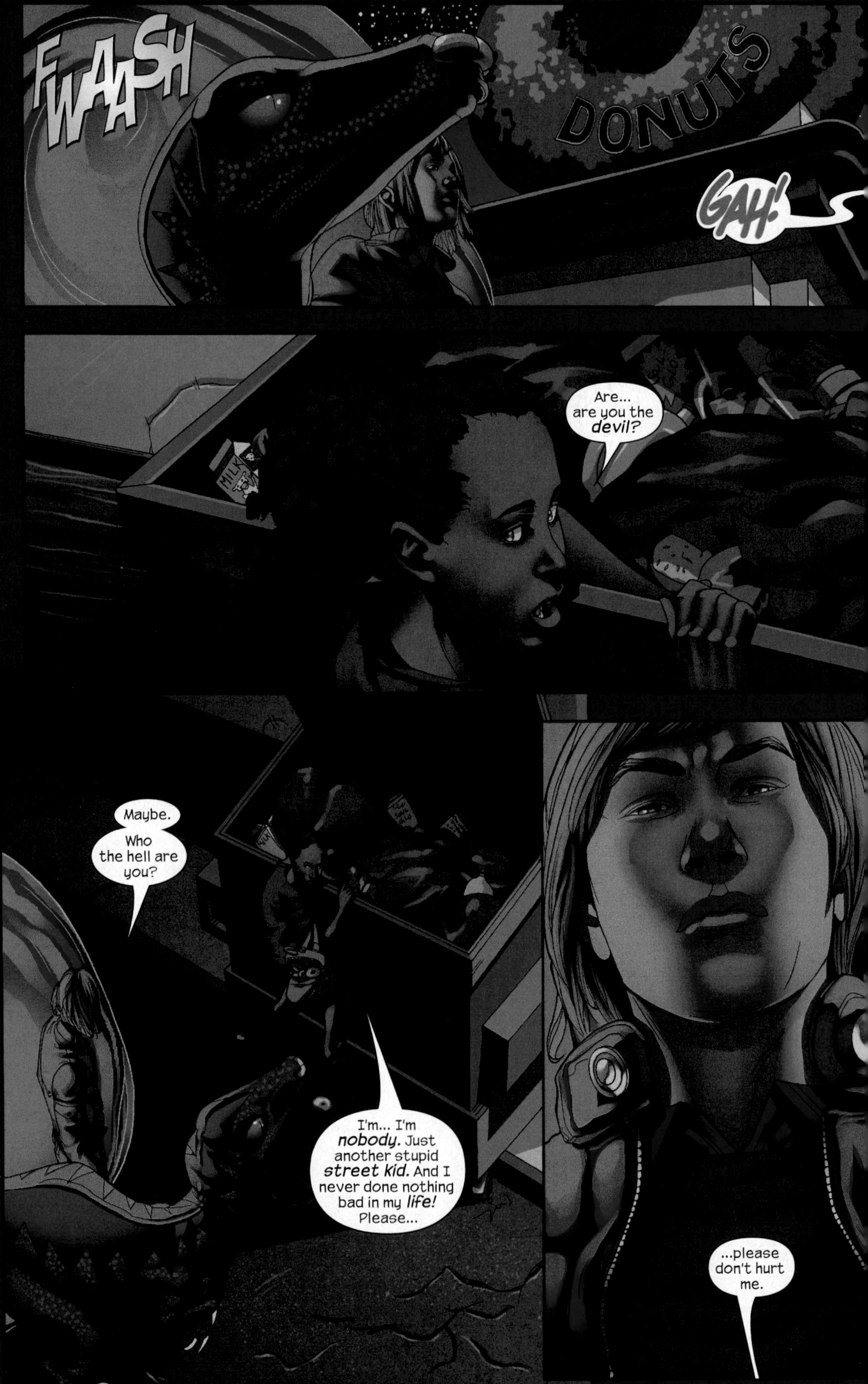
FWAASH
DONUTS
GAH!
Are... are you the *devil?*
Maybe.
Who the hell are you?
I'm... I'm *nobody.* Just another stupid *street kid.* And I never done nothing bad in my *life!* Please...
...please don't hurt me.

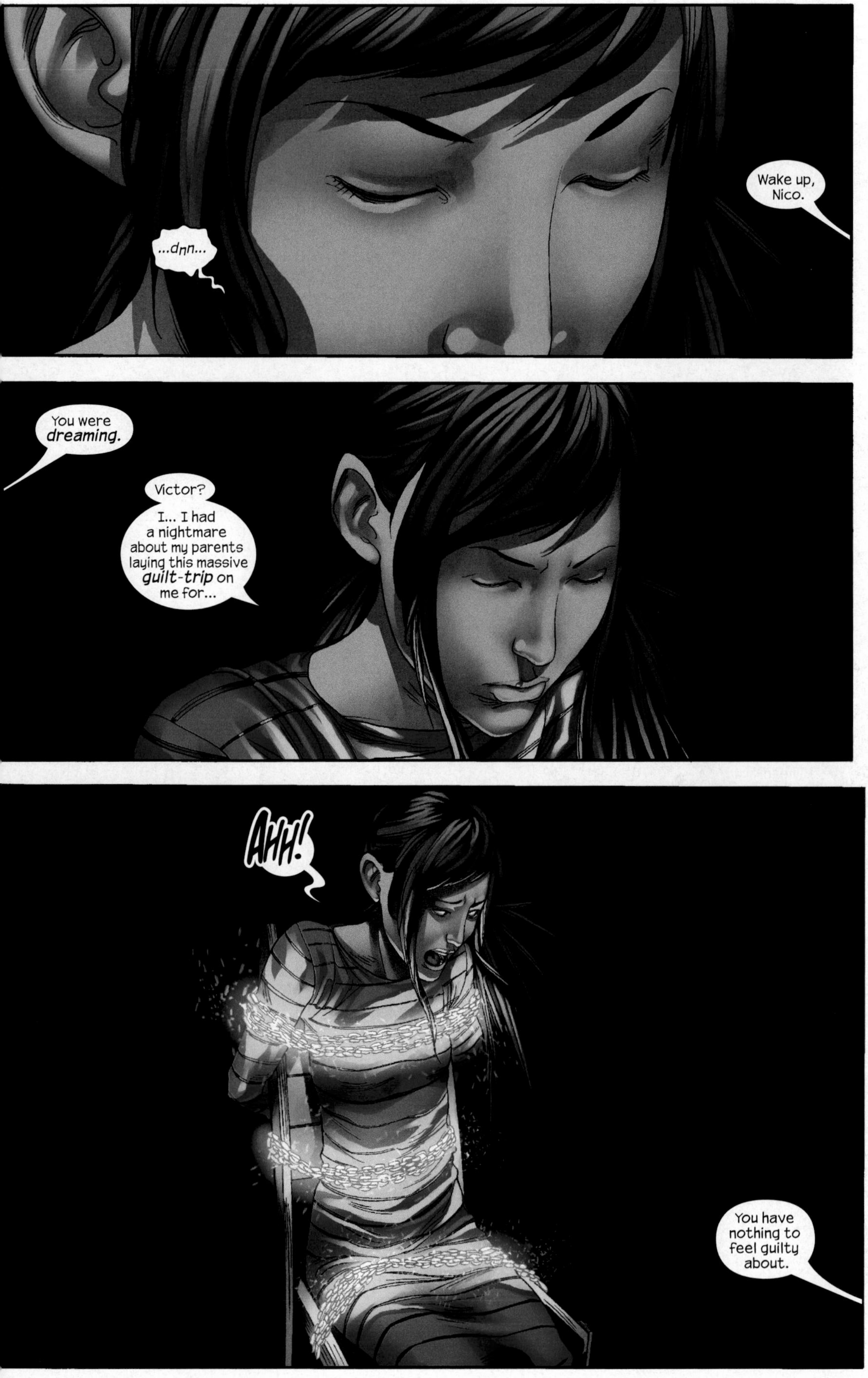

Wake up, Nico.
...dnn...
You were *dreaming.*
Victor?
I... I had a nightmare about my parents laying this massive ***guilt-trip*** on me for...
AHH!
You have nothing to feel guilty about.

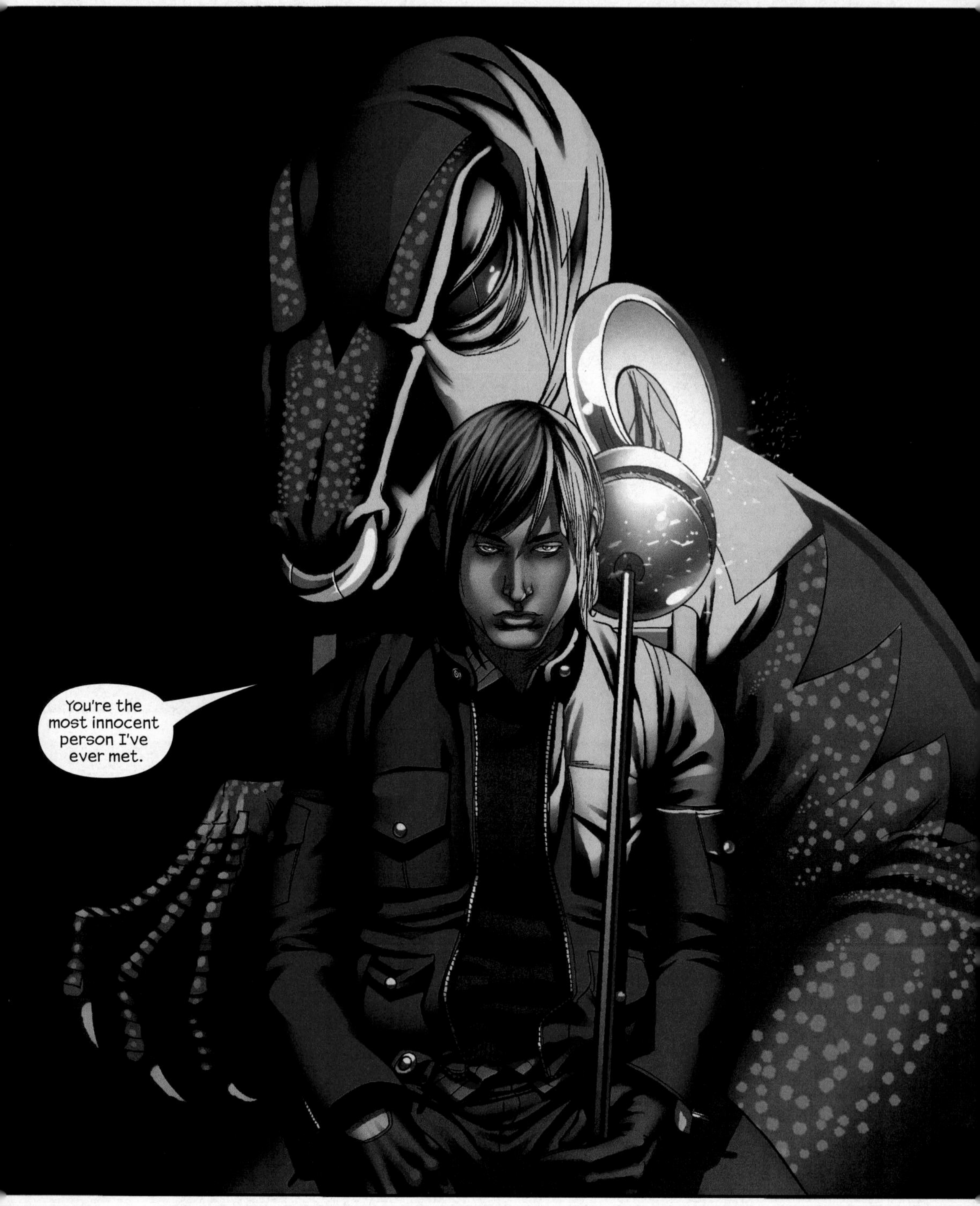
You're the most innocent person I've ever met.

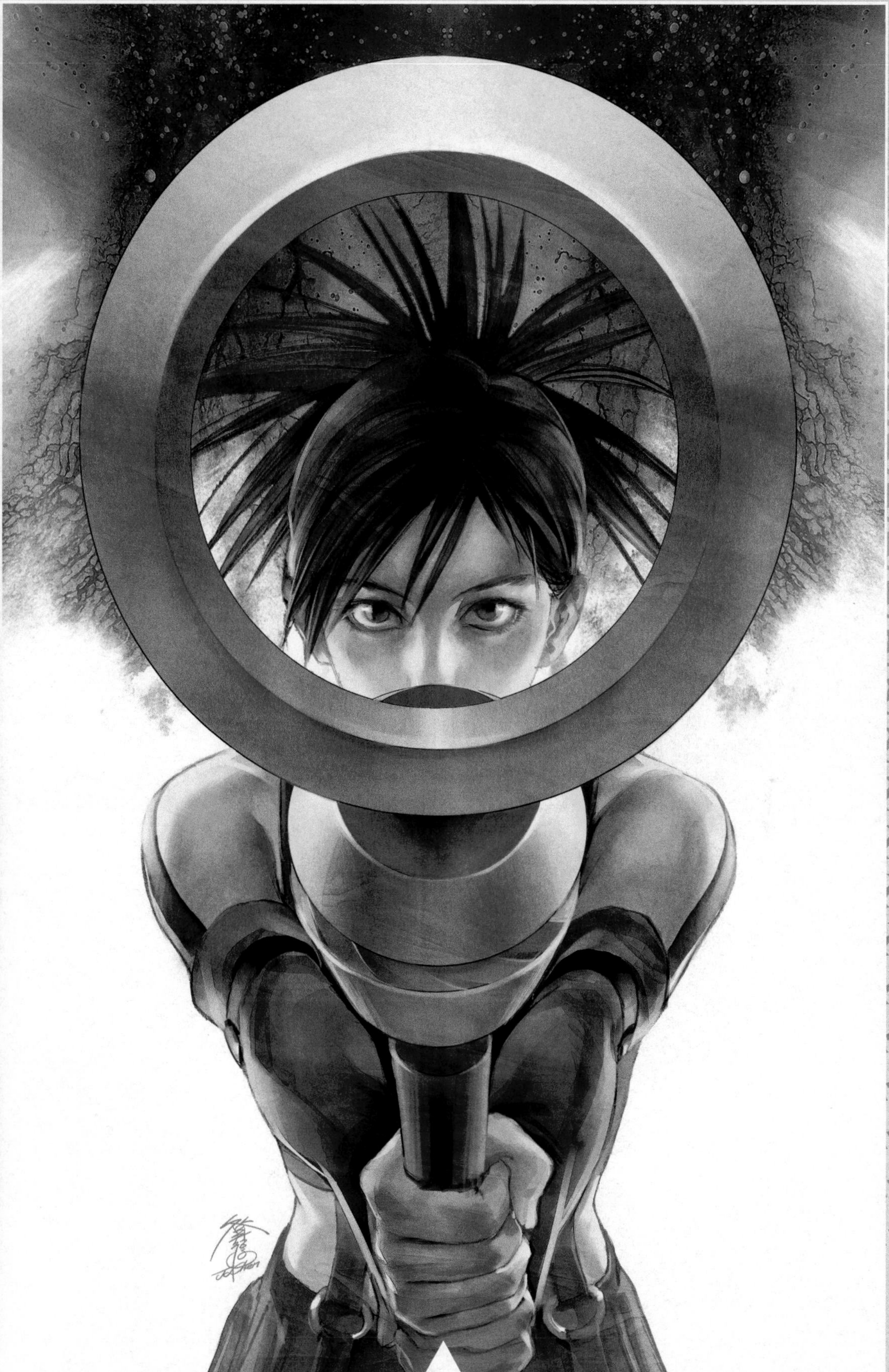

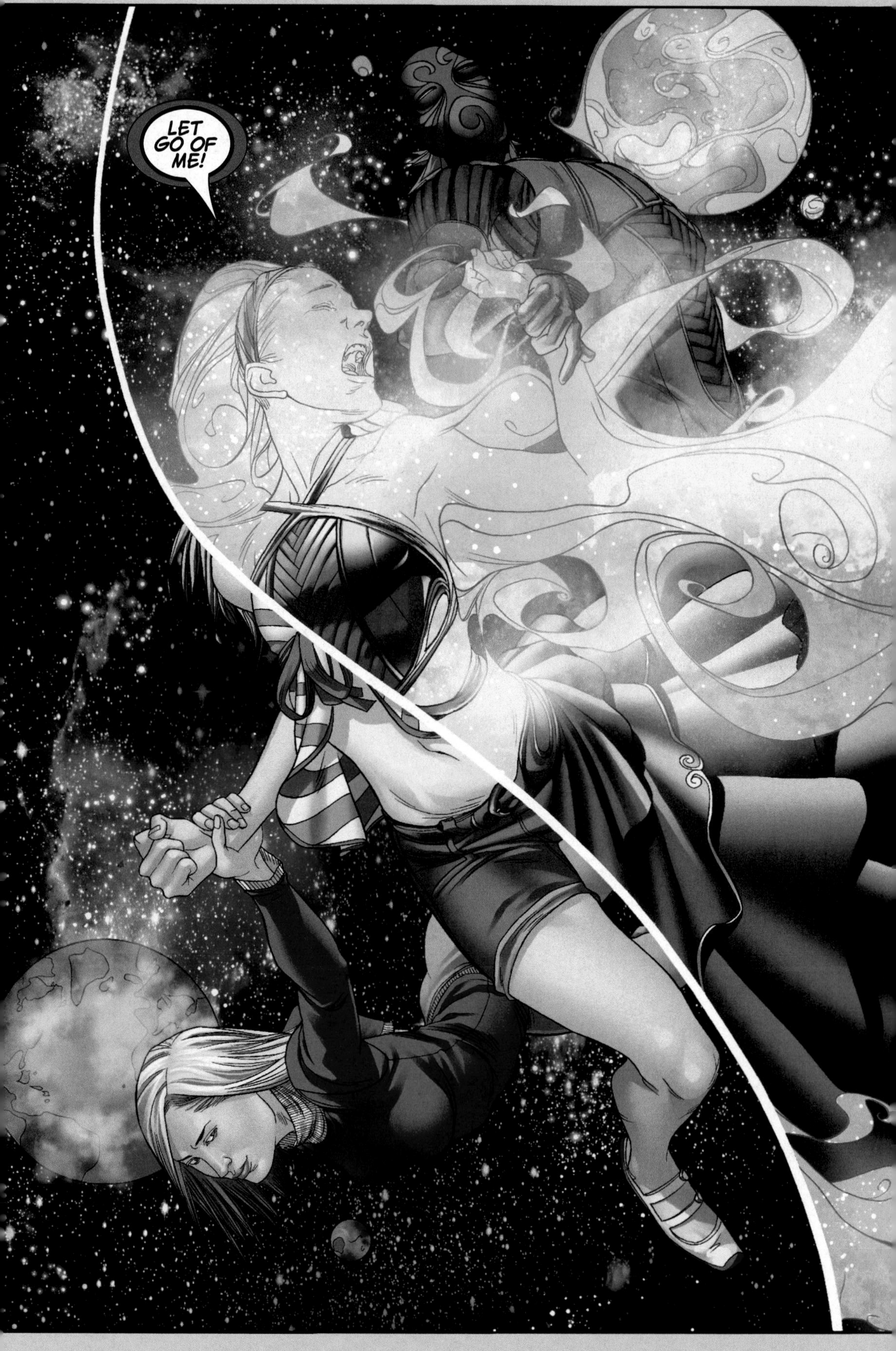
LET GO OF ME!

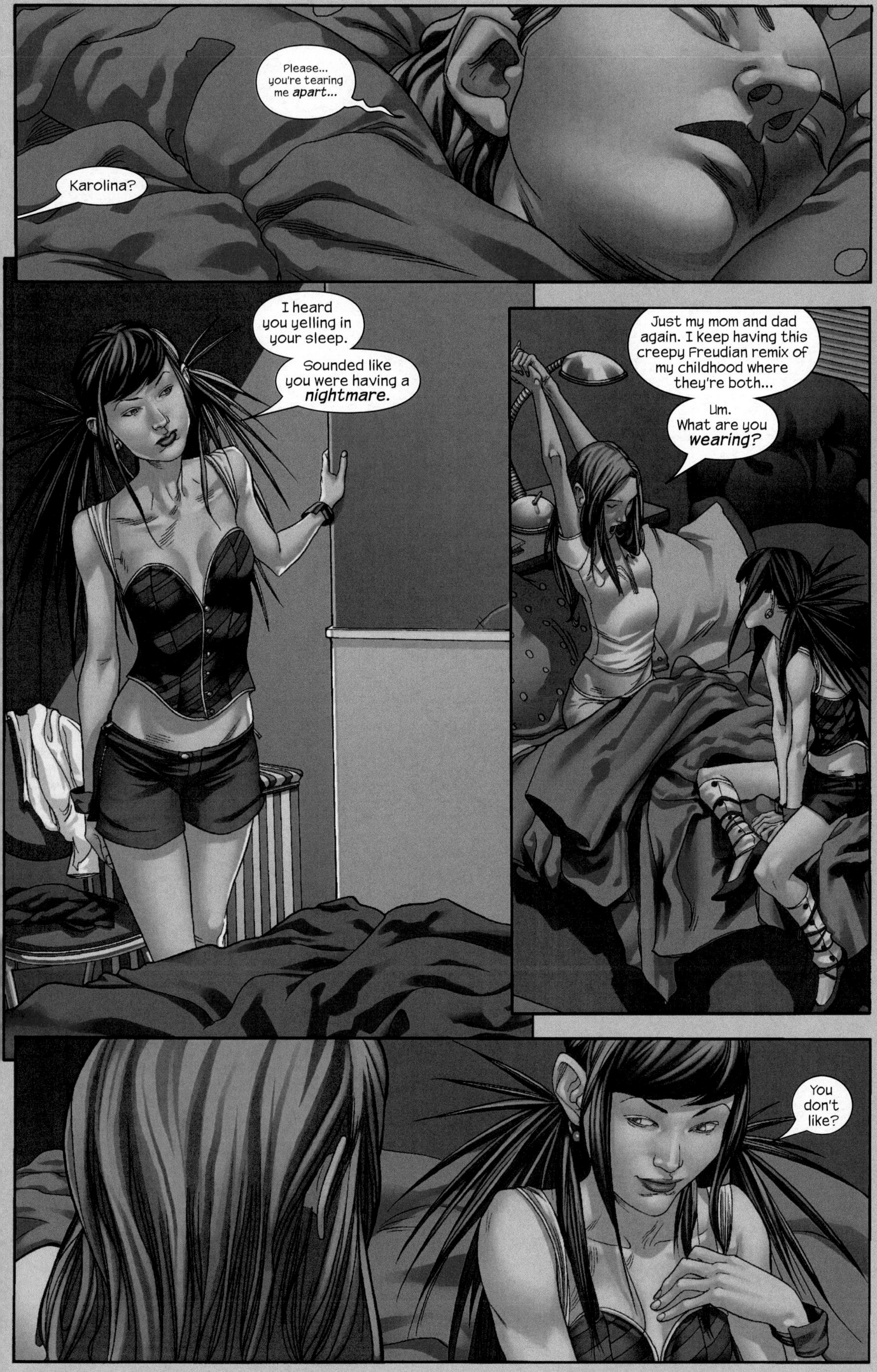
Please... you're tearing me apart...
Karolina?
I heard you yelling in your sleep.
Sounded like you were having a nightmare.
Just my mom and dad again. I keep having this creepy Freudian remix of my childhood where they're both...
Um. What are you wearing?
You don't like?

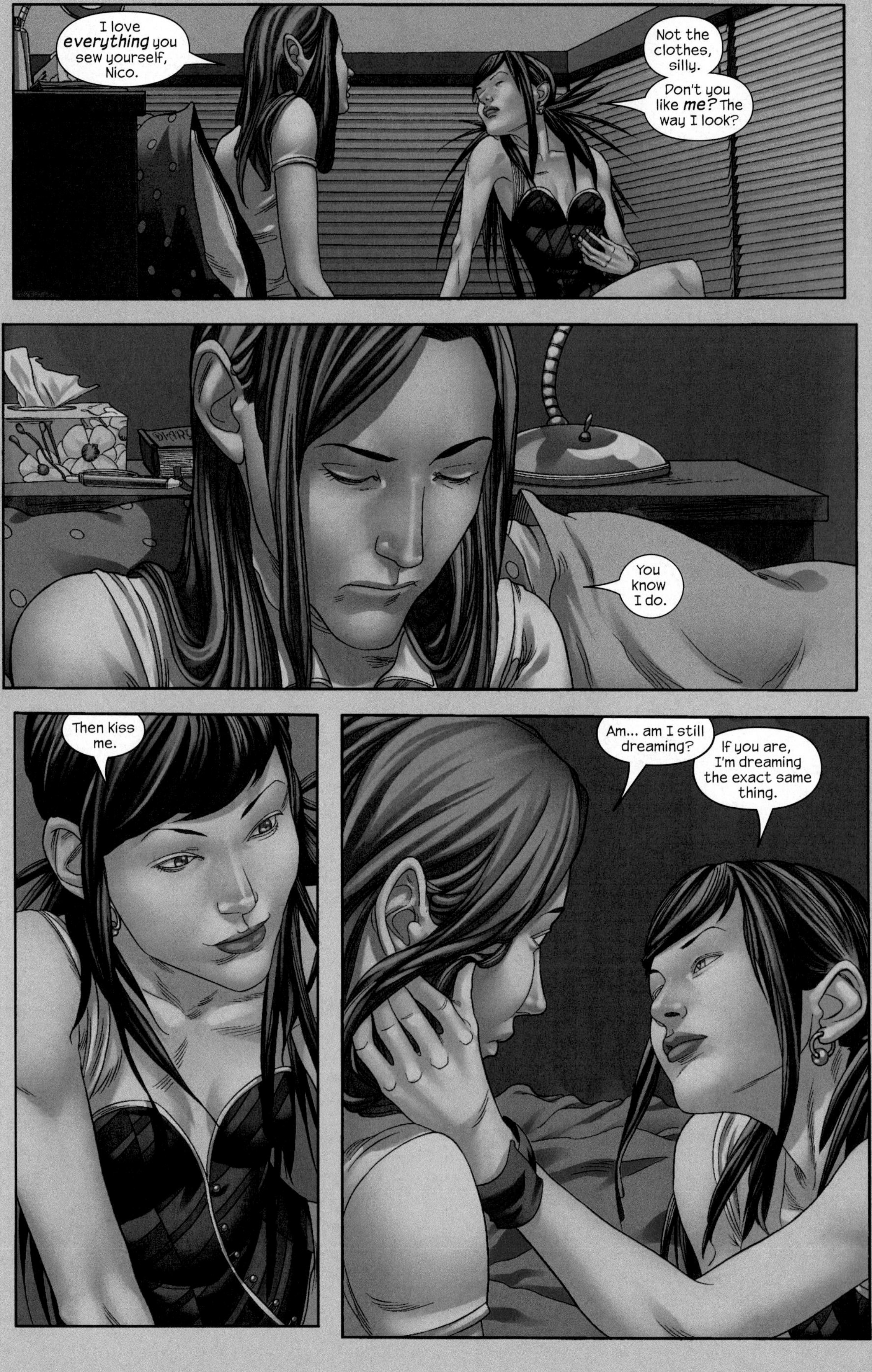
I love **everything** you sew yourself, Nico.
Not the clothes, silly.
Don't you like **me?** The way I look?
You know I do.
Then kiss me.
Am... am I still dreaming?
If you are, I'm dreaming the exact same thing.

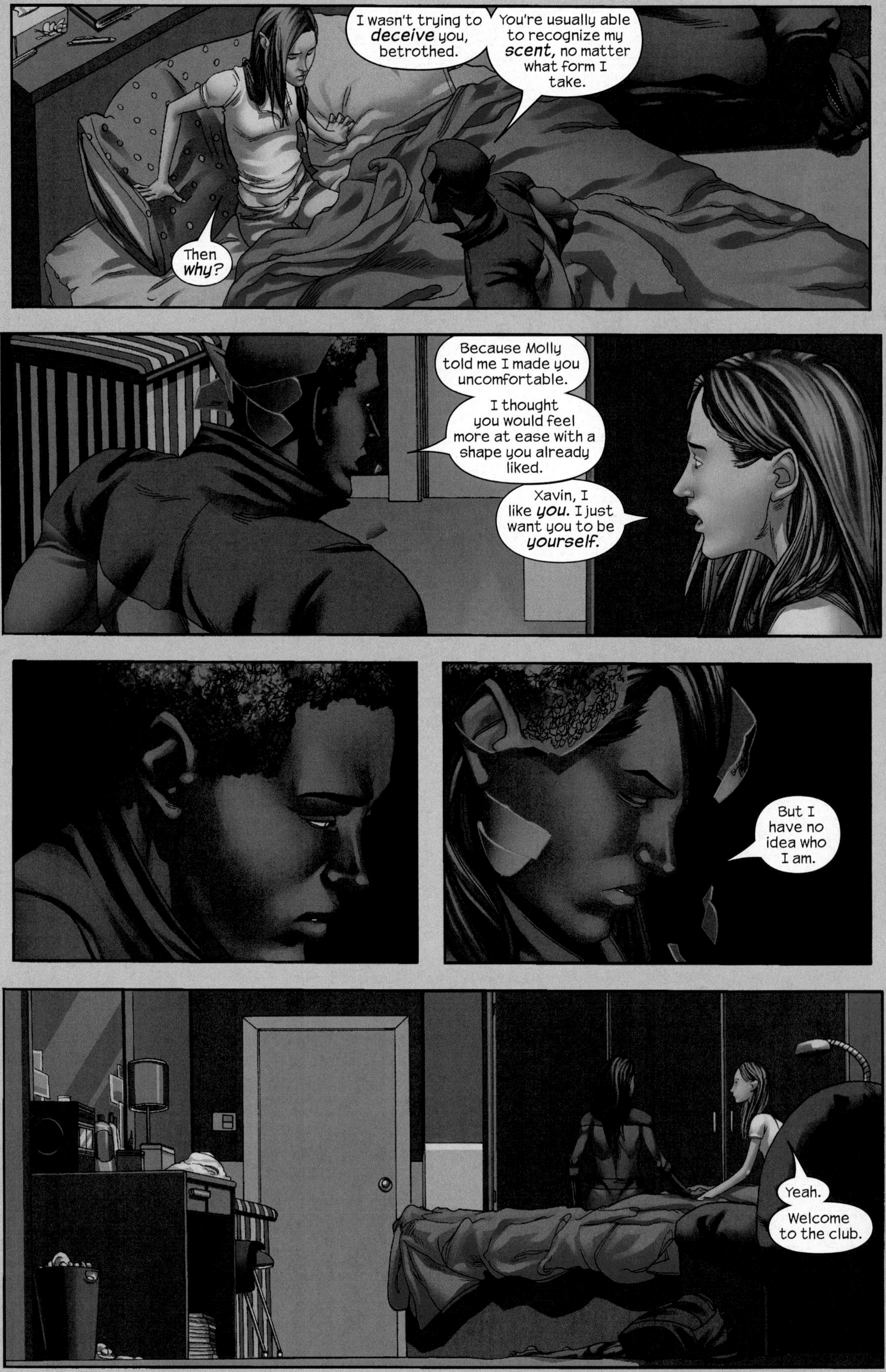
I wasn't trying to deceive you, betrothed.
You're usually able to recognize my scent, no matter what form I take.
Then why?
Because Molly told me I made you uncomfortable.
I thought you would feel more at ease with a shape you already liked.
Xavin, I like you. I just want you to be yourself.
But I have no idea who I am.
Yeah.
Welcome to the club.

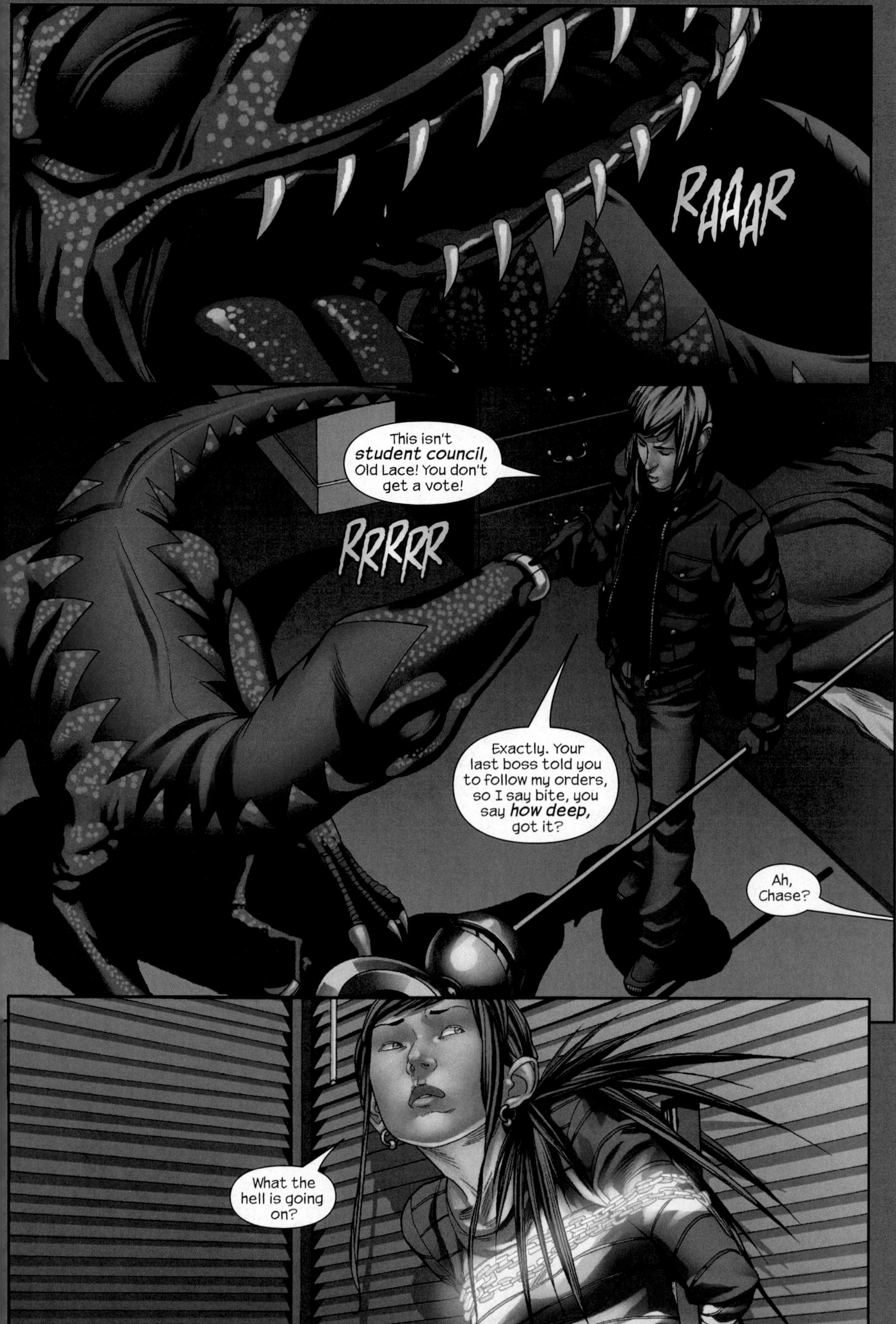
RAAAR
This isn't student council, Old Lace! You don't get a vote!
RRRRR
Exactly. Your last boss told you to follow my orders, so I say bite, you say how deep, got it?
Ah, Chase?
What the hell is going on?

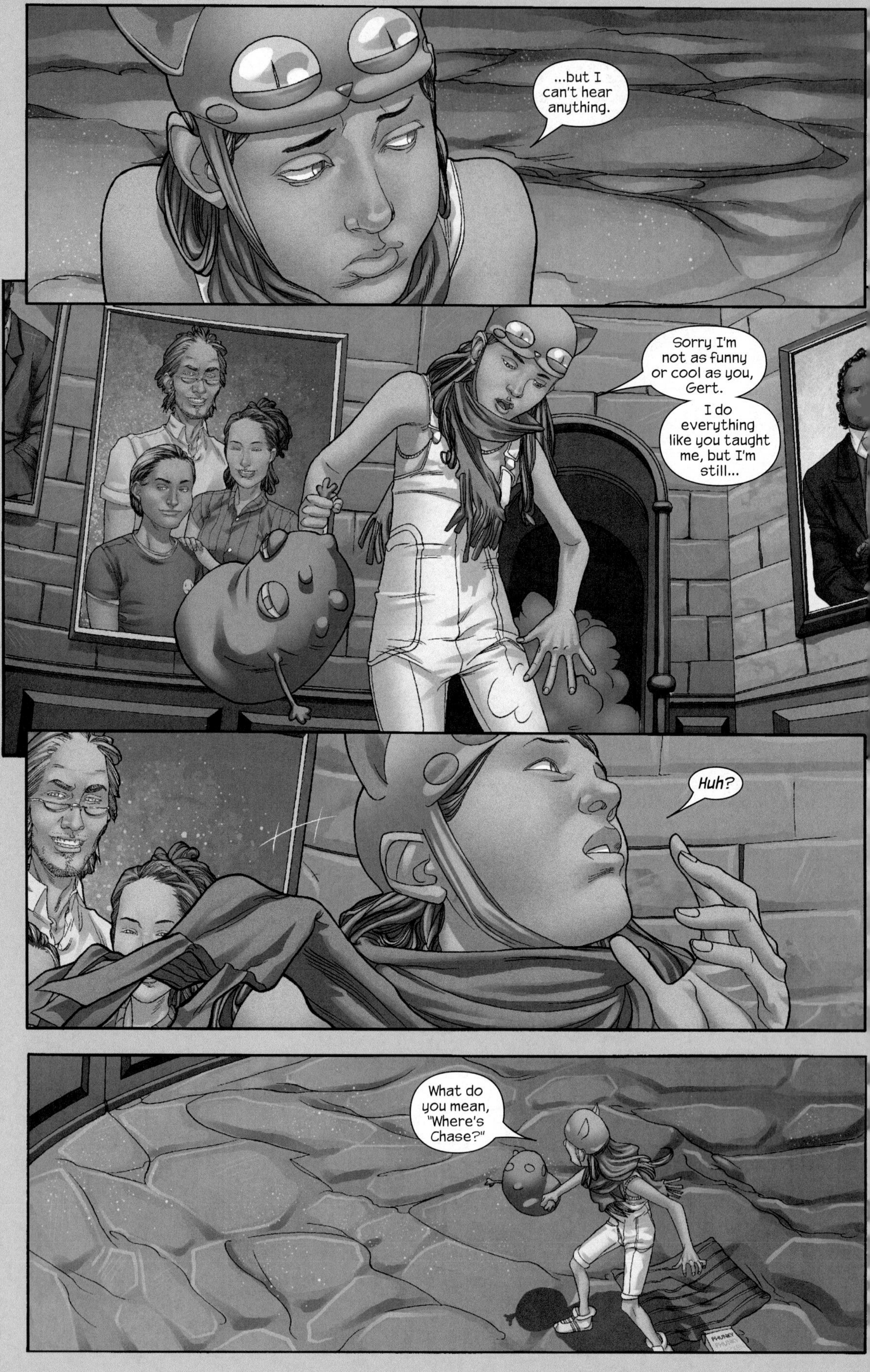
...but I can't hear anything.
Sorry I'm not as funny or cool as you, Gert.
I do everything like you taught me, but I'm still...
Huh?
What do you mean, "Where's Chase?"

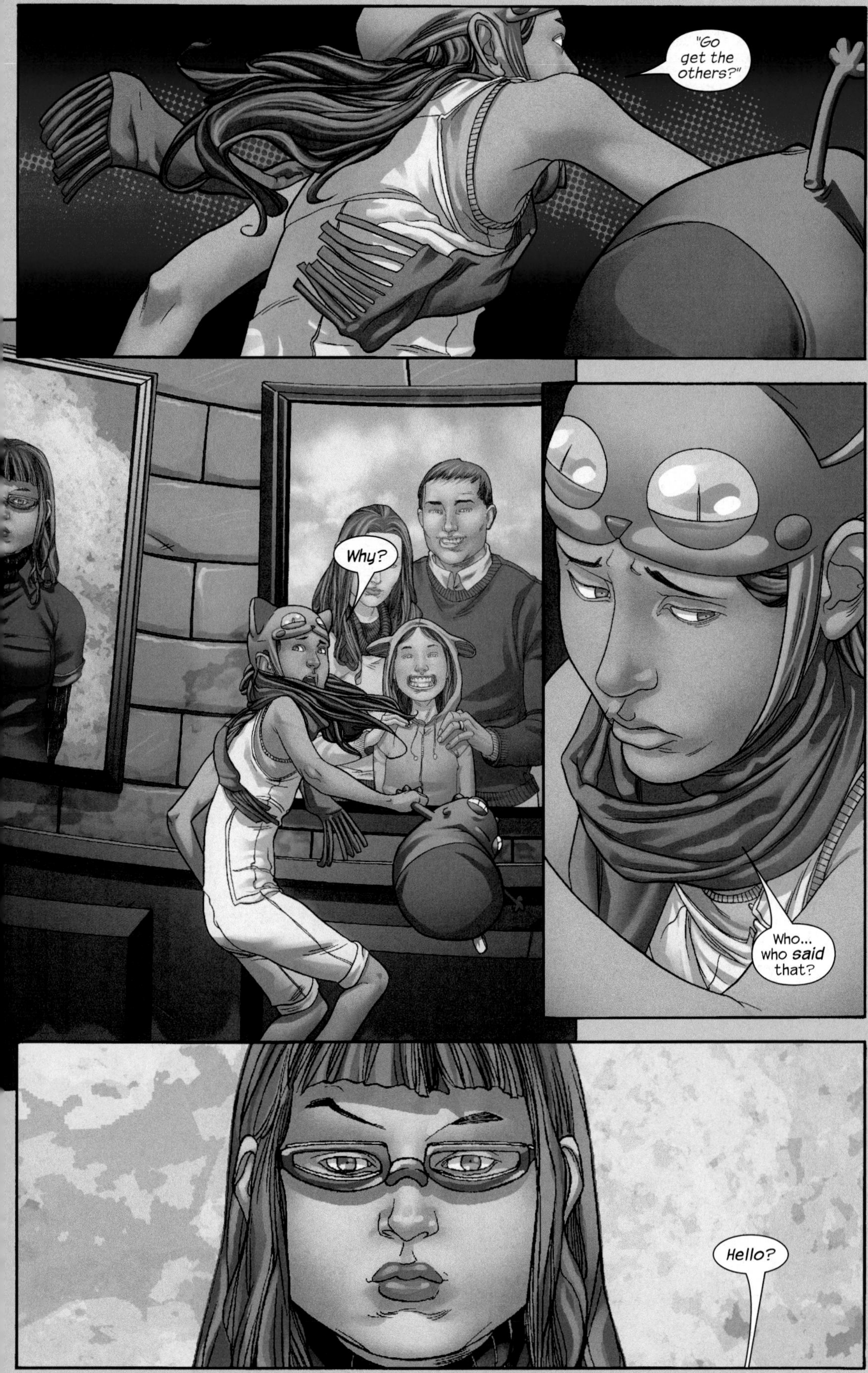
"Go get the others?"
Why?
Who... who said that?
Hello?

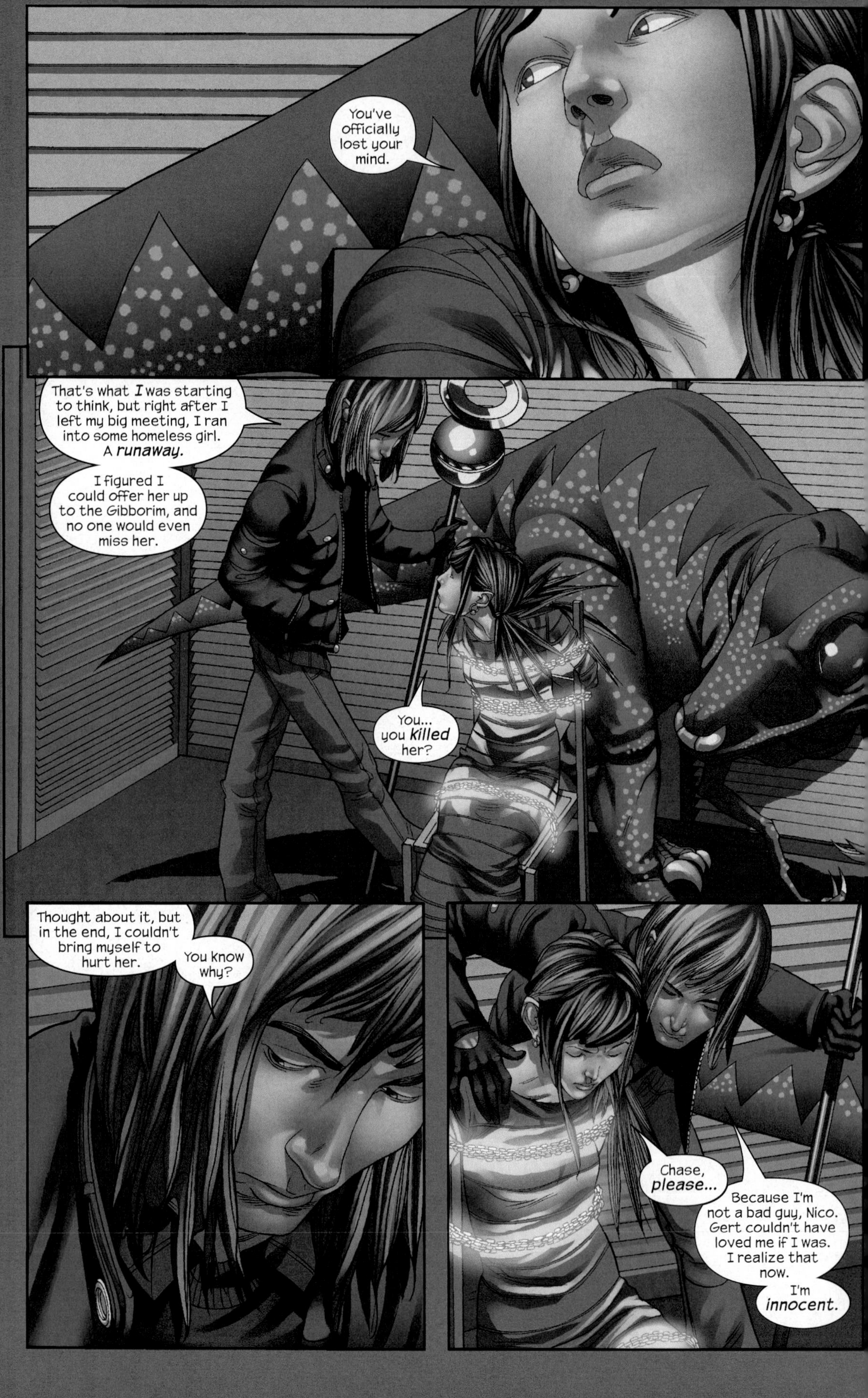
You've officially lost your mind.
That's what I was starting to think, but right after I left my big meeting, I ran into some homeless girl. A runaway.
I figured I could offer her up to the Gibborim, and no one would even miss her.
You... you killed her?
Thought about it, but in the end, I couldn't bring myself to hurt her.
You know why?
Chase, please...
Because I'm not a bad guy, Nico. Gert couldn't have loved me if I was. I realize that now.
I'm innocent.

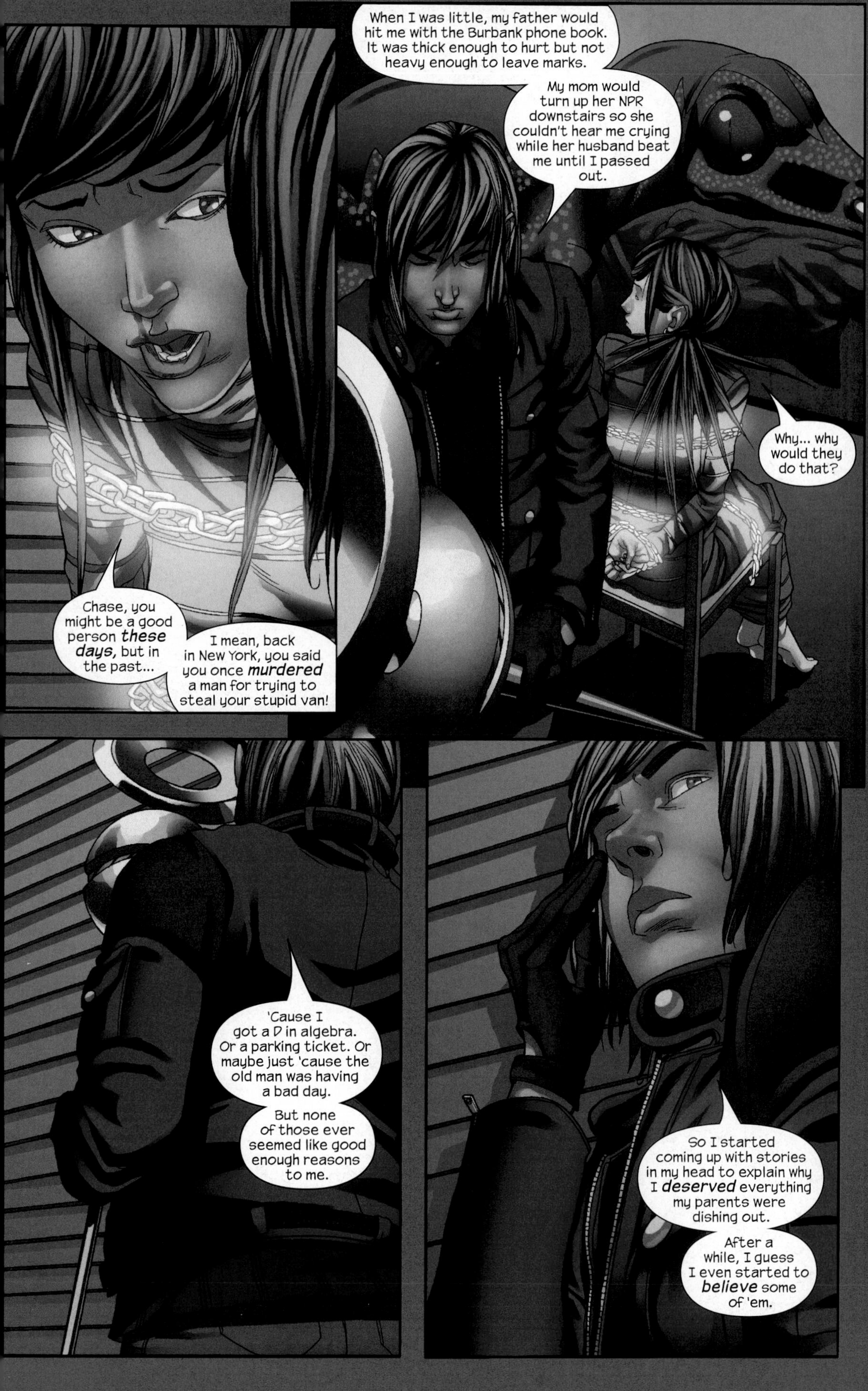
When I was little, my father would hit me with the Burbank phone book. It was thick enough to hurt but not heavy enough to leave marks.
My mom would turn up her NPR downstairs so she couldn't hear me crying while her husband beat me until I passed out.
Why... why would they do that?
Chase, you might be a good person *these days,* but in the past...
I mean, back in New York, you said you once *murdered* a man for trying to steal your stupid van!
'Cause I got a D in algebra. Or a parking ticket. Or maybe just 'cause the old man was having a bad day.
But none of those ever seemed like good enough reasons to me.
So I started coming up with stories in my head to explain why I *deserved* everything my parents were dishing out.
After a while, I guess I even started to *believe* some of 'em.

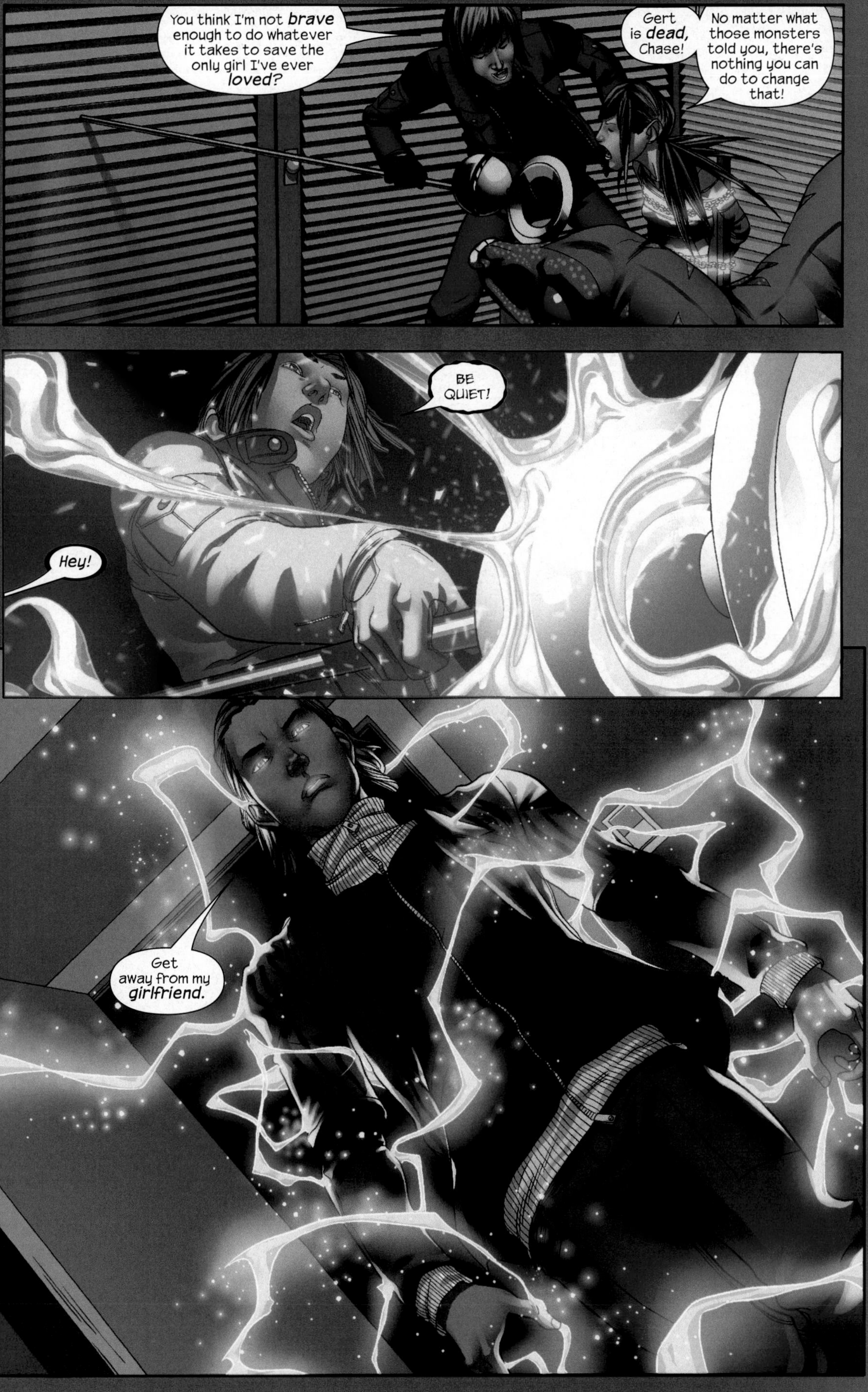
You think I'm not brave enough to do whatever it takes to save the only girl I've ever loved?
Gert is dead, Chase!
No matter what those monsters told you, there's nothing you can do to change that!
BE QUIET!
Hey!
Get away from my girlfriend.

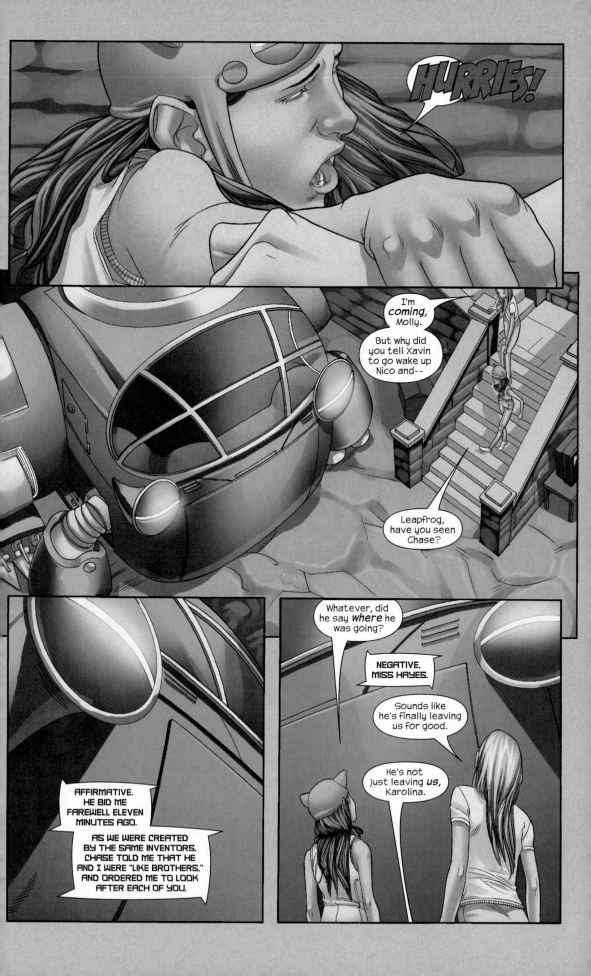

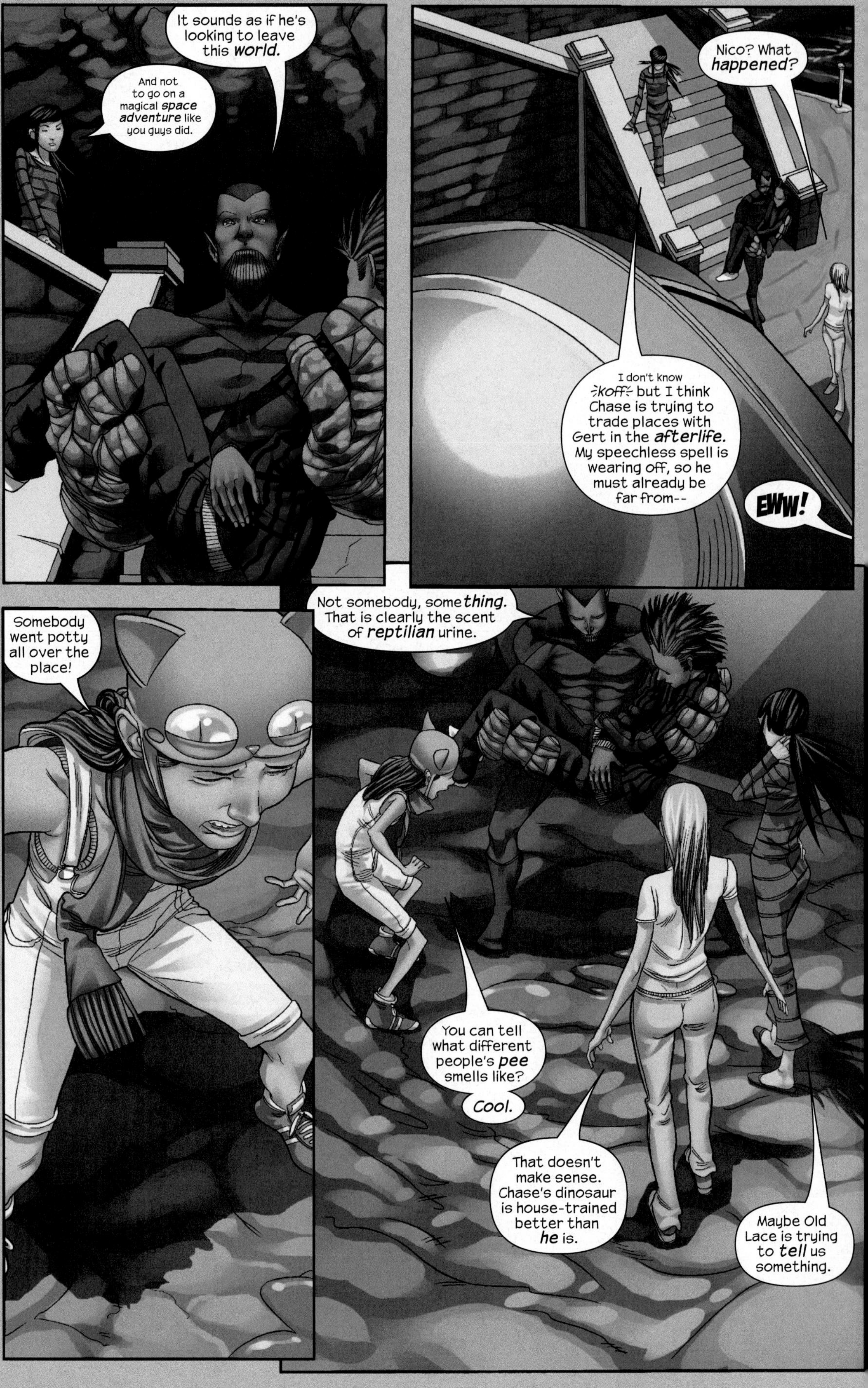

It sounds as if he's looking to leave this *world.*
And not to go on a magical *space adventure* like you guys did.
Nico? What *happened?*
I don't know *koff* but I think Chase is trying to trade places with Gert in the *afterlife.* My speechless spell is wearing off, so he must already be far from--
EWW!
Somebody went potty all over the place!
Not somebody, some*thing.* That is clearly the scent of *reptilian* urine.
You can tell what different people's *pee* smells like?
Cool.
That doesn't make sense. Chase's dinosaur is house-trained better than *he* is.
Maybe Old Lace is trying to *tell* us something.

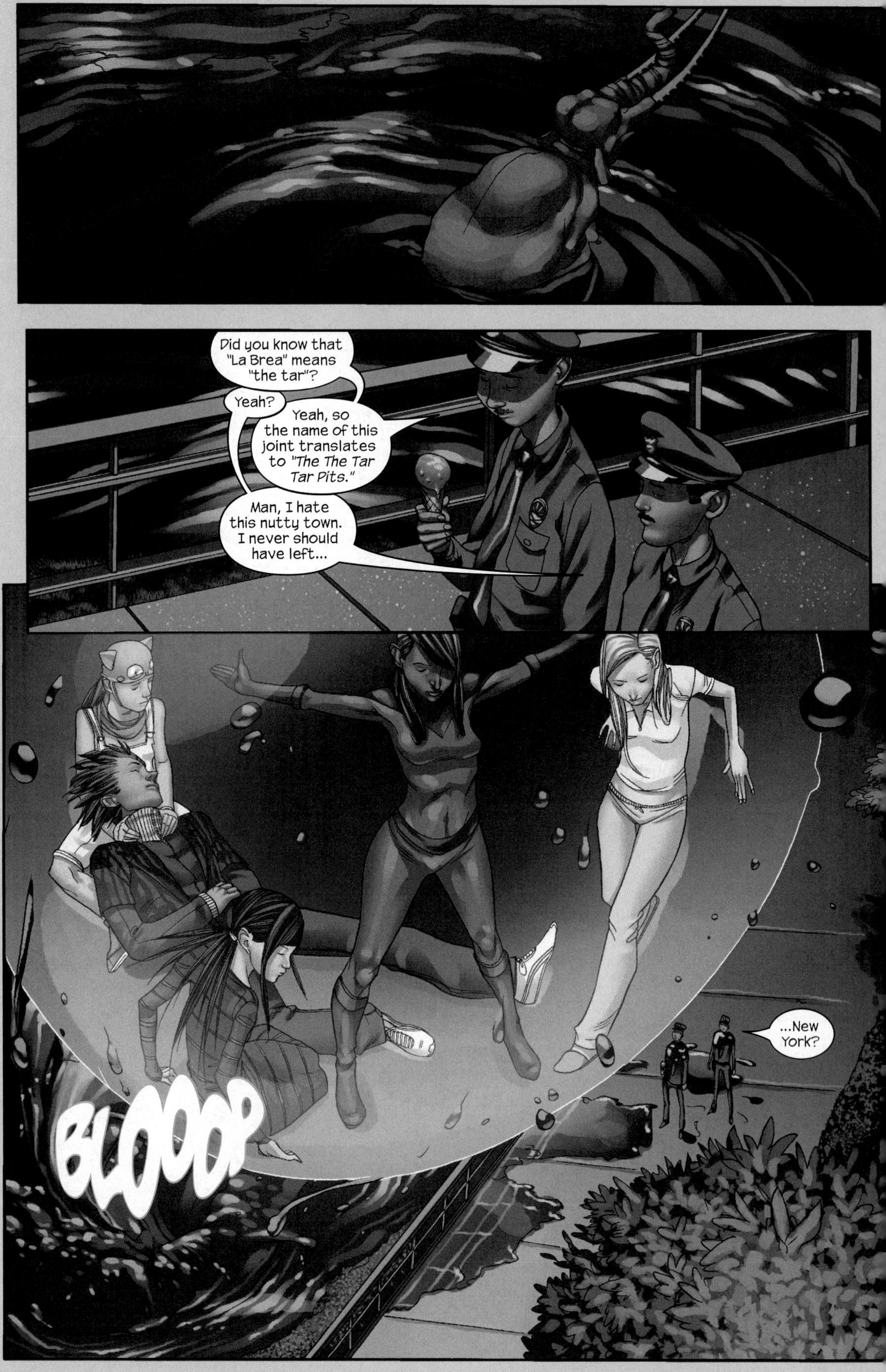
Did you know that "La Brea" means "the tar"?
Yeah?
Yeah, so the name of this joint translates to "The The Tar Tar Pits."
Man, I hate this nutty town. I never should have left...
BLOOOP
...New York?

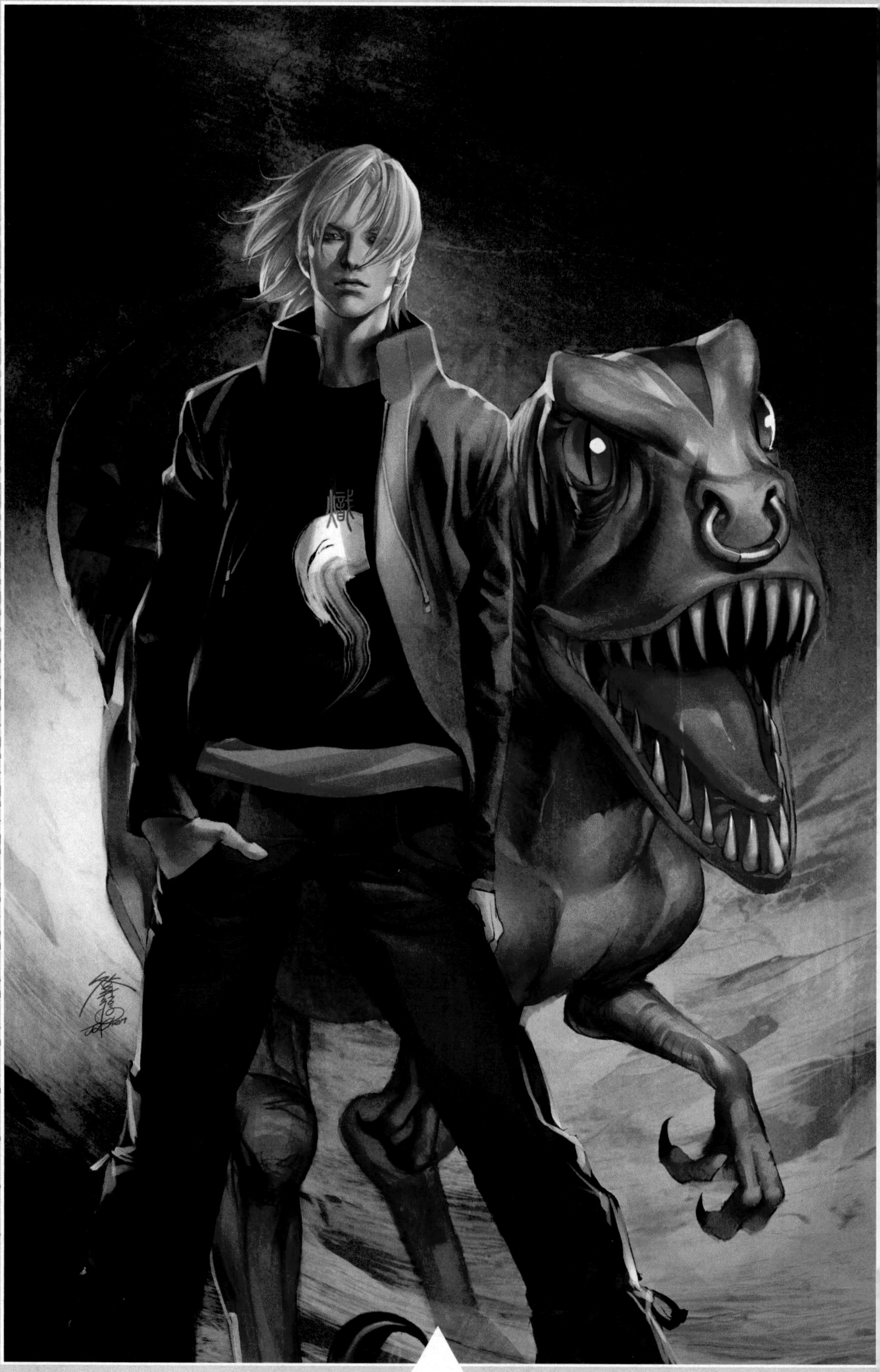

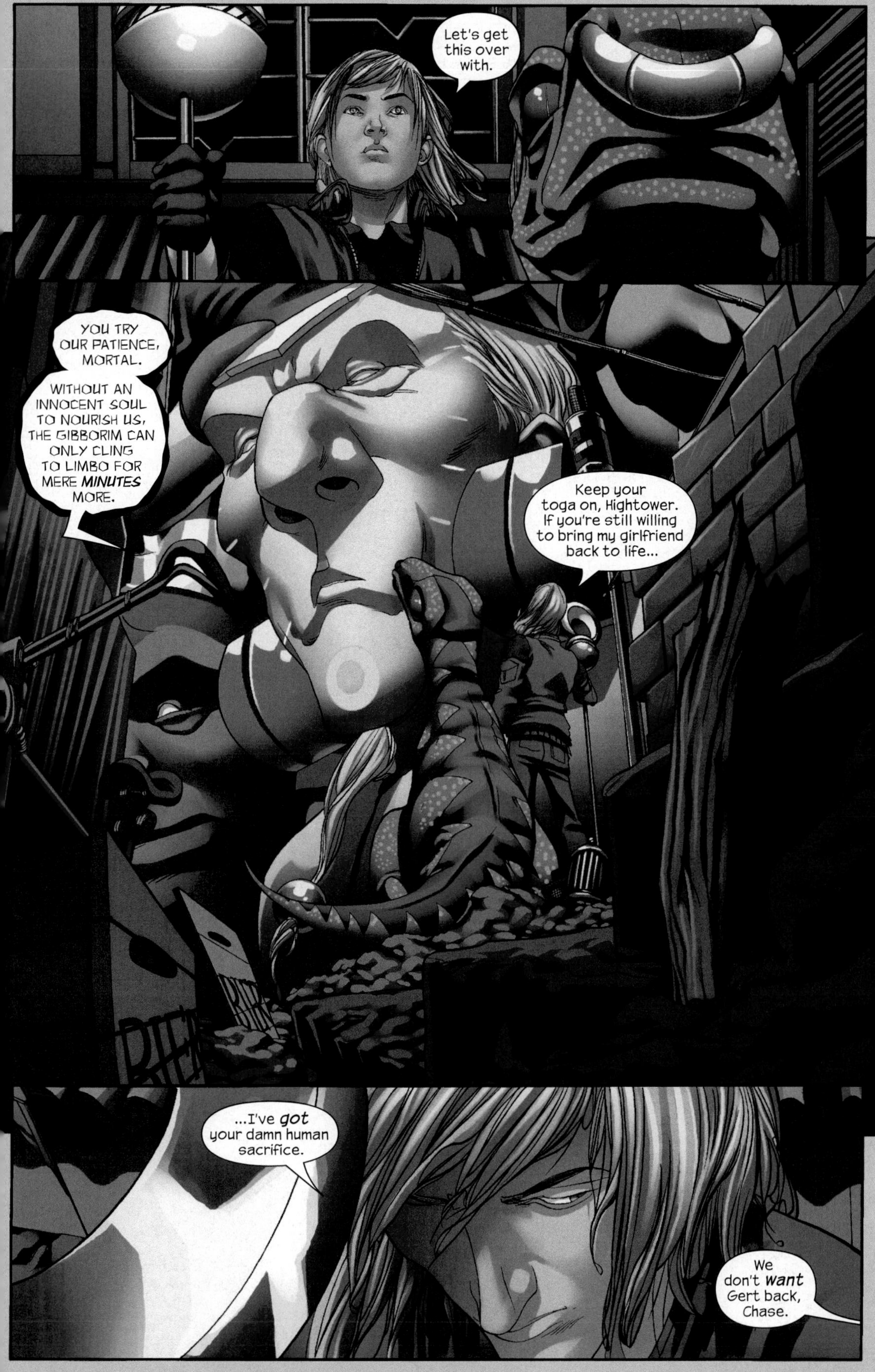
Let's get this over with.
YOU TRY OUR PATIENCE, MORTAL.
WITHOUT AN INNOCENT SOUL TO NOURISH US, THE GIBBORIM CAN ONLY CLING TO LIMBO FOR MERE *MINUTES* MORE.
Keep your toga on, Hightower. If you're still willing to bring my girlfriend back to life...
...I've *got* your damn human sacrifice.
We don't *want* Gert back, Chase.

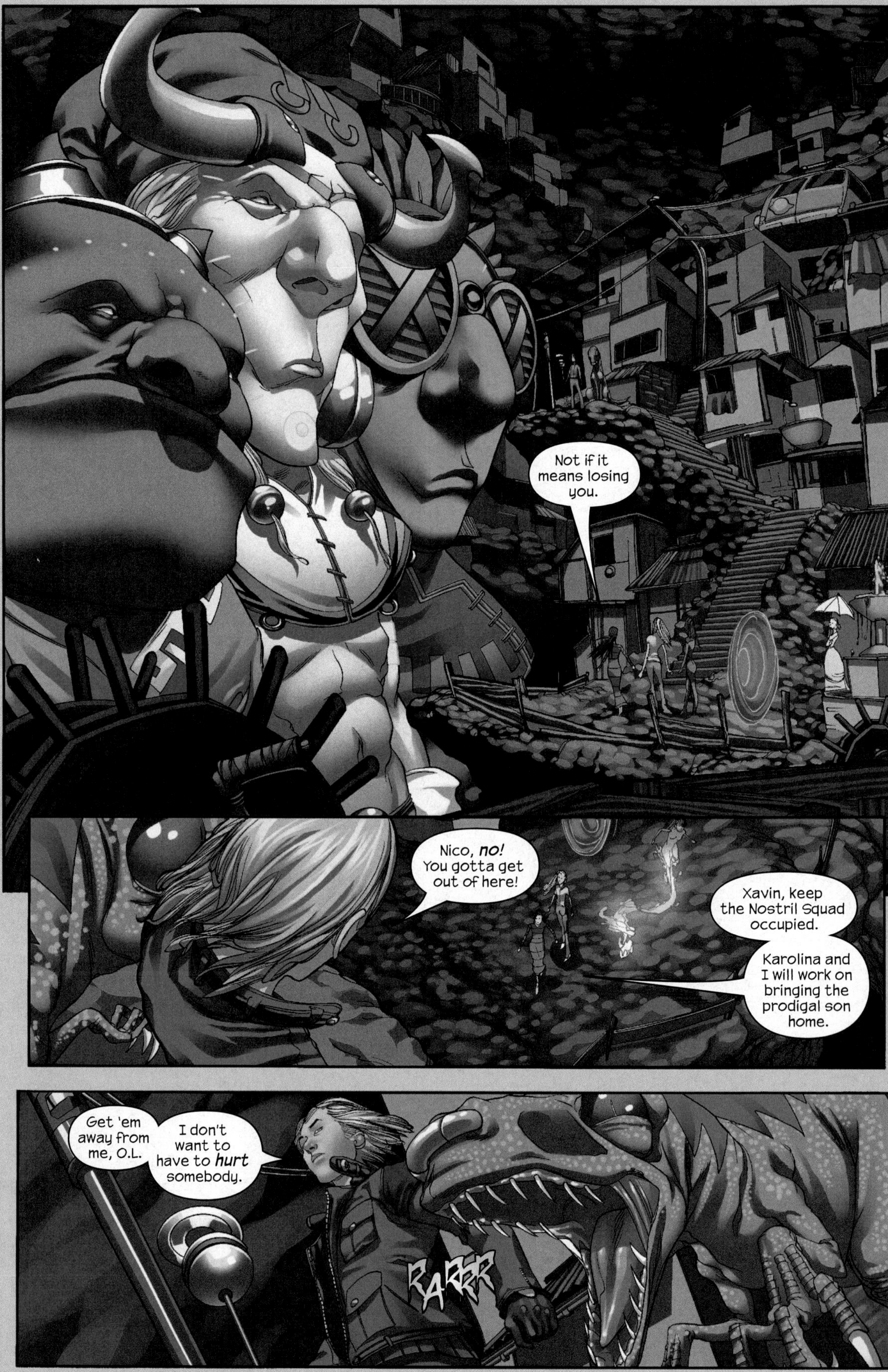

Not if it means losing you.
Nico, *no!* You gotta get out of here!
Xavin, keep the Nostril Squad occupied.
Karolina and I will work on bringing the prodigal son home.
Get 'em away from me, O.L.
I don't want to have to *hurt* somebody.
RARRR

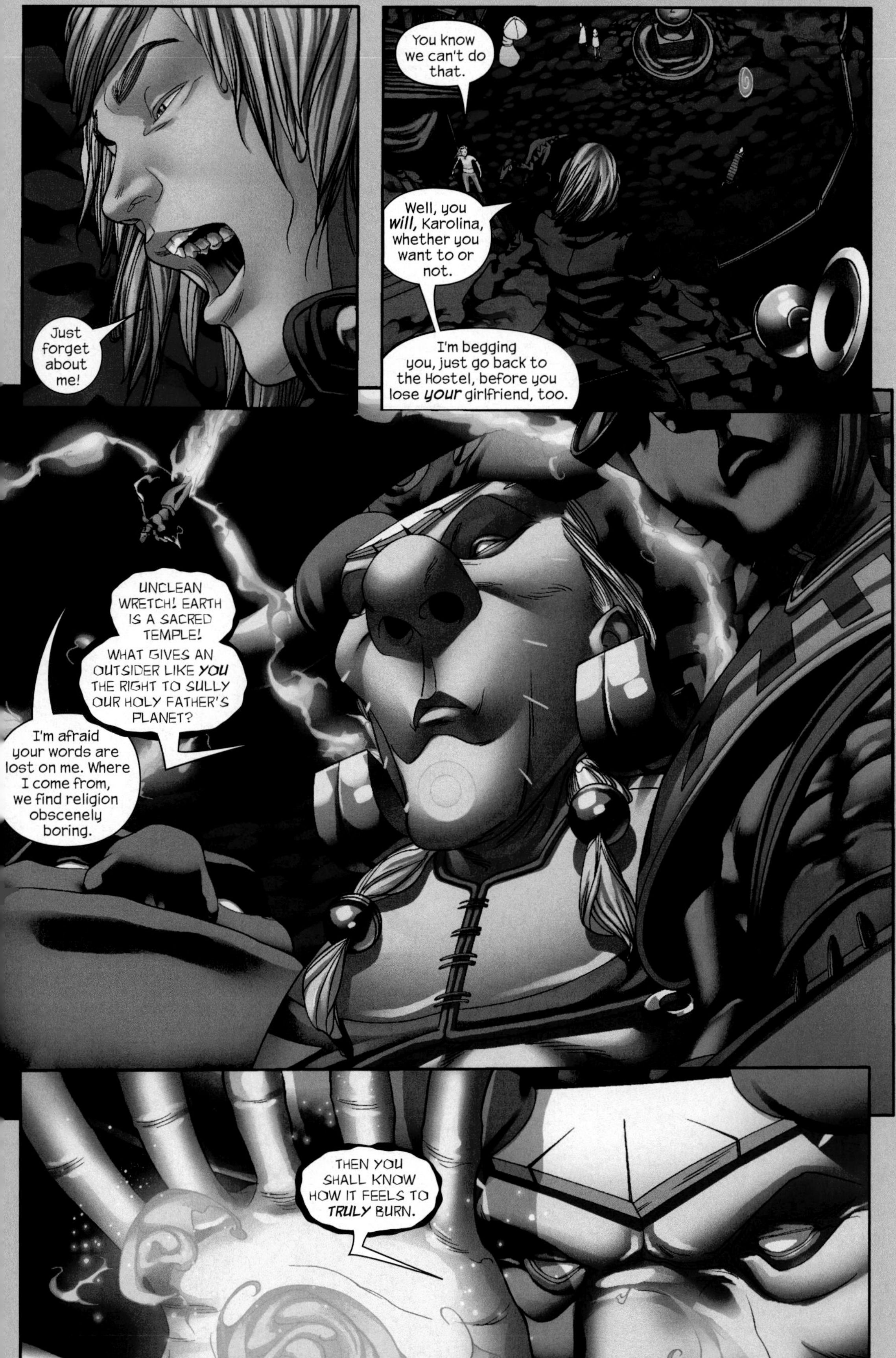
Just forget about me!
You know we can't do that.
Well, you *will,* Karolina, whether you want to or not.
I'm begging you, just go back to the Hostel, before you lose *your* girlfriend, too.
UNCLEAN WRETCH! EARTH IS A SACRED TEMPLE!
WHAT GIVES AN OUTSIDER LIKE *YOU* THE RIGHT TO SULLY OUR HOLY FATHER'S PLANET?
I'm afraid your words are lost on me. Where I come from, we find religion obscenely boring.
THEN YOU SHALL KNOW HOW IT FEELS TO *TRULY* BURN.

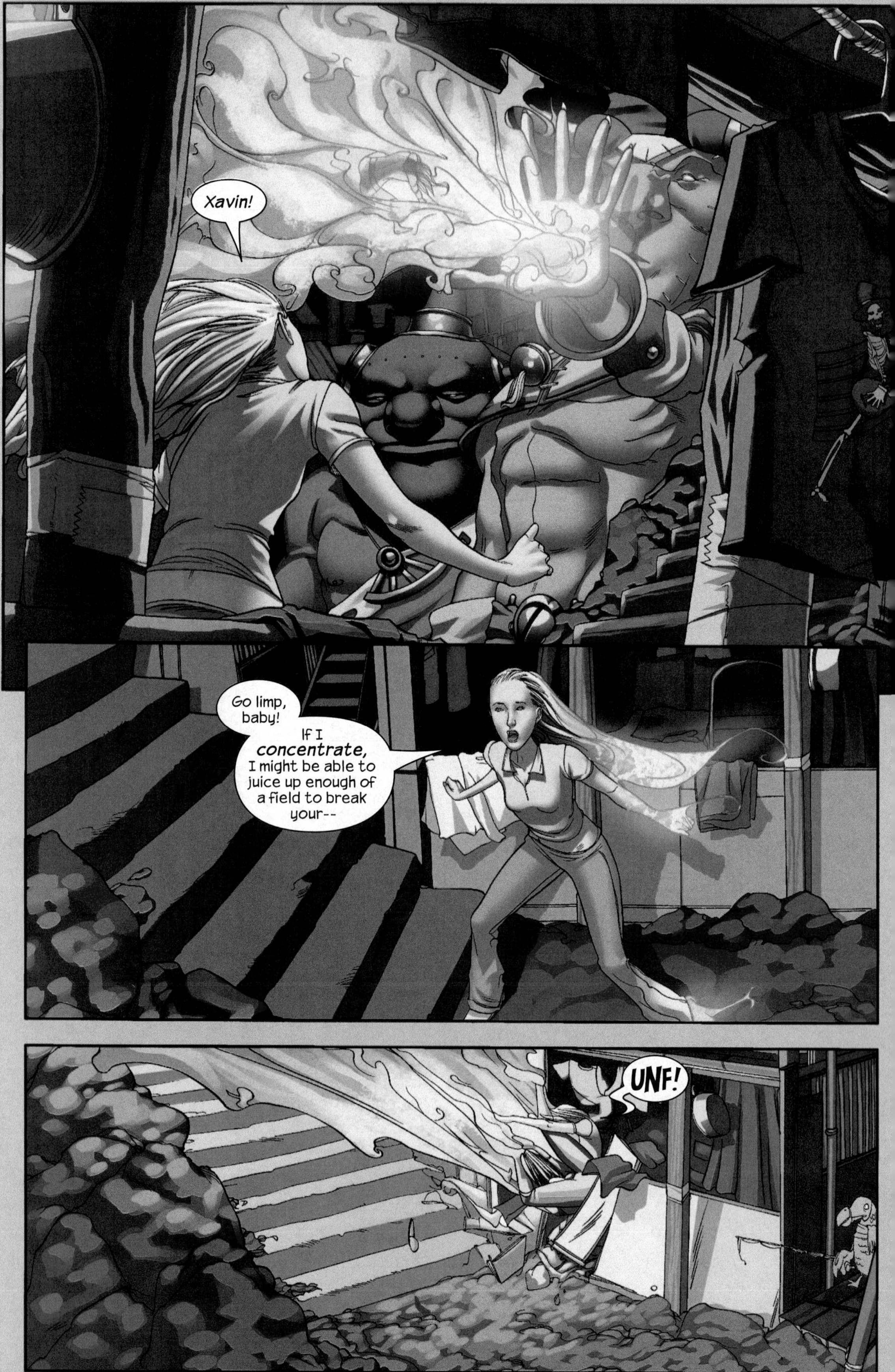
Xavin!
Go limp, baby!
If I concentrate, I might be able to juice up enough of a field to break your--
UNF!

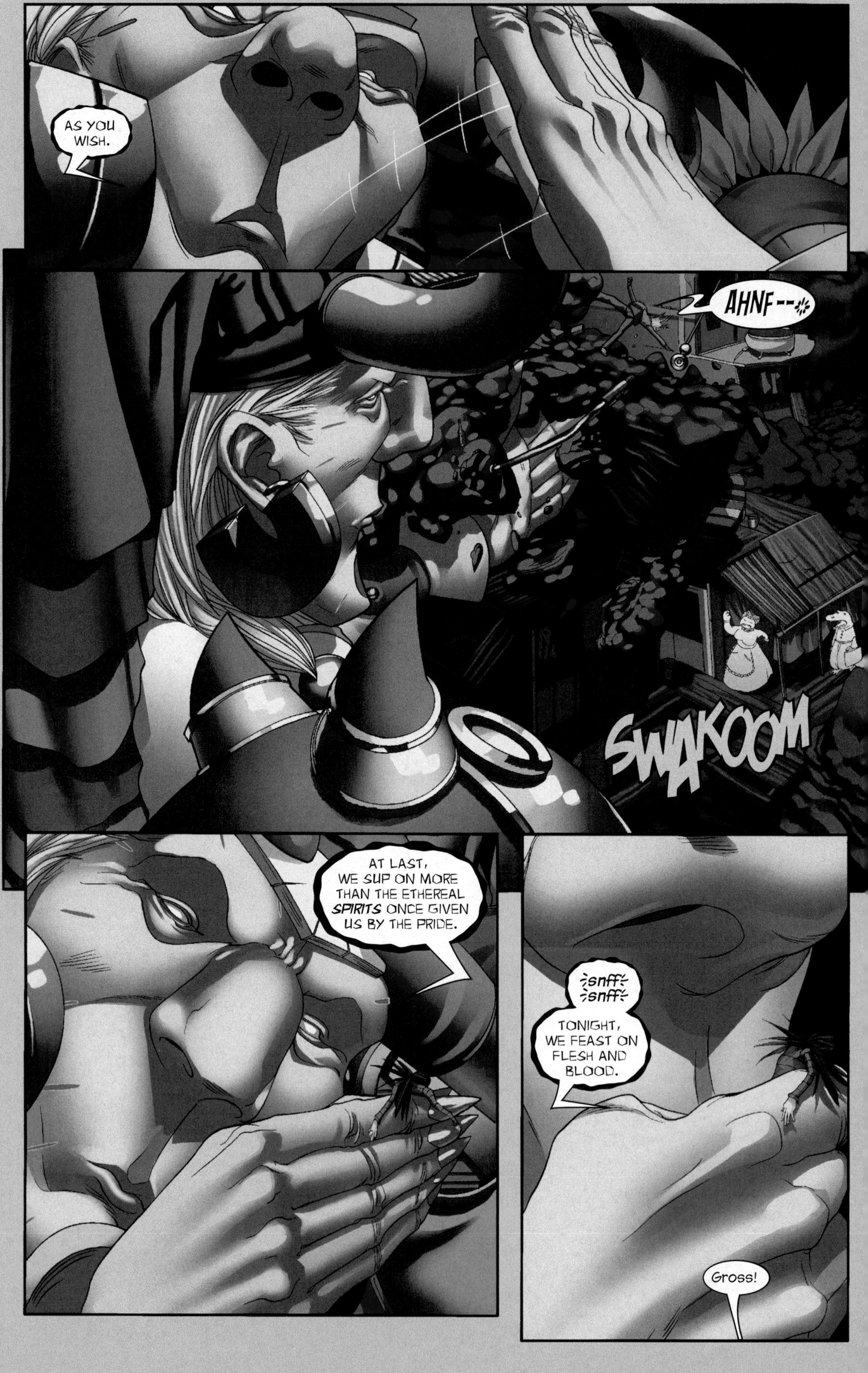

AS YOU WISH.
AHNF--
SWAKOOM
AT LAST, WE SUP ON MORE THAN THE ETHEREAL SPIRITS ONCE GIVEN US BY THE PRIDE.
snff snff
TONIGHT, WE FEAST ON FLESH AND BLOOD.
Gross!

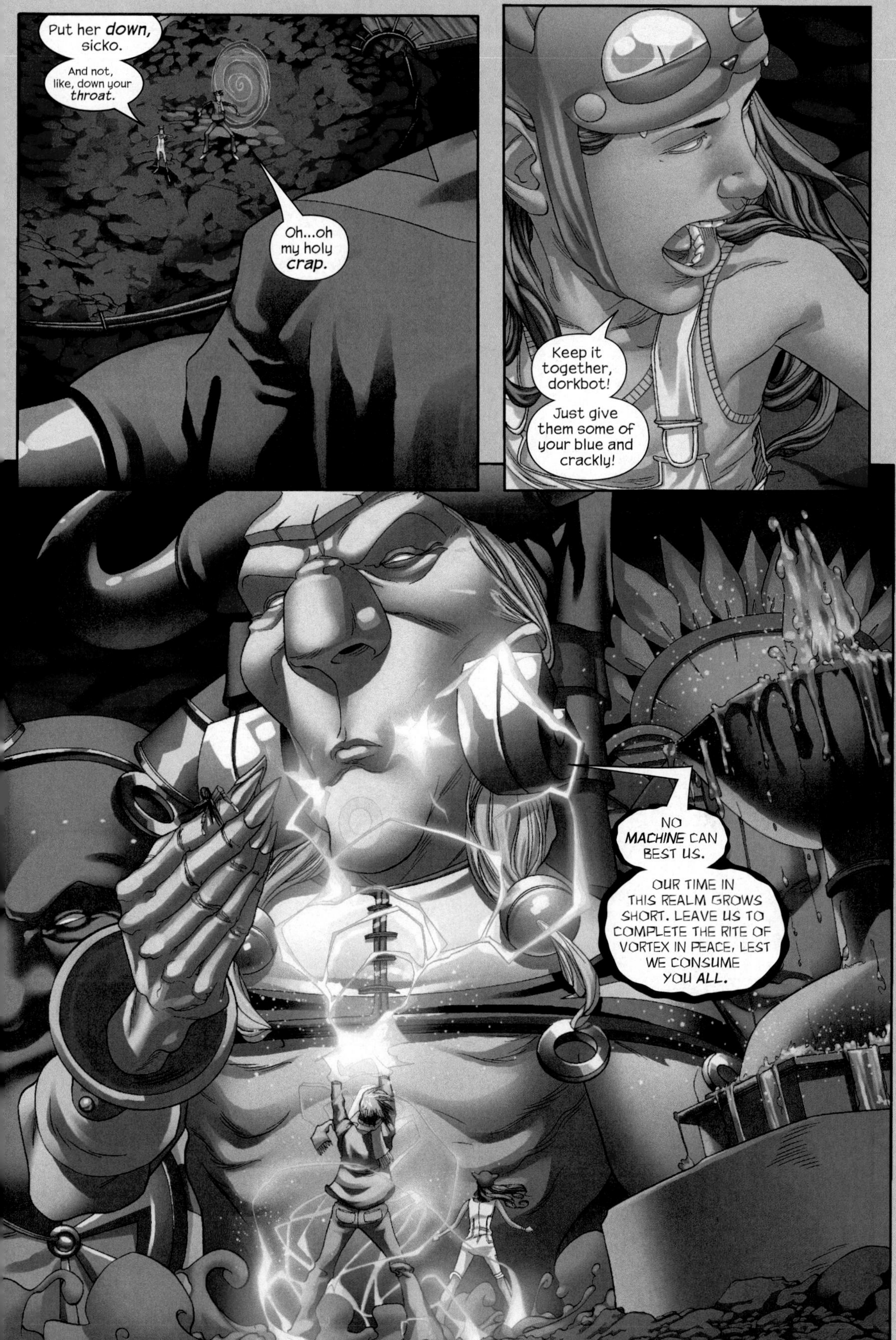
Put her *down,* sicko.
And not, like, down your *throat.*
Oh...oh my holy *crap.*
Keep it together, dorkbot!
Just give them some of your blue and crackly!
NO *MACHINE* CAN BEST US.
OUR TIME IN THIS REALM GROWS SHORT. LEAVE US TO COMPLETE THE RITE OF VORTEX IN PEACE, LEST WE CONSUME YOU *ALL.*

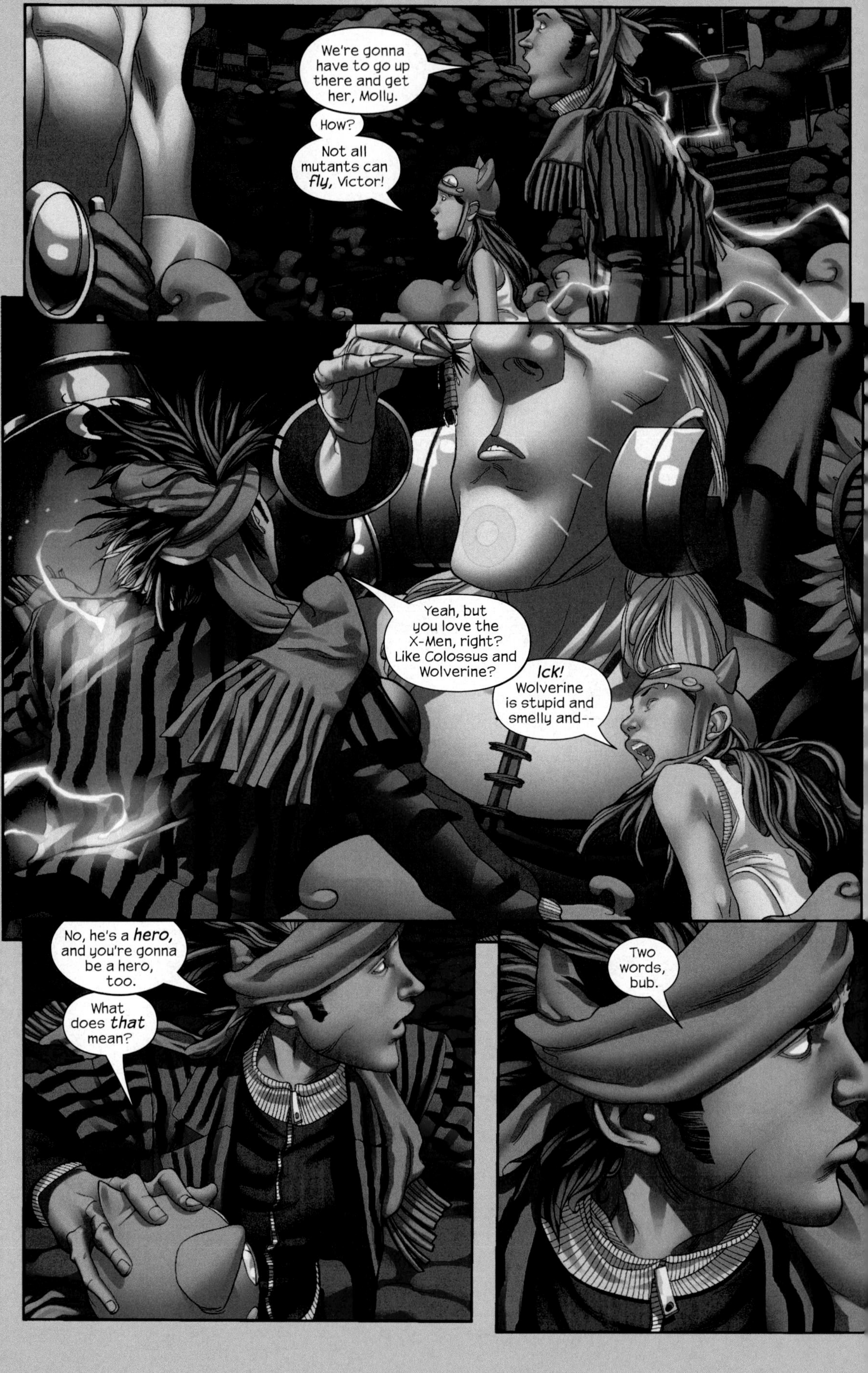

We're gonna have to go up there and get her, Molly.
How?
Not all mutants can *fly,* Victor!
Yeah, but you love the X-Men, right? Like Colossus and Wolverine?
Ick! Wolverine is stupid and smelly and--
No, he's a **hero,** and you're gonna be a hero, too.
What does **that** mean?
Two words, bub.

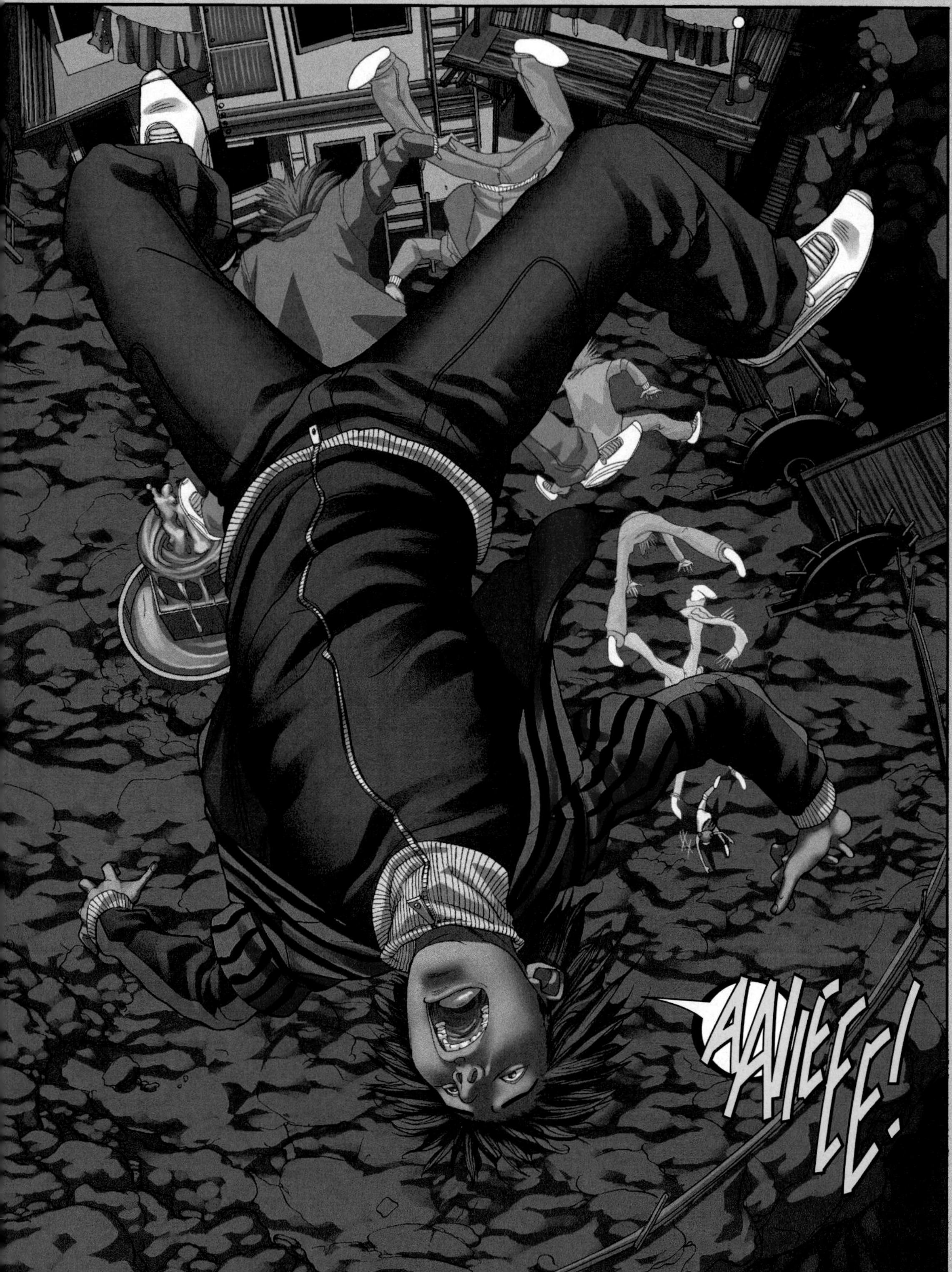
AAIIEEEE!

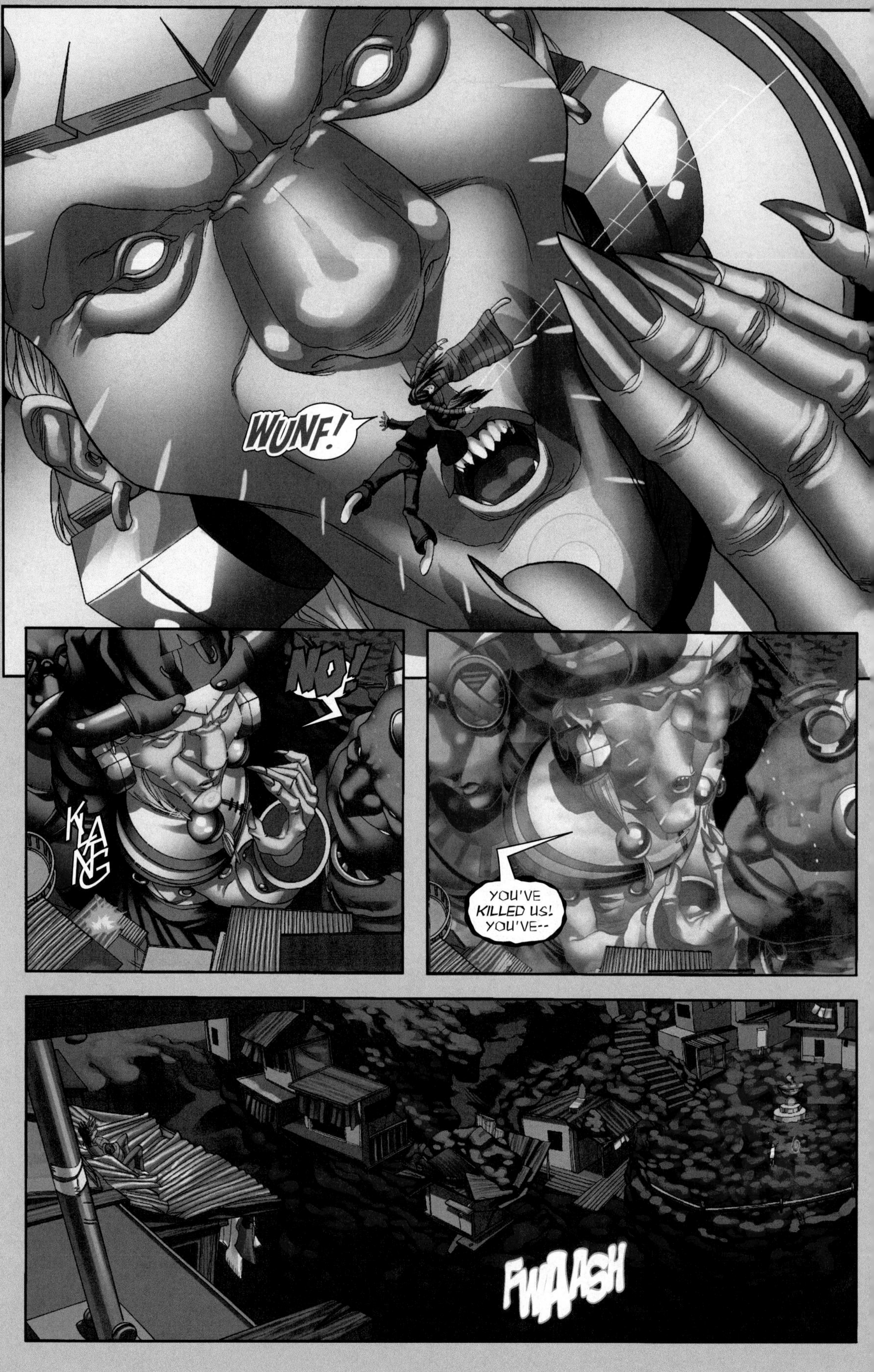
WUNF!
NO!
KLANG
YOU'VE KILLED US! YOU'VE--
FWAASH

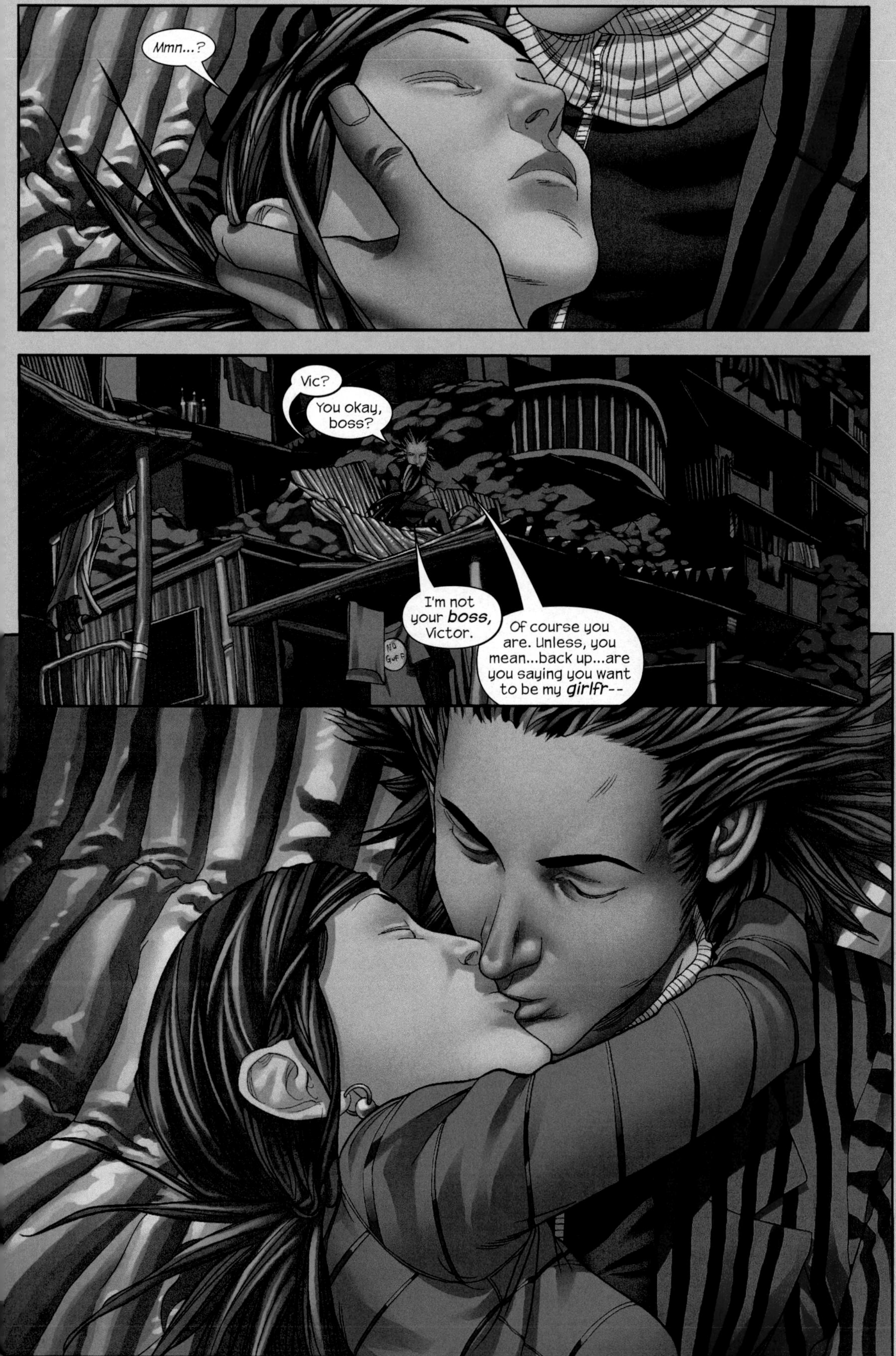
Mmn...?
Vic?
You okay, boss?
NO GUFF
I'm not your *boss,* Victor.
Of course you are. Unless, you mean...back up...are you saying you want to be my *girlfr*--

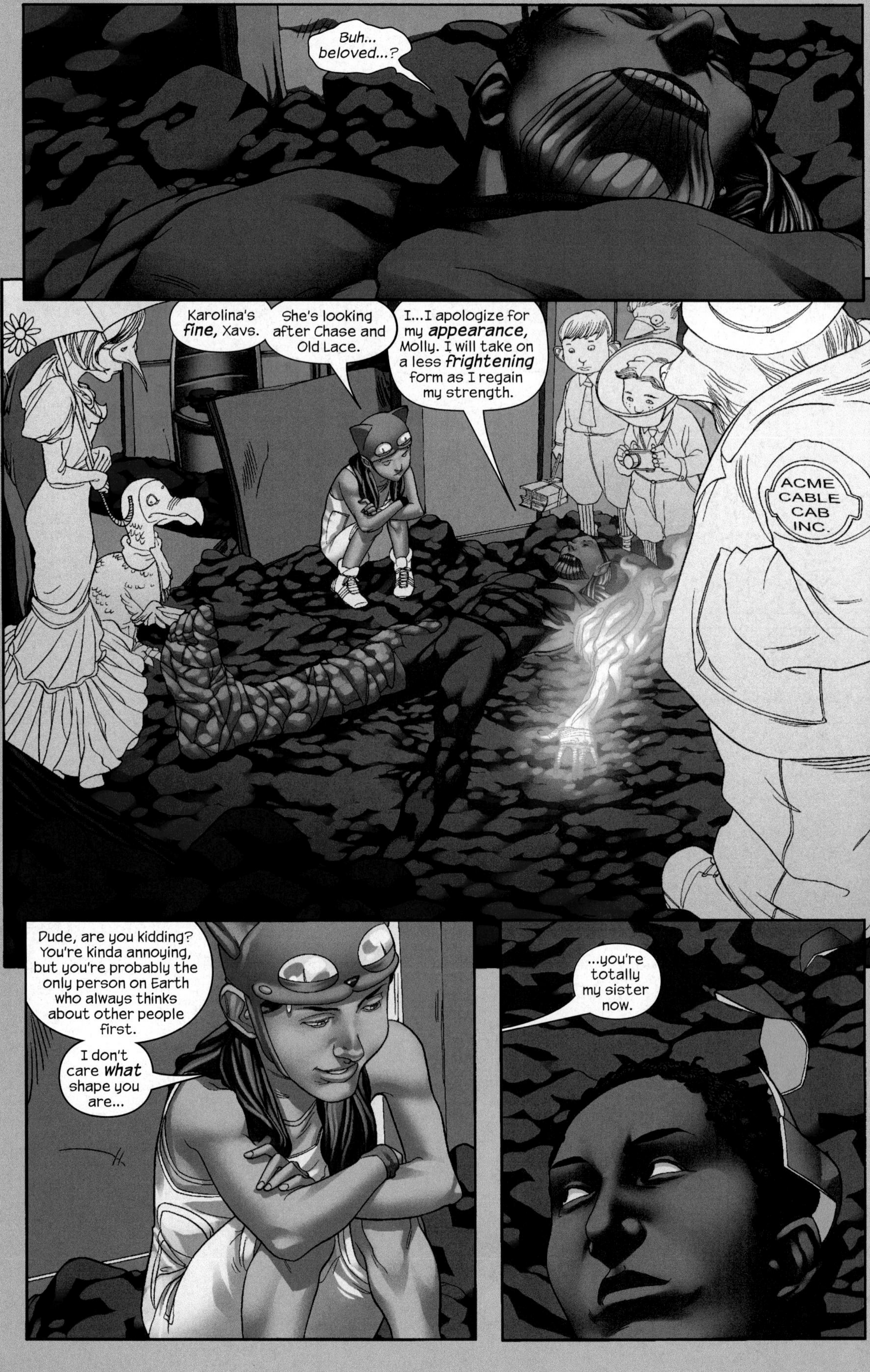
Buh... beloved...?
Karolina's *fine,* Xavs.
She's looking after Chase and Old Lace.
I...I apologize for my *appearance,* Molly. I will take on a less *frightening* form as I regain my strength.
ACME CABLE CAB INC.
Dude, are you kidding? You're kinda annoying, but you're probably the only person on Earth who always thinks about other people first.
I don't care *what* shape you are...
...you're totally my sister now.

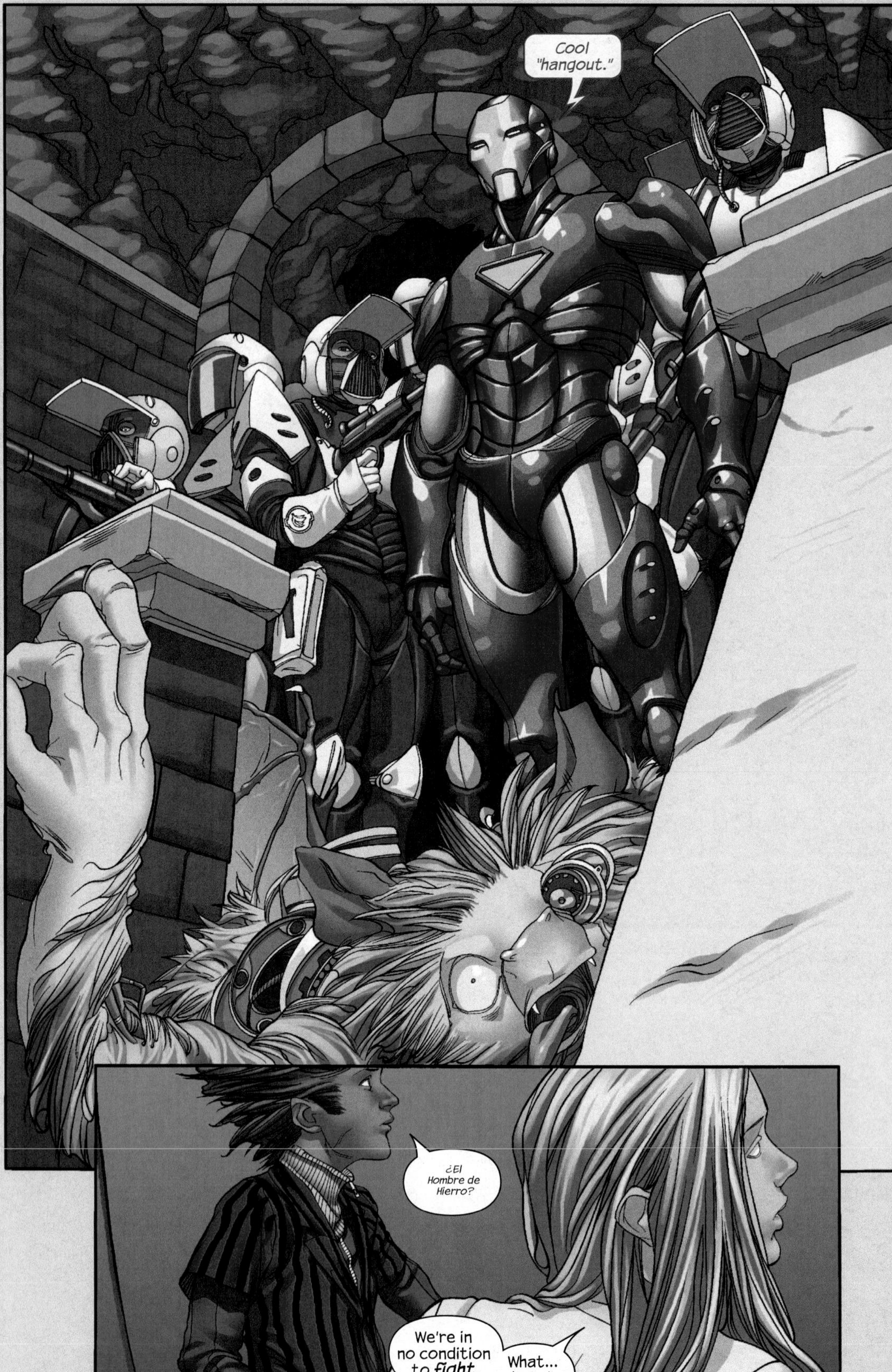
Cool "hangout."
¿El Hombre de Hierro?
We're in no condition to *fight.*
What... what do we *do?*

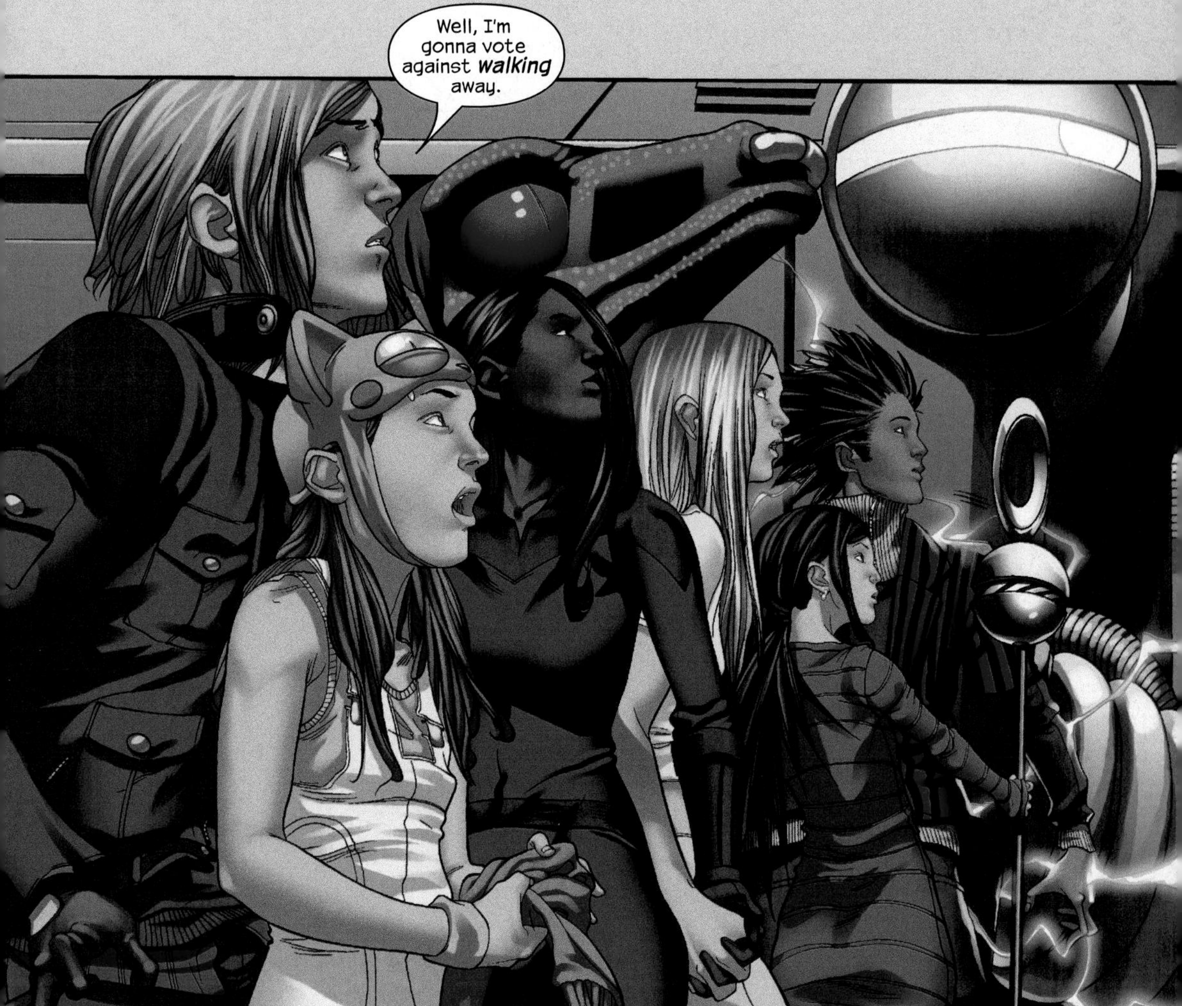
Well, I'm gonna vote against *walking* away.

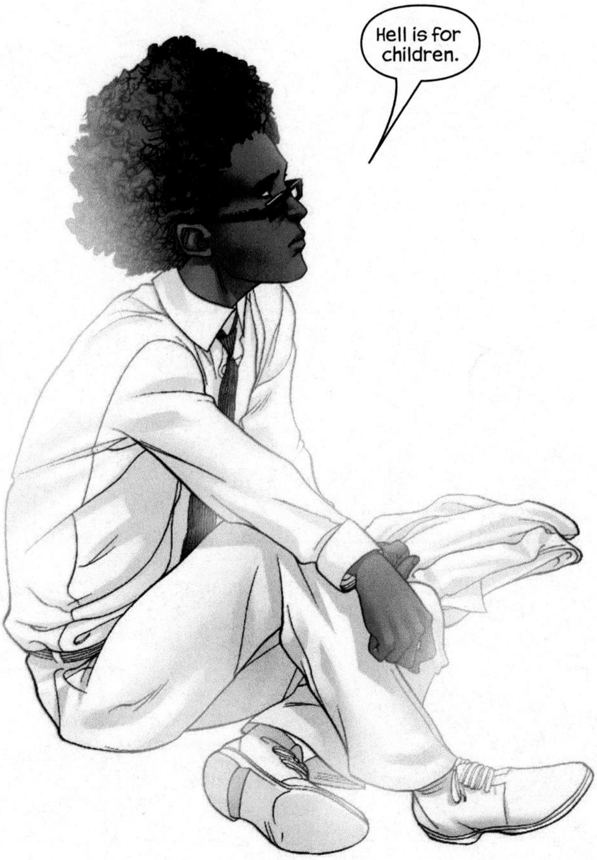
Hell is for children.

MIKE NORTON SAMPLE PAGES

(RUNAWAYS #15, PAGES 14-15)

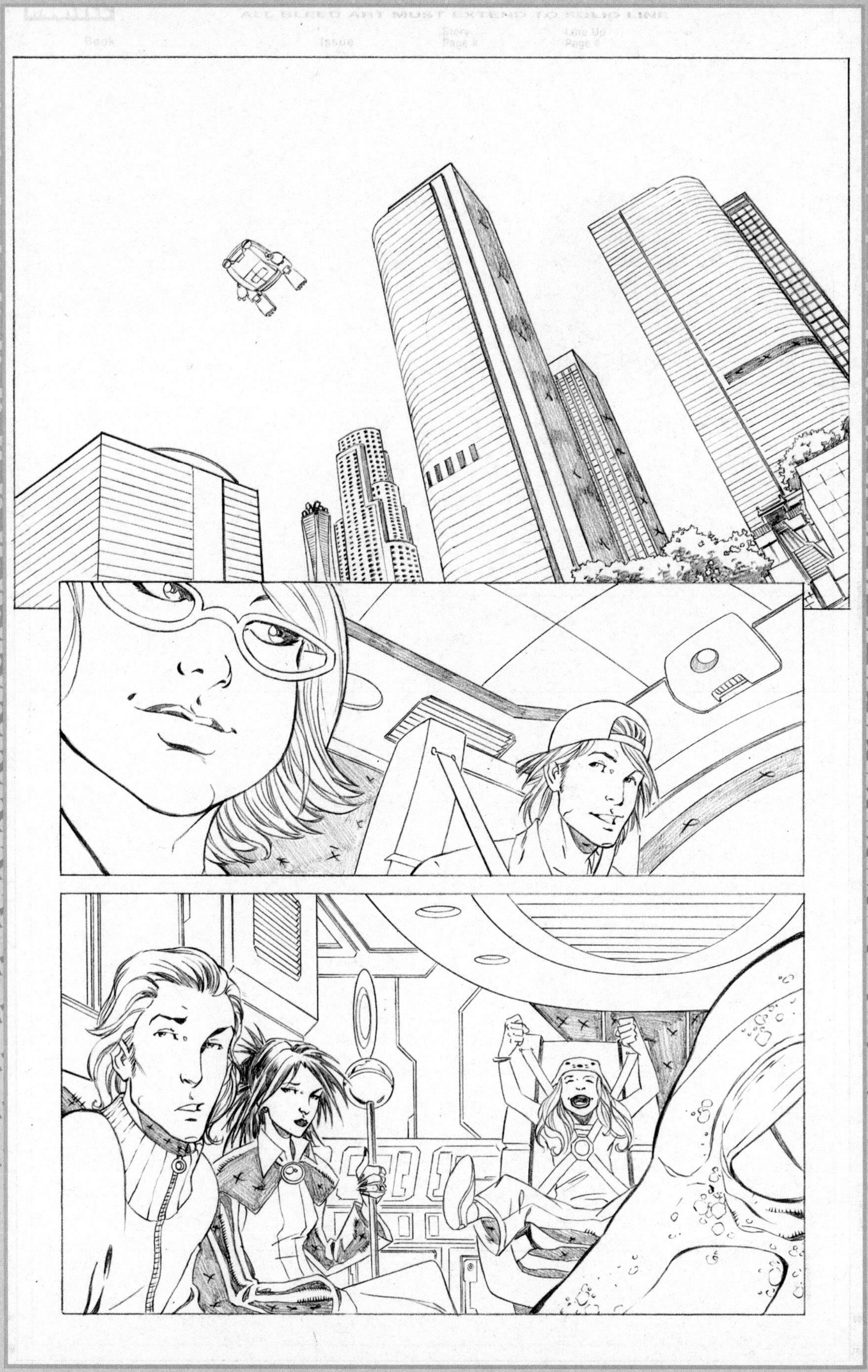

ALL BLEED ART MUST EXTEND TO SOLID LINE
Book
Issue
Story Page #
Line Up Page #

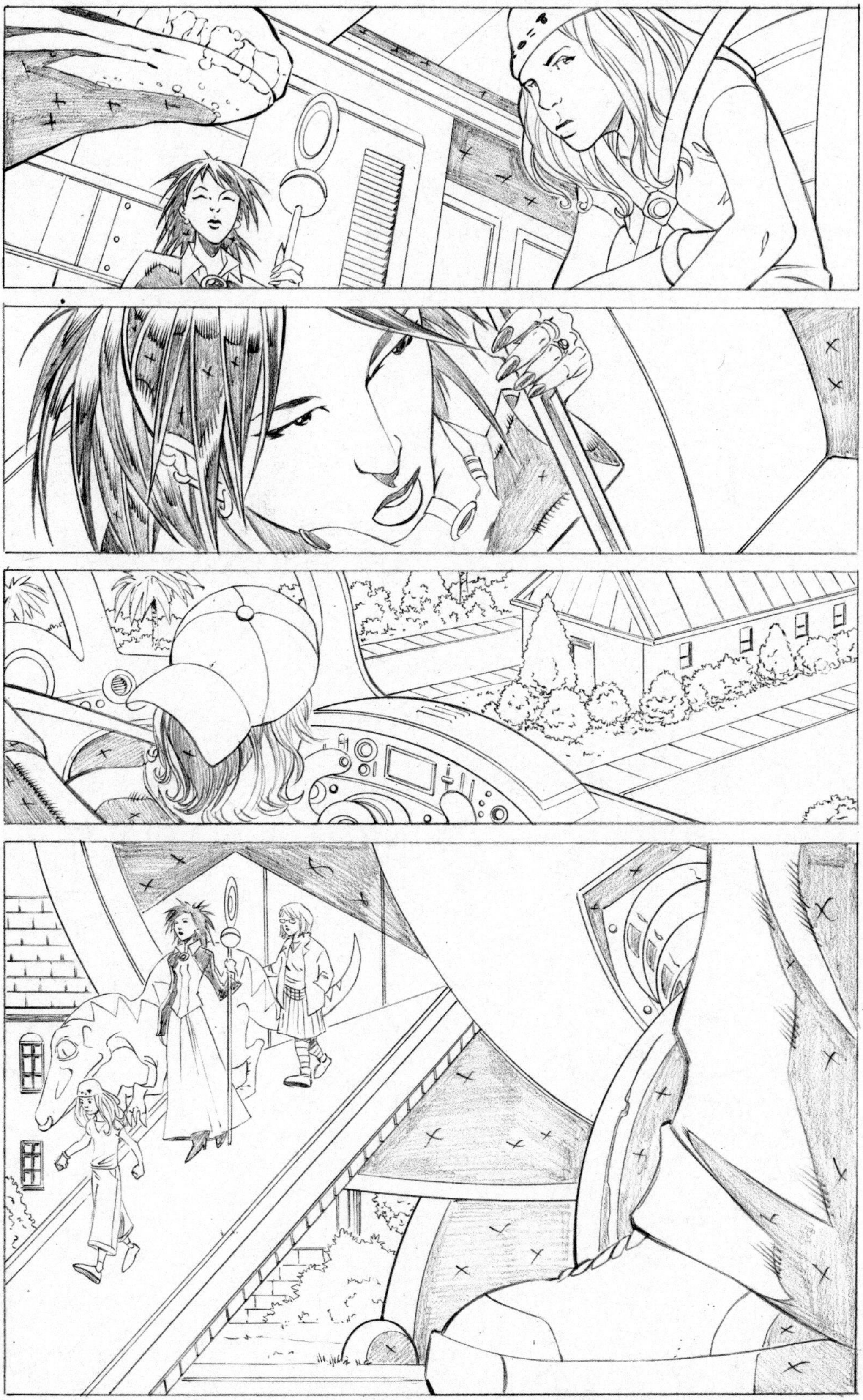

PIN-UP BY MIKE NORTON

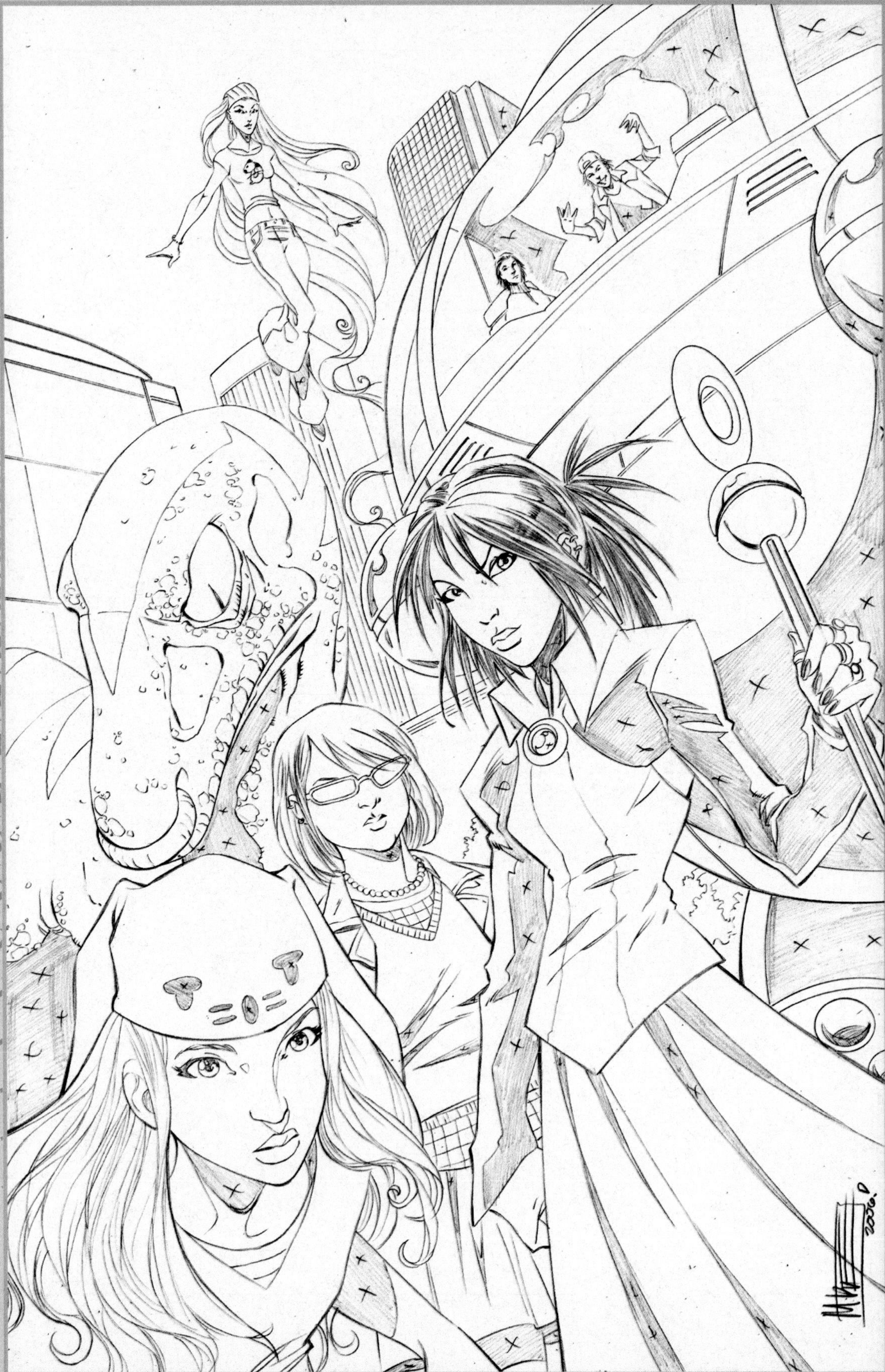

VOL. 3 HARDCOVER ART BY
ADRIAN ALPHONA, CRAIG YEUNG & CHRISTINA STRAIN

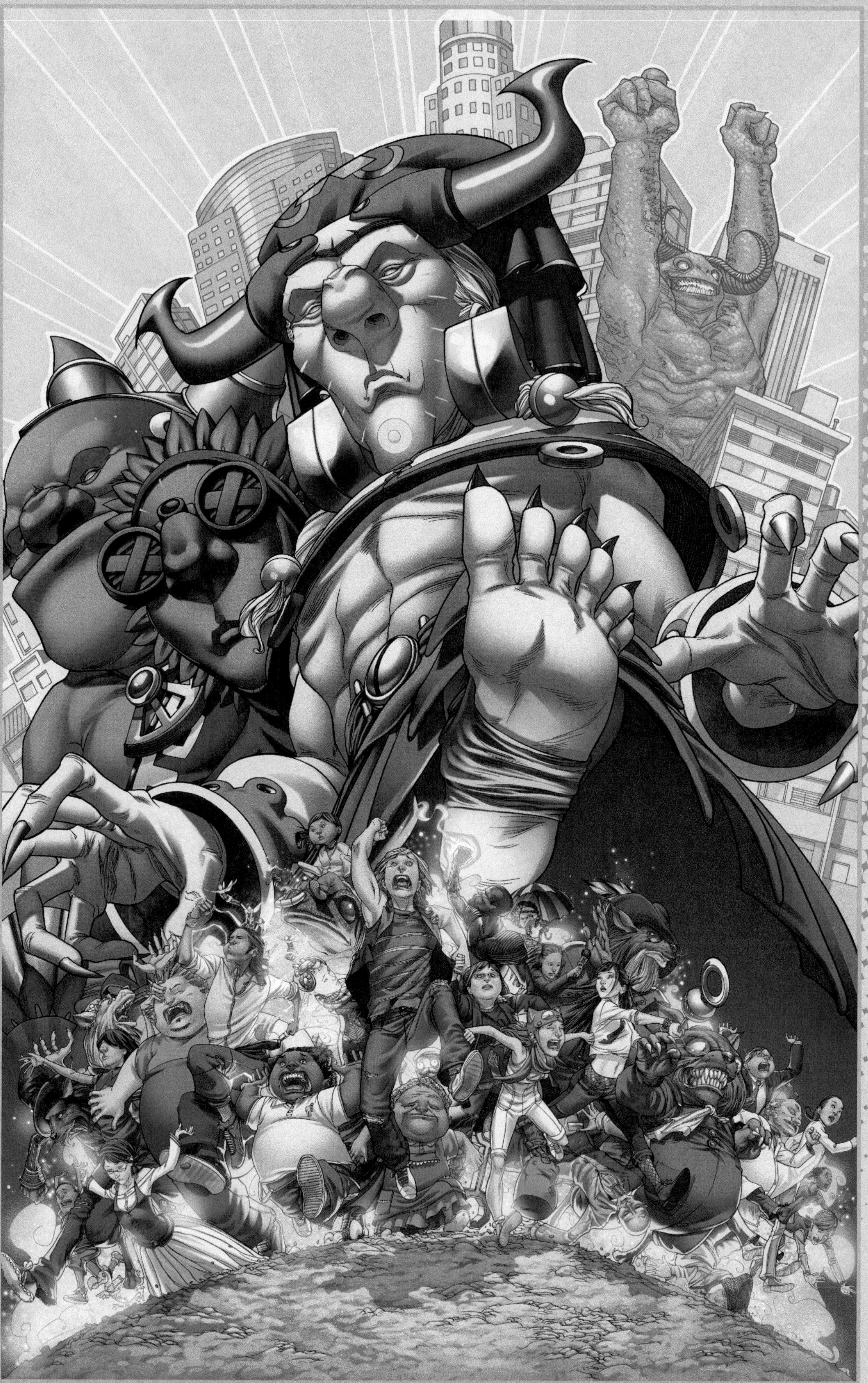

VOL. 3 HARDCOVER CONCEPTS AND LAYOUTS BY ADRIAN ALPHONA

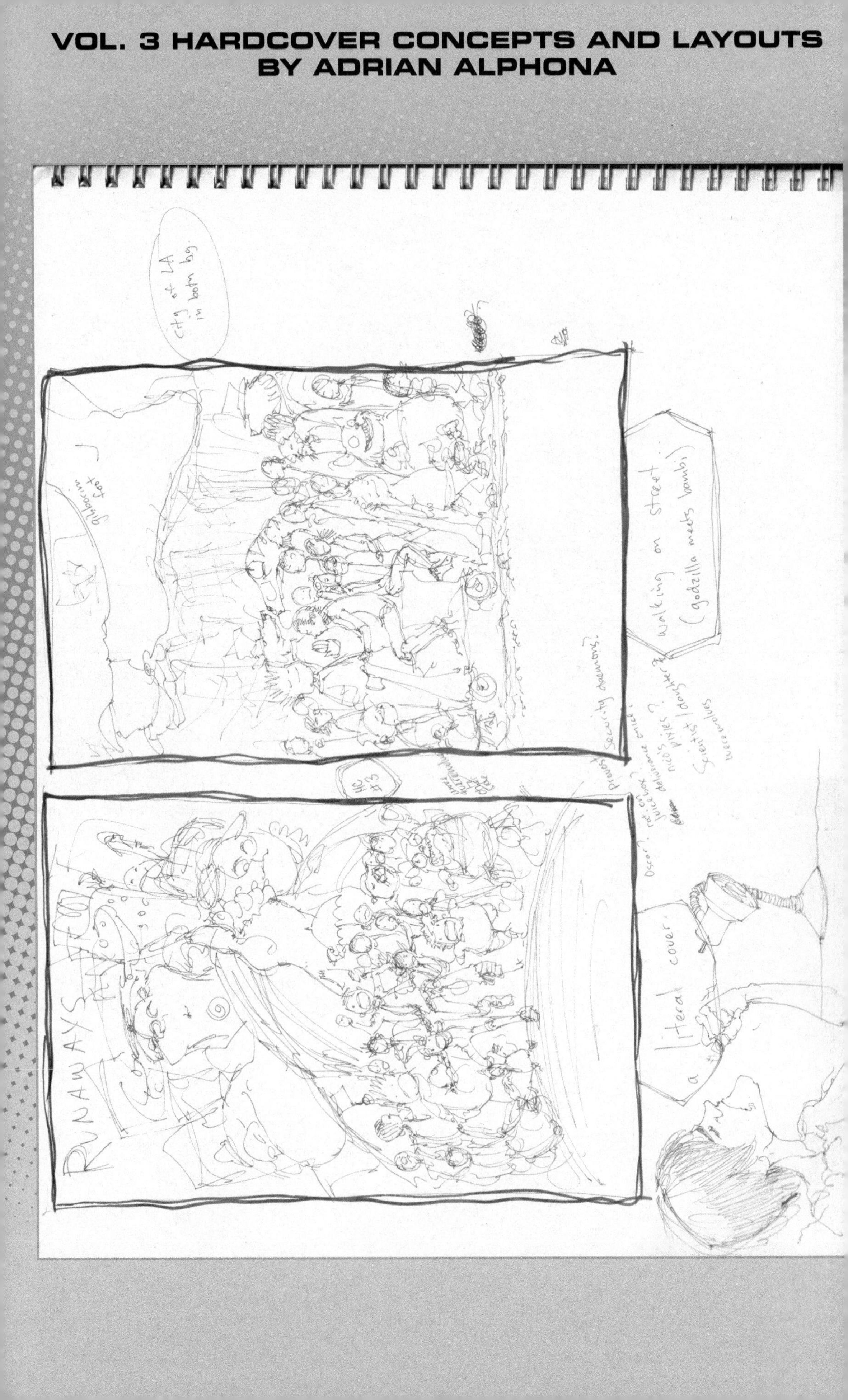
city of LA in both bg
walking on street
(godzilla meets bambi)
RUNAWAYS
HC #3
Security daemons?
a literal cover.

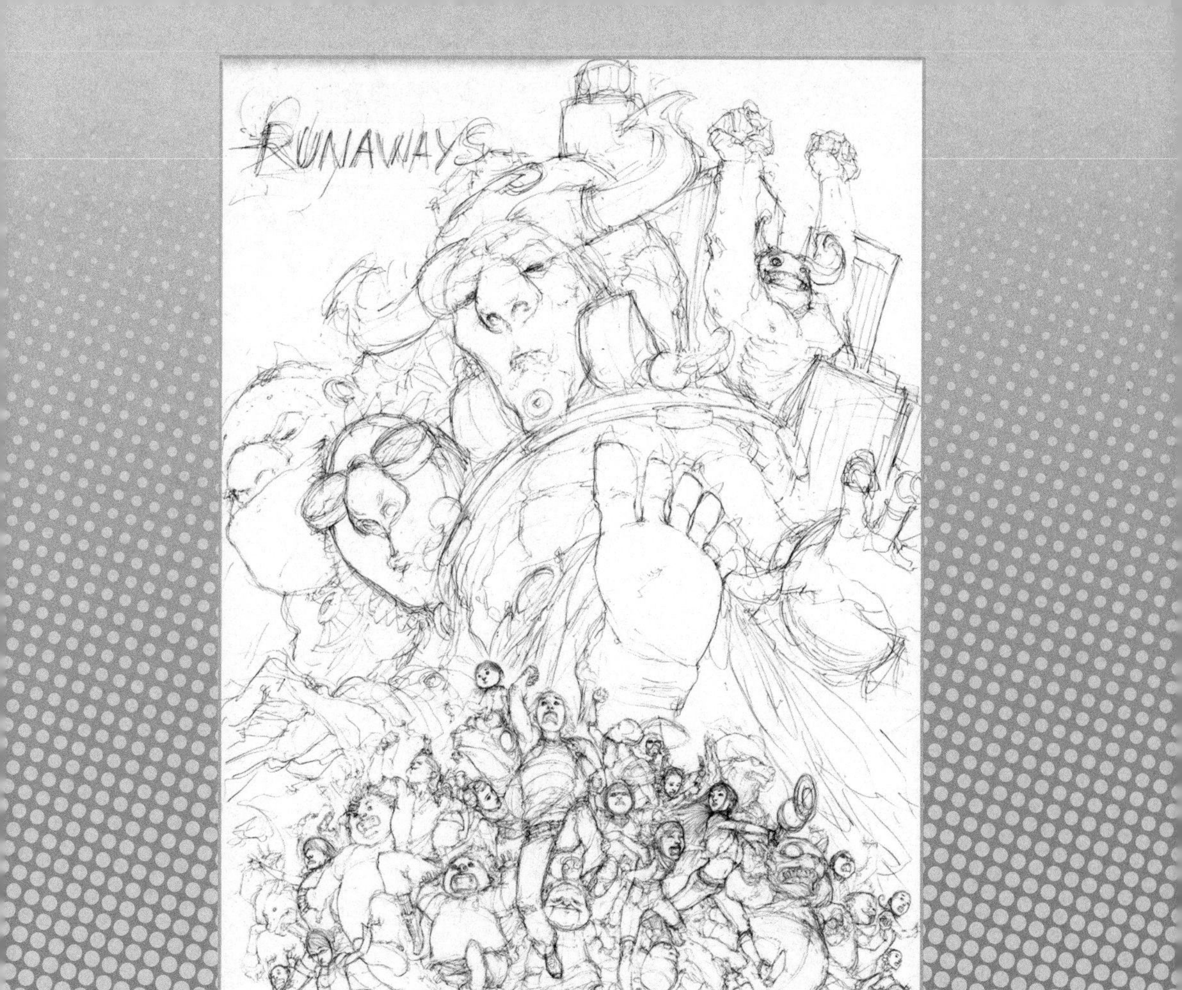
RUNAWAYS

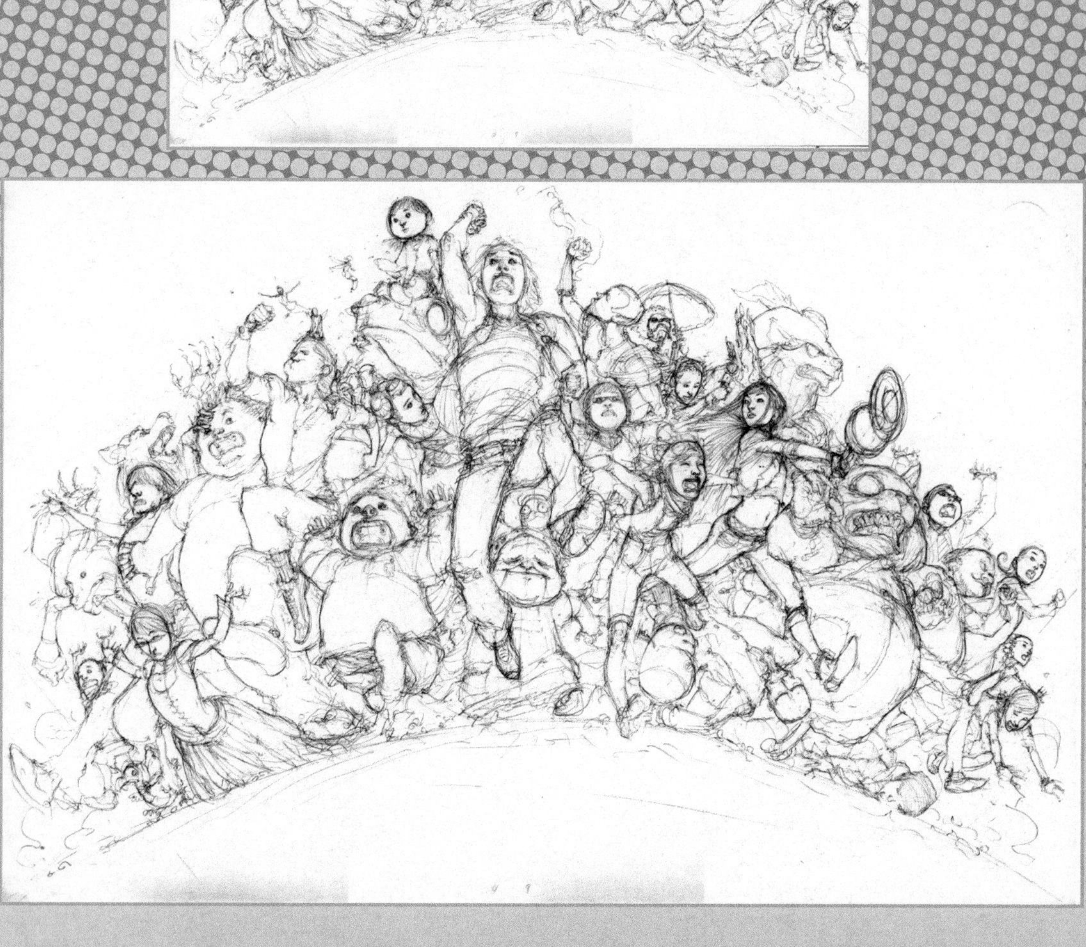

VOL. 3 HARDCOVER PENCILS BY ADRIAN ALPHONA

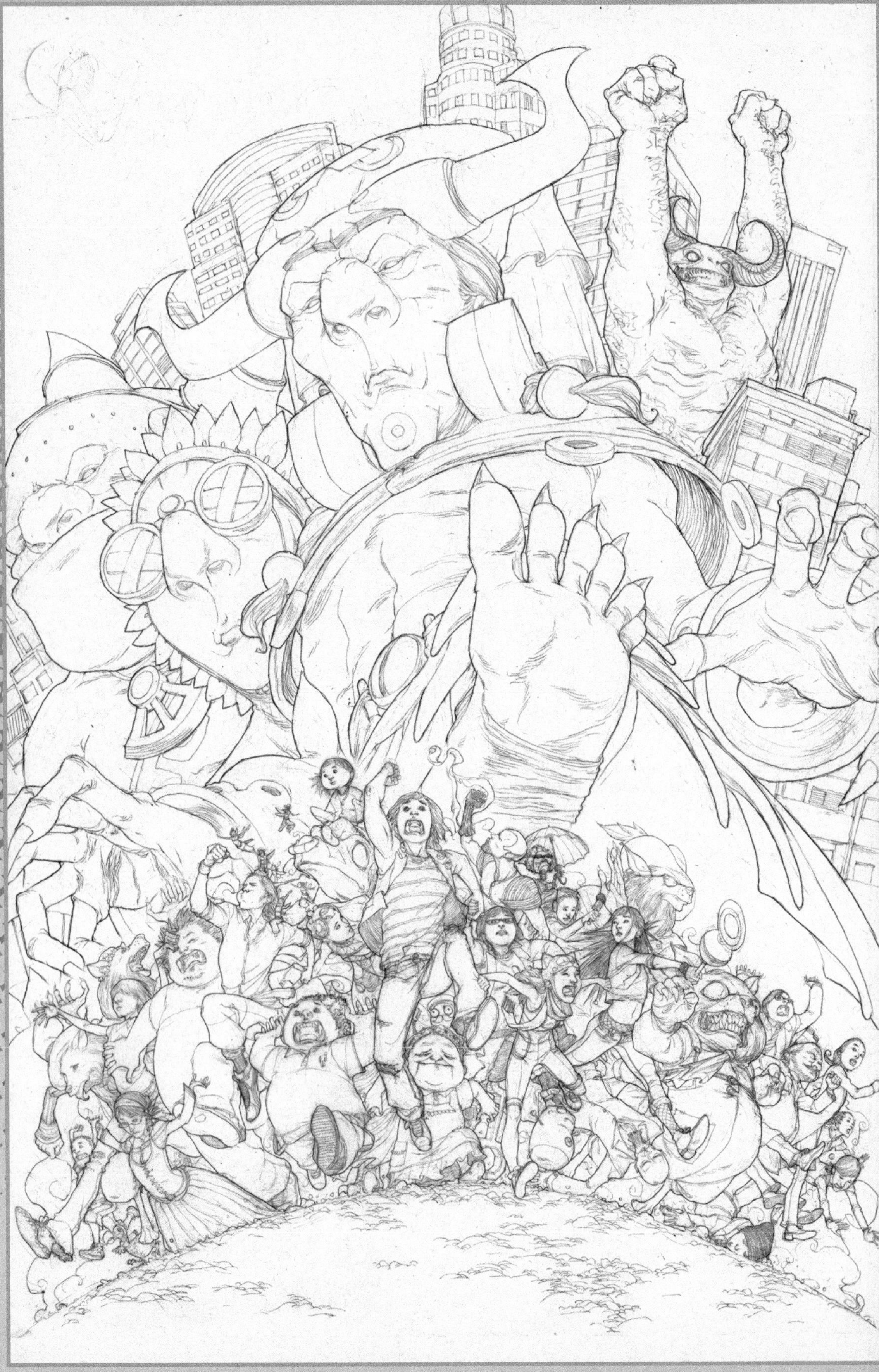

VOL. 3 HARDCOVER DETAILS BY ADRIAN ALPHONA, INKS BY CRAIG YEUNG

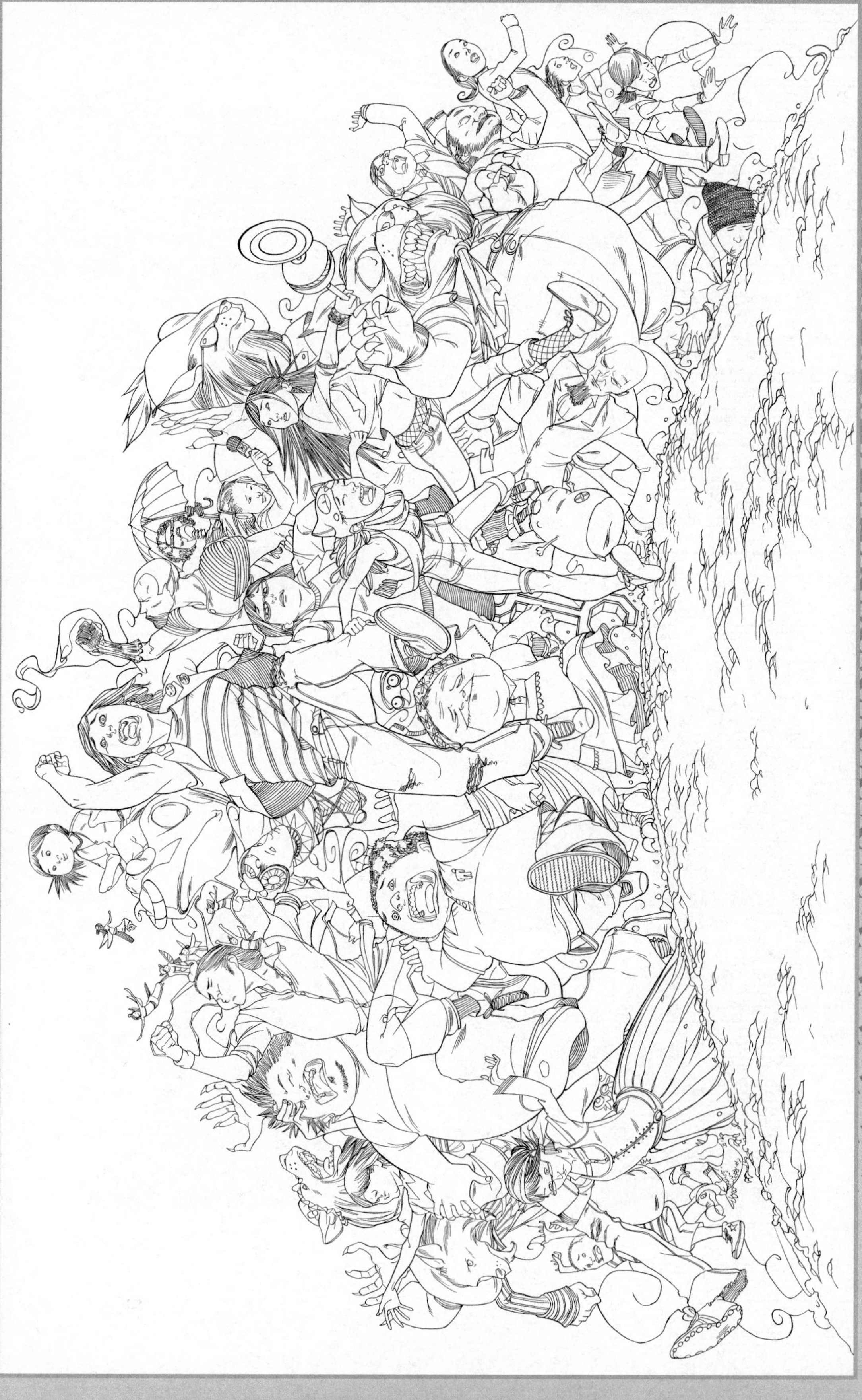

MOLLY'S HATS!

COLORIST CHRISTINA STRAIN AND EDITOR JENNIFER GRÜNWALD LOVE MOLLY'S HATS SO MUCH, THEY GOT SOME OF THEIR OWN!

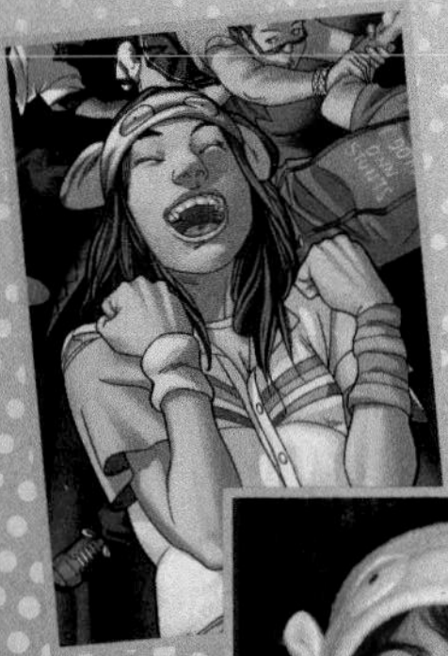
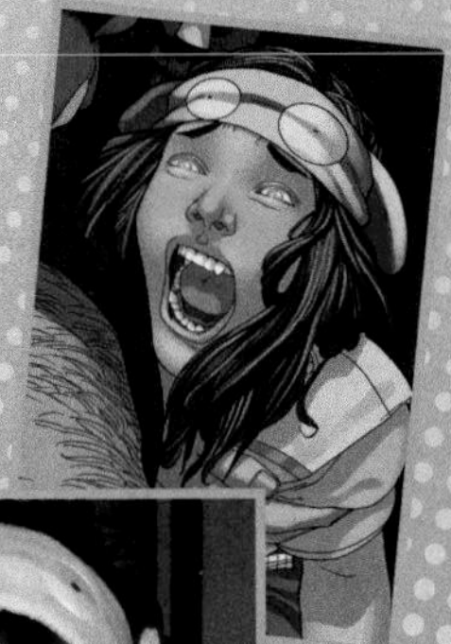
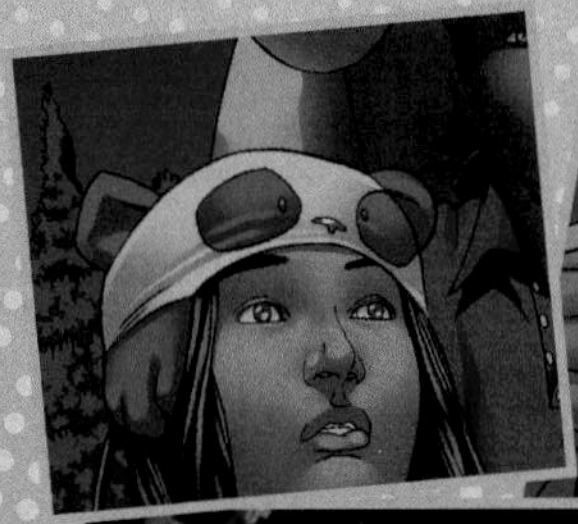
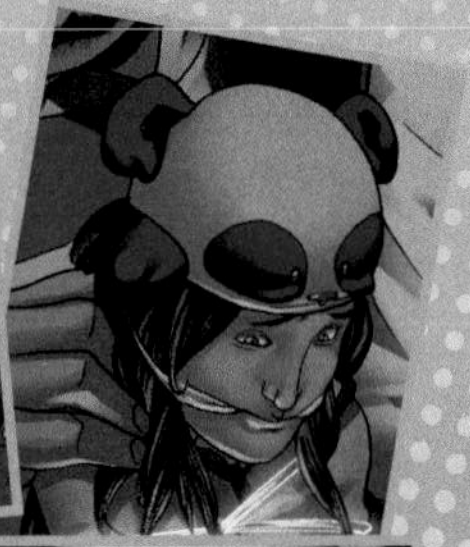
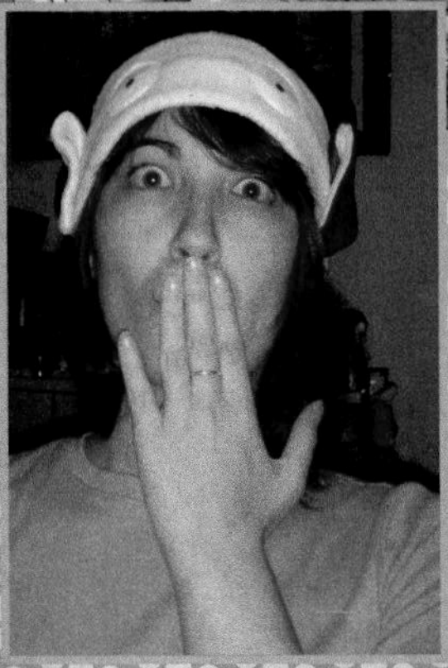
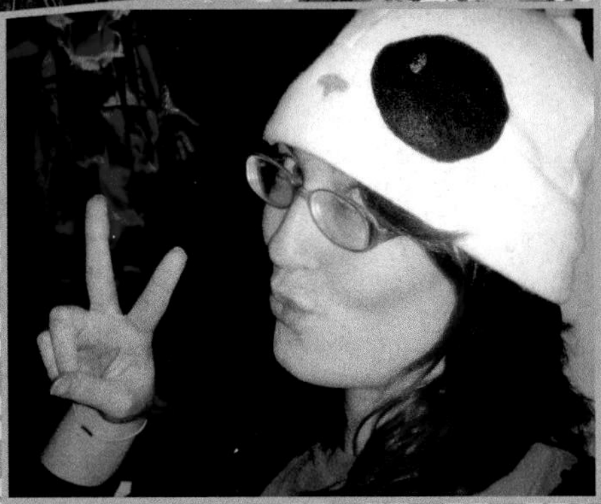
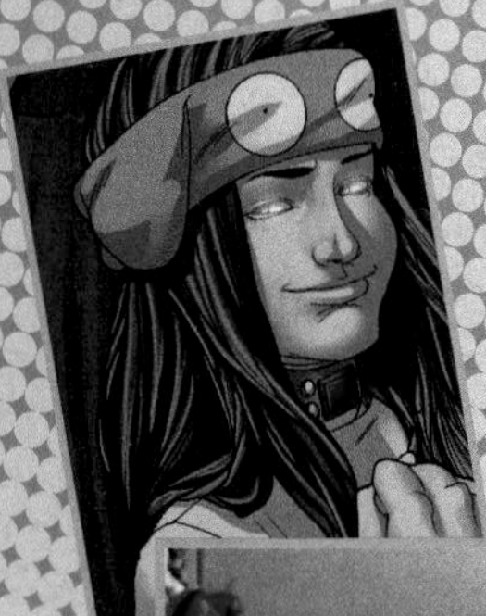
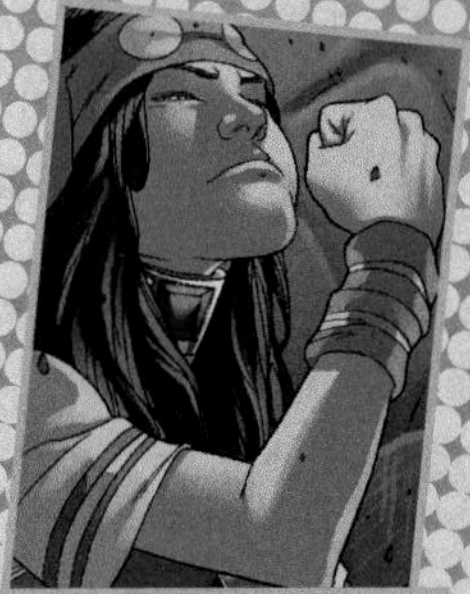
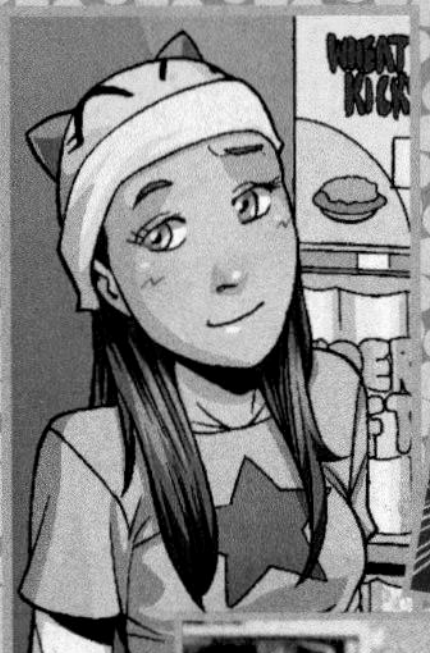
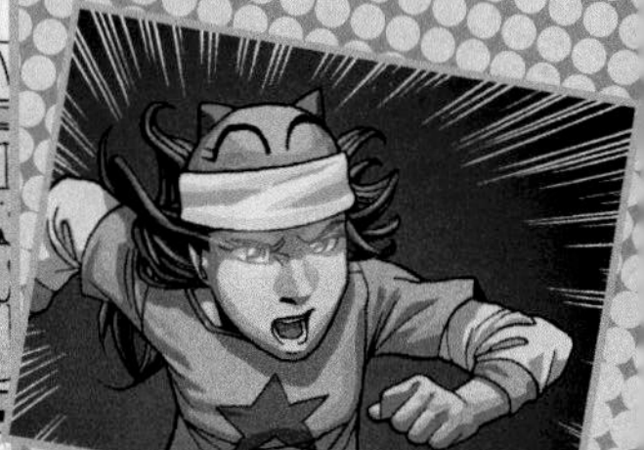
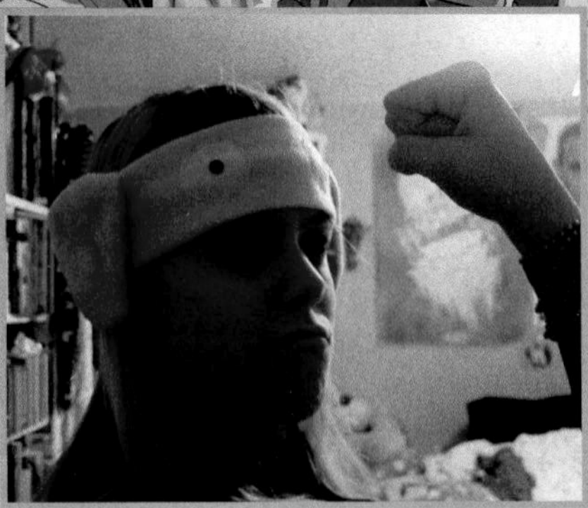
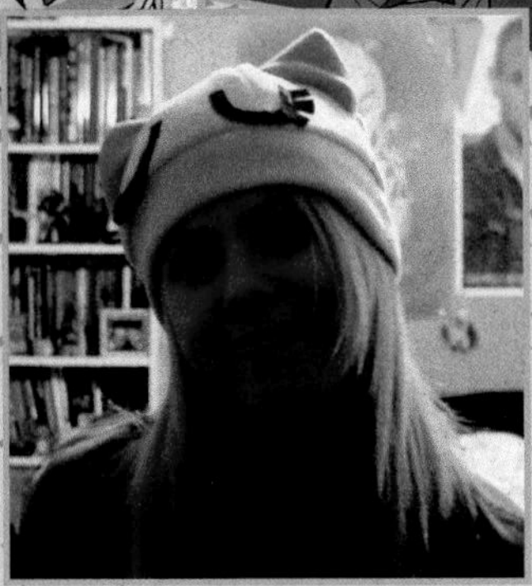

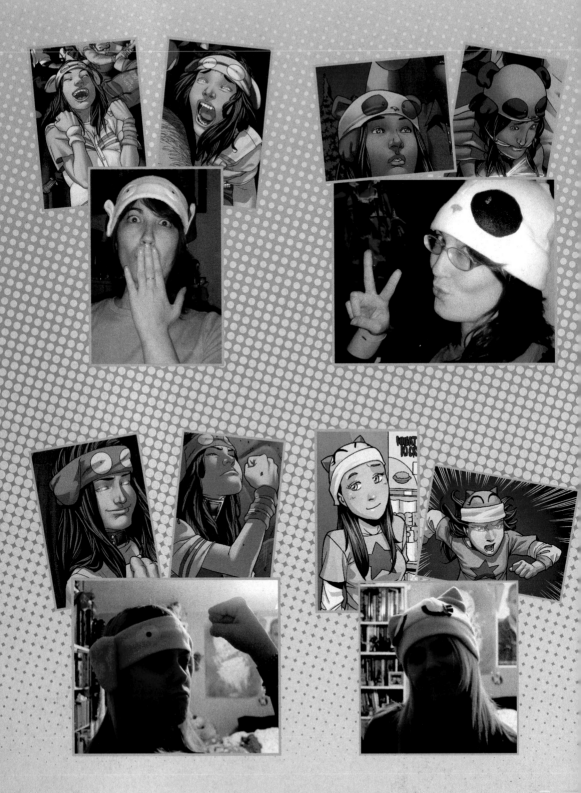

SPECIAL THANKS TO THE HAT MAKERS OVER AT GENKI HATS!